For

LOUIS L. STEIN, Jr.

ALICE MARSH CAMRON   LLS

THE HISTORY OF

ORINDA

Gateway to Contra Costa County

MUIR SORRICK

regards -
Muir Sorrick

With A Prologue By CHARLES L. CAMP

PUBLISHED BY THE ORINDA LIBRARY BOARD, INC.
FRIENDS OF THE ORINDA LIBRARY · ORINDA, CALIFORNIA
MCMLXXVI

SECOND PRINTING BY THE FRIENDS OF THE ORINDA LIBRARY
IN 1976 AS A CONTRIBUTION TO THE
BICENTENNIAL CELEBRATION OF THE BIRTH OF OUR NATION

Library of Congress Catalogue Card No. 74-149338

PRINTED IN THE UNITED STATES OF AMERICA

COVER DESIGN

CATTLE BRANDS OF VICTOR CASTRO, ALICE MARSH, AND JOAQUIN MORAGA

1000 COPIES

DESIGNED AND PRINTED BY LAWTON AND ALFRED KENNEDY

SAN FRANCISCO

Foreword and Acknowledgments

The purpose of this book is twofold: to provide for the student, in detail, an accurate record of the development of Orinda, and to stimulate interest in the rich history of the area.

In searching for true facts, dependence has been placed on the written record left behind by the early citizens, such as: deeds, inventories, assessment books, tax sale and court records, newspapers with articles of the day, and maps. Some personal letters, memoirs, and interviews with older citizens also have been very helpful.

Many individuals dropped hints as to where some material could be located or answered letters of inquiry, and their help is gratefully appreciated. The cooperation of the following is especially acknowledged: Nancy Macomber Skinner, Charlotte Chapple Meyer, Florence Sullivan, Carmel Martinez, Brother Dennis (St. Mary's College), June Hadden, Charles R. Allen, Josephine Dawson, Myrtle Lovdal Rosenthal, Kenneth L. Courtright, W. E. (Ed) Wallace, Clark Wallace, Gladys Shally, Dorothy Roos, Allen P. Winsor, Ezra E. Nelson, Harrison Sigworth, Edward L. deLaveaga, and the families of Antonio J. Marshall and James Miner.

Without the assistance of Louis L. Stein, Jr., this book would have been less complete. Mr. Stein was ever willing to tramp the fields to point out an old site and to share without reservation his life-long collection of illustrations and memorabilia of Contra Costa County. Much credit is accorded to him.

Finally, a particular debt is owed for the contributions made by Charles L. Camp, who provided the Prologue; Lauramay Dempster, who contributed the list of plants; and Harry Curieux Adamson, who donated his list of birds of the area.

Dr. Camp, an Orindan for most of the last twenty-five years, was, before his retirement, head of the Department of Paleontology and Director of the Museum of Paleontology at the University of California, Berkeley. Outstanding, also, are his contributions in the field of Western American History. The beautiful volume, "Earth Song," reveals his roles as both paleontologist and historian. For his work as author, historian, bibliographer, and editor, Dr. Camp has been chosen by the California Historical Society to be honored with the 1970 Henry R. Wagner Memorial Award.

Lauramay Dempster majored in Botany at the University of California and took a Master's Degree under W. L. Jepson. She worked as his research assistant before having her family. In 1952 she went back to work in the botany department and has done research ever since, specializing for the most part on one genus. Her list of plants was gathered during walks taken over the local countryside, while a resident for twenty-five years, and not solely from her technical knowledge. As a result the list is not intended to be complete or to distinguish between wild flowers in the strict sense and weeds or other introductions, but includes those plants from this area which have impressed her as common or beautiful.

Harry Adamson is a wildfowl artist who does original oil portrayals of native American game birds; he is a member of the Audubon Society and a highly respected bird authority. He lives in neighboring Lafayette, and this is his personal list from field trips in Orinda, including the San Pablo Dam. Mr. Adamson says that a half-dozen other species probably have been in the area—Lawrence's Goldfinch is one—but as there seem to be no certain observations, they are not included.

The reader, then, may wish to add to the list of plants and birds, as well as fill in the inevitable omissions in the history.   M.S.

The following organizations and individuals provided the illustrations used in this book:

ADB	Andrew D. Blalock	IM	Irene Moylan
AF	Art Fleuti	JH	June Hadden
AM	Albert Marshall	KC	Kenneth Courtright
BRAD	Donald Bradley	LAV	Edward L. deLaveaga
CC	Catherine Campbell	LLS	Louis L. Stein, Jr.
CDH	California Division of Highways	MCS	M. C. Sorensen
CL	Cliff Lightner	MS	Margaret Symes
CR	Contra Costa County-Recorder's Office	OFD	Orinda Fire Department
DB	Deliah Bender	OT	Oakland Tribune (Les Sipes Photo)
EB	Elizabeth Badgley	RB	Mrs. Robert Barnes
EP	Ewart J. Phair	RE	Ruth Enos
FL	Frances Lax	RLC	R. L. Copeland
FS	Florence Sullivan	SKR	Mrs. Sidney K. Rosenthal
GK	Grace Kendall	WH	Warren Harrold
GS	Gladys Shally		

Pictures not credited are from the files of the Friends of the Orinda Library. A portion of the poem "Camp Camron" is courtesy of The Bancroft Library.

Table of Contents

Prologue

We live in a changing world. Even the rocks and landscapes are changing. Natural forces in the earth, as well as unceasing human activities, alter the land. Nothing remains the same for long. We have to find ways to adjust to changes in the earth's surface; therefore, we need to know what these changes are and what their effects may be.

In selecting a site for a new house, we must try to avoid places in the hills where earth-slides have occurred, or are likely to occur, during heavy rains, or when the surface soil is disturbed. We lay out plans for a tunnel, but we may forget to find out beforehand what kind of soft, slippery clay is likely to be encountered deep in the rocks. We should anticipate such dangerous conditions. Road cuts, swimming pools, retaining walls and heavy buildings must be constructed with regard and respect for instabilities in the earth.

After the man with the bull-dozer has come to excavate for your new house in Orinda, he will probably send you a bigger bill than you had anticipated. Many a softly-rounded, innocent-looking hillslope in our district is nothing more than a mass of gravelly rock (conglomerate) containing hard boulders full of water-worn pebbles firmly cemented together with lime. This means they may have to dynamite an excavation for your basement or swimming pool. If you have a choice, place your house or swimming pool on this rock. Then you will not be troubled with cracks due to settling of the ground. It is worth the time and money to have such a solid foundation.

Then, too, the excavated gravel is good to mix with our stiff adobe soils to lighten them and make them more workable. It also makes good driveway surfaces and pathways. The hard, rough boulders are decorative in rustic walls and rock gardens. They have been so used at the Orinda Country Club, especially in the high wall above the swimming pool and along the parapet of the dam.

This curious conglomerate, resistant to weathering and erosion, forms the hills and ridges throughout most of Orinda. It occurs in local layers which were tilted up at various angles during movements of the earth's crust in past ages. The ravines and valleys between the high ridges have been scooped out of the softer sandstones and clays that lie between the beds of conglomerate. The soft yellow clays decay near the surface of the ground to produce a tough, rubbery soil, difficult to cultivate during the dry season. This soil absorbs water and expands during the rainy months. When it dries, it shrinks about one-tenth of its volume and develops deep surface cracks. The seasonal expansion and shrinking of the adobe soil creates a flow of the surface layers down steep hillsides. This down-hill creeping sometimes develops into quickening earth slides. These slides fortunately are not numerous in Orinda, but anyone planning to build should be careful to avoid this shifting ground.

A recent slide looks like a big thumb-print on the hillside. It starts in a series of crescent-shaped cracks with the arcs curving upslope. These cracks allow the surface water to gain access rapidly to the slippery clay beneath. The clay becomes a wet pudding and will no longer bear the heavy weight of the sod above. So, during a rainstorm the whole area may move down slope a hundred feet or more to pile up in a soft mound—a tempting yet treacherous knoll upon which to build a house.

One of the largest mud glaciers in our region used to cut across the Tunnel Highway in the Siesta Valley, a mile southwest of the Orinda-Moraga crossroads. This great slide, nearly a mile long, sent its nose out over the highway during wet winters and has been pouring into the West Branch of San Pablo Creek for thousands of years. The slide involves the whole floor of upper Siesta Valley and is moving slowly toward the southeast. Remnants of old slides are to be found throughout Orinda, but not many of them are active. They tend to begin moving again when roads and other excavations are cut through them.

The Orinda conglomerate is interesting to study. When you drive a pick into it, the pebbles fly out and hit your shins and pepper your eyes with gravel. Most of the pebbles are smaller than your fist and are finely smoothed and rounded as though they had been shaped and polished in a stream bed or on a beach. Some of them are quartz; some are glassy red, brown, or greenish chert. Similar siliceous rocks occur in place in the ancient chert beds laid down 150 million years ago in an arm of the sea over what is now San Francisco Bay and the peninsula.

Some of the pebbles are of hard sandstone similar to the sandstones deposited on the old California sea floor fifteen million years ago. A few of the pebbles are of granite, and the nearest source of this granite appears to have been the mass now forming Montara point, the Farallones and the tip of Point Reyes. Our gravels could hardly have come from the Sierra Nevada for several reasons: The larger cobbles and pebbles lie in the western part of the deposit; the eastern areas toward Mount Diablo consist mainly of sand, silt and mud; the red and green chert pebbles seem to come from sources to the west in the much older Franciscan formation; gold is practically absent in our deposits, indicating that the material was not derived from the gold bearing rocks of the Sierra Nevada. Therefore, our gravels were probably transported from the west. Were they carried along an ancient beach by the ocean currents, or were they washed in and dumped along the terraces and channels of streams flowing from the west?

A small part of the lowermost beds of the Orinda formation was laid down in a shallow arm of the sea, an embayment that extended inland across most of Contra Costa County, as is shown by the shells and other marine fossils to be found here. The much thicker and higher beds, laid down in later years, contain land animal remains, and no sea shells are found in these beds.

When you dig into an unweathered bed of Orinda conglomerate, a fossil turns up occasionally. A bit of the foot bone of an extinct species of camel was found on the property at 39 Ardilla Road. Another large bone, unidentified, came from the gravels along the northern end of Haciendas Road. Many bones were found in the excavation made for the Orinda schoolground. Small shells of fresh water shrimps (ostracodes) are numerous. Pieces of charcoal and remains of tree trunks and branches, usually badly decayed, are common. No one has ever discovered sea shells in this upper part of the Orinda formation, although the sea did invade the area further northeast for short intervals. Shells occur in older rocks south of the Cotton Tract.

These findings seem to prove that the upper part of the Orinda formation—the conglomerates and interbedded shales and sandstones—was laid down in fresh water, probably by a river, or rivers, issuing from ancient highlands lying west of the Berkeley Hills. These waters dumped the coarser gravels and cobbles to the west of our region in what are now the Berkeley Hills. The smaller pebbles occur in our area; still further east, toward Moraga, the sediments are fine sands, silts, and muds with ripple-marked lake bottoms still preserving the tracks of mastodonts, horses and geese. These have been found in the road cut alongside the lake at St. Mary's College.

Along the south base of Mount Diablo are rocks similar to those of Orinda. A great variety of animals have been found there in the rich bone bed on the Black Hawk Ranch, and these have been studied at the Museum of Paleontology on the Berkeley Campus.

The animals living during Black Hawk time show that those rocks were laid down about ten to twelve million years ago. There were herds of long-jawed mastodonts (*Gomphotherium*), elephant-like animals with short legs, long heads, and carrying four tusks—two in the lower jaws as well as the two upper tusks. The lower tusks may have been used like forks or scoop shovels to dig up vegetation in soft, swampy ground.

The camels were numerous, delicately built, with long, slender necks. The horses were smaller than those of today. Some of them had three hoofs on each foot—two small side hoofs and a larger one in the middle. Others had a single hoof and may have been the ancestors of our modern horses.

There was a wild dog with powerful jaws and blunt teeth, almost like the teeth of a hyena. Herds of antelopes, something like our prong horns of today, roamed the open country. There were pig-like peccaries and the extinct deer-pigs called oreodonts. There were also small beavers, rabbits, and a host of the lesser animals similar to those of today.

The plants found at various places, particularly in the Mulholland deposits near St.Mary's College, in the Orinda and Black Hawk beds, and at other localities, include the manzanita, sycamore, oak, poplar, willow, and hackberry. These plants were not so different from those of today.

Ten million years ago, according to these records in the rocks, the landscape in our region contained low rolling hills with a bay between Berkeley Hills and Mount Diablo. The rivers drained toward the San Joaquin Valley and the Sierra Nevada where smoking volcanoes might be seen on a clear day. Highlands to the west cut off the breezes from the distant sea. Mount Diablo, the Berkeley Hills, and San Francisco Bay had not yet been formed. Streams, full of frogs and fishes, flowed in pebbly channels eastward across what is now Orinda to spread out over marshy bottoms and into lakes and swamps near Moraga and on beyond what is Mount Diablo now. Herds of antelope, horses and camels browsed in the hilly savanna. Mastodonts waded in the shallow lakes and marshes, scaring up geese and other water fowl. Sabre-toothed cats, smaller than the big smilodons which came much later, preyed on the herbivores, and hyena-dogs (*Osteoborus*) chewed up the bones when the cats were through.

Before the time of deposition of the Orinda formation, from fifteen to thirty million years ago, our district lay, for much of the time, beneath shallow sea ways. It was a coastal region, and the fossils found in those earlier deposits include whale bones, great numbers of shellfish—clams and huge oysters—brittle starfish, spines of sea urchins and the like. The most peculiar animal of the time was a sort of sea-going elephant—a big, splay-footed, short-legged, long-jawed monster who lived along the sea shore and probably swam like a hippopotamus. His bones and teeth have been found in various places in Contra Costa County, up and down the coast and in Japan. His strong teeth were like bundles of old-fashioned cigars. His jaws had small tusks above and below. He may have been a clam dredger or possibly a seaweed eater like the modern sea cows. Some bones of this mammal have been obtained near San Pablo reservoir and another skeleton, known since Spanish days, lay on the top of a hill near the Cresta Blanca winery below Livermore. It was thought to be a whale until its teeth were studied.

The hills about us were formed later, pushed up by strong movements in the earth crust. Lavas poured out in fissures along what is now the ridge of the Berkeley Hills, and the western highlands sank beneath the sea. This great recent revolution, three million years ago, created the Orinda landscape much as it is today.

The movements in the rocks still continue, causing earthquakes which have not been severe in our district. The great earthquake belt is just to the west of us along the Hayward-San Andreas fault zone.

The great animals of the past lived here until at least ten thousand years ago, after the first pre-Indians came over from Asia. Among these animals was a mammoth elephant with tusks ten feet long and nearly a foot in diameter. A tusk of that size was found in a road cut at the South Gate of the Mount Diablo Park. Alongside was the jaw of a long-horned bison of great size. The smaller animals of today, the foxes, coyotes, skunks, raccoons, bobcats, rabbits and mice were much the same in those old days.

We live in a young landscape that is rapidly changing, wearing down, and being carried away by the slides and streams. But we can hardly see these changes in our short lives, and we must look to the rocks and fossils to learn the story.

I

Explorers and Indians

The story of the two land grants on which the community of Orinda is located has its origin in the Spanish Empire's explorations of the California Coast. Soldier-explorers, Jose Joaquin Moraga, Juan Francisco Bernal, and Joaquin Ysidro Castro helped to found a mission and a presidio near San Francisco Bay. It was the grandsons of these men who later received the land grants—Laguna de los Palos Colorados and El Sobrante.

Expeditions to the Bay Area

The members of Don Gaspar de Portolá's exploring party on a land expedition up the coast in 1769 were first to see the beautiful San Francisco Bay. With the Spanish explorers was Father Juan Crespi who kept a diary that is a "veritable guidebook"[1] of their travels. Here, in the diary, is the first historical mention of the redwood tree. Seeing some huge new trees that they did not recognize, the men named them the palos colorados for the color of their wood.[2] Later, Joaquin Moraga used the name in the title of his rancho because of the many redwood trees growing there.

On a later expedition in 1772, Don Pedro Fages and Father Crespi mapped the Golden Gate and explored the inland country around the bay. They climbed to the summit of Willow Pass near Concord and camped on the banks of the stream near Martinez.[3]

When the overland expedition of Juan Bautista de Anza came from Mexico in 1775–76 to establish a colony, with it were the men whose descendants later owned the land where Orinda is now located. The diaries of this trip document the episodes of the expedition, and Father Pedro Font as the chronicler kept an excellent account of the travels. Jose Joaquin Moraga, who also kept a diary, was Anza's lieutenant, and one of the soldiers who accompanied the group was Joaquin Ysidro Castro.[4]

Font and Anza further explored the region of the bay and the interior. Both mention the redwoods on the Oakland hills. One area where they speak of camping for the night was on Walnut Creek not far from where it empties into the Carquinez Straits.[5]

Moraga Founds San Francisco

Shortly after returning to Monterey, Anza turned over his command of the colony to Lieutenant Moraga. Commandante Fernando de Rivera soon gave orders to Moraga to return to the region of San Francisco Bay to build a presidio. Moraga made a temporary camp on the site that had been selected by Anza for a mission. About this site Father Font had written on March 29, 1776, "We arrived at a beautiful arroyo which because it was Friday of Sorrows, we called Arroyo de los Dolores."[6] Here by the river Dolores, Moraga ordered a shelter of branches built to serve as a chapel in which to celebrate Mass. The first

Indian utensils uncovered near eleventh green of Orinda Country Club golf course   LAV
Ranchos El Sobrante, Acalanes, and Boca de la Canada del Pinole meet above Sleepy Hollow   RB

Mass was said by Father Palou on June 29, on the spot which became the Mission San Francisco de Asis, popularly called Mission Dolores.[7]

Camp was moved to where the new presidio was constructed and on September 17, 1776, this task was completed and possession taken in the name of the sovereign. On October 3 the Mission Dolores also was completed, blessed and, five days later, formally dedicated.[8]

Indians

When the explorers arrived, they found the Costanoan Indians occupying the area around the bay and parts of Contra Costa County. Ethnographers have assigned some of the more interior regions of the county to Bay Miwok Indians.[9] Although the exact locations of their villages are obscure, there was probably a main village, Ahala-n, near Lafayette.[10] It is from the name of this village that the Spanish are believed to have derived the word Acalanes. Near this center and over the countryside were scattered many smaller rancherias.

A number of recent archeological surveys have been made in Contra Costa County, but none has been made of the Orinda area. Relics have been found that date back about 5,000 years in a site in Stone Valley and about 2,500 years in one at Grayson and Reliez Roads in Pleasant Hill.[11] Arrowheads, mortars, skeletons and shells were unearthed near Miner Road when the California and Nevada Railroad was graded through Orinda in 1892.[12] During the building of the golf course in 1924, an extensive burial ground was found in the location of the eleventh green which is not far from the first discovery. Some of this material went to the Department of Anthropology at the University of California.[13] The site of this rancheria is near the joining of Lauterwasser Creek with the San Pablo Creek.

Four stone mortars were discovered during excavations on adjacent properties on Glorietta Boulevard, and a burial site was discovered at the nursery on Moraga Way.[14]

Characteristics

The local Indians were reported to be dark, often bearded and long-haired, but some were seen with scant beards and short hair.[15] They were flat-nosed and generally short of stature and occasionally mentioned as having an oriental look.

Moraga, while on the Anza expedition, said of the Indians near Carquinez, "It is certain that these and the rest of the Indians whom I encountered while my exploration lasted I found affable, generous, and not at all doubtful of communication with us."[16]

The Costanoans had their burial customs, games, rituals, songs, "medicine men," and their myths individual to their tribe. Besides the sun, their sacred objects included the large redwood trees.[17] Generally, they buried their dead in a flexed position in the Contra Costa area.[18]

Food and Clothing

The culture of the Costanoans is supposed to have been rather primitive when compared to that of the Indians from many other areas. The mild climate and the abundance of game, fish, roots, seeds, and the dependable acorn crop made life busy but not difficult.

Acorns which had been gathered and carefully stored were leached to remove the tannic acid, and a meal was made from them which was a staple of the Indian diet. The country was often burned over to gather acorns more easily and to foster the growth of seed-bearing

3

annuals.[19] Moraga noticed this treatment of the land south of San Francisco, and he wrote to the Commandante in 1776: "I saw the heathen had burned many patches, which doubtless would produce a good pasturage."[20]

Local Indians went to the coast and traded for shellfish and caught the steelhead salmon that ran up the San Pablo Creek every winter. All available game was caught and eaten, and rabbits were hunted with a rabbit stick which the men possessed. Father Font saw that the Indians on the Carquinez Strait were "fishing with nets and that they anchored the raft with some very long slim poles."[21] Alfred L. Kroeber, an authority on California Indians, writes that although the only boats which the Costanoans had were made from tules, on these they were able to cross San Francisco Bay.[22]

Kroeber describes the dress customs: "The men were accustomed to go naked when the weather permitted. The women wore the usual two short skirts, one before and one behind, made either of deerskin, tule or bark fiber. The rabbit-skin blanket served both as mantle and as bedding. A common custom of the men was to coat themselves thickly with mud in the morning until the sun shone warm."[23]

Dwellings

Costanoan houses were simply constructed of poles covered with bark, mud or tules, sometimes shaped like a tepee, sometimes rounded and covered with grass. The social and ceremonial center was the temescal or sweat house, partially dug out of the ground; the smaller portion above was a round, earth-covered and almost air-tight structure. The entrance was small and close to the ground, and there was an outlet at the top for the smoke. A fire was lighted, and the Indians confined themselves in the extremely hot interior until they were dripping with perspiration; then they would come out and plunge into a nearby supply of cold water. The temescal was used for maintaining good health as well as a cure-all for any illness.

Indian Problems

Jose Moraga's son, Gabriel, not only became a famous explorer, but led some forty-six campaigns against the Indians. Contra Costa Indians, their lives uprooted when they were sent by the Spanish Americans to missions at Sonoma, San Rafael, San Francisco and San Jose, often ran away.[24] Sometimes, they would join hostile groups. Indian forays also occasionally took place on the rancho of the white man.

Candelario Valencia acquired the landgrant, Acalanes, in 1834. When he transferred his rancho to William Alexander Leidesdorff, he wrote of the nearby area that is presently Lafayette, "This place was occupied by my family and myself during a period of five years. When it had been harried by the Indians up to a point where my life and the lives of my family were endangered, I abandoned it for a time."[25]

In 1847 Elam Brown was sawing lumber in the San Antonio Redwoods and shipping it to Leidesdorff, who was engaged in the lumber business as well as land speculation. Brown purchased the Valencia grant from Leidesdorff that year and became the founder of the neighboring town of Lafayette.[26] Leidesdorff and Jose Joaquin Moraga are both buried in Mission Dolores.

4

The Indians learned many trades and did much of the work in the early days of white occupation. Later, some went to work on the large ranchos where they lived under comparatively protected circumstances. Olivette Moraga, a great-granddaughter of Joaquin Moraga, grantee of the Laguna de los Palos Colorados, remembered hearing that Joaquin had brought 300 Mission Indians to his ranch to help build the adobe.[27]

It is estimated there were 7,000 Costanoans in 1770, but within sixty years the unremitting mortality reduced the number greatly.[28] Although the mission period was a severe shock to the Indians, after secularization their condition deteriorated at a greater rate. By 1910 the group was, for all practical purposes, extinct.[29] Many of the causes of this decline are obscure. Kroeber says that although new diseases and alteration of diet, clothing, and dwellings contributed to the rapid decrease of California Indian population, the primary cause may have consisted of undetermined cultural factors.

As the large grants of land passed to new owners, by one means or another, the Indians no longer had the protection that living on the rancho had afforded. When the Americans arrived in great numbers, the story was about over. Of the local Indians there remains nothing except a few mission records, some relics and the place names derived from the names of their villages or their language.

The Joaquin Moraga adobe was restored after one hundred years and a memorial plaque
placed on the building in 1954 OT

II

The Land Grants

Land grants had been made under Spanish rule since 1775 and under Mexican rule from 1822 until the beginning of the American occupation in 1846.[1] Governors were authorized, in 1828, to make grants of land, and they often did to the men of families who had served their country and who, with their wives and children, would help populate the area and cultivate the land.[2]

Laguna de los Palos Colorados

Joaquin Moraga and his cousin, Juan Bernal, whose grandfather had also been a soldier with Anza's expedition, applied for the Rancho Laguna de los Palos Colorados on August 20, 1835.[3] This land was granted to them by Governor Castro on October 10th.[4] The grant consisted of three leagues of land or about 13,326 acres.

It was the job of Father Gomez, head of Mission San Jose, to investigate the petitions for vacant land, and, in expressing his approval of this grant, he mentions the hope that "at no time they hinder the mission in the cutting of wood it may need."[5]

On the eastern slopes of the hills above Moraga Valley were the tremendous redwood trees, the "Palos Colorados," which had been used in the construction of the Mission San Jose.[6] The "Laguna" was the lake in the area of the present Campolindo High School. The lake existed into the 1900's and was known by later residents as the tule pond.

Within a year after receiving the grant, the cousins are reported to have built some houses and corrals and to have ranged their cattle on the land.[7] The title was confirmed by Governor Juan B. Alvarado on August 10, 1841, with the specification "within one year they shall build a house and it shall be inhabited."[8]

The adobe which was built by Joaquin Moraga is located about four miles from Highway 24 on a knoll above the present Del Rey School and overlooks the valley. Bernal built his adobe nearer to the town of Lafayette.

The Moraga adobe was restored in 1941 by Mrs. James Irvine. It was purchased in 1964 by Donald Manuel who further remodeled it into a lovely private home which kept much of the original character. No definite proof of the construction date of the building has been found, but estimates range from 1841 to 1845.[9] The Contra Costa Historical Society marked the historic house with a memorial plaque in 1954, designating it as California Historical Landmark No. 509.

Joaquin Moraga lived with his sons and daughters and their families on the Laguna de los Palos Colorados and was one of the great and hospitable landowners in California. James Lamson in his diaries gave a glimpse of the home and life when he wrote in 1855 to tell of attending a fandango at Senor Moraga's. He wrote of the comfortable home, his gracious host, the family, and the guests, among whom were other Mexicans, Americans from the

THE JOAQUIN MORAGA ADOBE - 1841

JOSE JOAQUIN MORAGA - MEMBER OF THE JUAN BAUTISTA DE ANZA
1776 EXPEDITION. FOUNDER AND FIRST COMMANDANTE OF THE
PRESIDIO OF SAN FRANCISCO - WAS THE GRANDFATHER OF
DON JOAQUIN MORAGA WHO WITH HIS COUSIN DON JUAN BERNAL
WAS AWARDED THIS GRANT IN 1835 WHICH THEY CALLED RANCHO
LAGUNA DE LOS PALOS COLORADOS. IN AUGUST 1841 THIS
PROPERTY WAS ACQUIRED AND RESTORATION MADE BY KATHARINE
BROWN WHITE IRVINE OF OAKLAND. LATER OWNERSHIP WAS
BEQUEATHED TO HER GRANDSON WILLIAM THORNTON WHITE III.

CONTRA COSTA COUNTY HISTORICAL SOCIETY
1954   CALIFORNIA   STATE   REGISTRATION   NO.509

redwoods, and Indian women and their papooses. He described the dances, the orchestra playing, the merriment that went on, and the bountiful supper that was served. He concluded, "Thus pleasantly passed the evening until eleven o'clock, when, giving my Mexican friends a cordial shake of the hands, I bade them *a dios*, and winded my way back again over the mountain to my lodging. The company continued dancing until morning."[10]

El Sobrante

The families of many of the owners of the large grants in this area were related. Joaquin Moraga's wife was Maria Francisca Castro, whose father was the grantee of Rancho San Pablo. Her brothers, Victor and Juan Jose, applied in 1841 for all of the surplus land lying between the Ranchos San Antonio, San Pablo, Pinole, Valencia and Moraga. They received this grant from Governor Alvarado on April 22, 1841.[11] In the grant Alvarado made a specification that was to cause litigation and confusion for years to come. He said that the land must be regulated and bounded by the boundaries of the neighboring ranches. The land grant was called El Sobrante (the surplus). It was estimated at approximately five leagues of land or about 22,000 acres.

Victor Castro married Luisa Martinez, and Juan Jose was married to Petral Bernal. One of the Moraga girls, Guadalupe, was married to Vicente Martinez, and Maria Moraga married a member of the Briones family. These marriages made close family ties between the owners of the ranches in this area of Contra Costa County.

The two-story adobe that Victor and Juan Jose Castro built was near the county line in El Cerrito and not in the Orinda area.

Victor Castro, who lived to be eighty years old, was elected on June 14, 1852, as one of the five men to serve on the first Board of Supervisors of Contra Costa County. The county was formed by an act of the legislature on February 18, 1850, and confirmed on April 25, 1851. At that time Contra Costa County included most of the present Alameda County. In March 1853 Alameda County was formed from part of Contra Costa County and part of Santa Clara County, and, from that time on, the name Contra Costa, "opposite coast," was rather a misnomer.

A fifth generation of the Castro family are now on a ranch of about 100 acres near El Sobrante and have a meat business there. Patricio, the son of Victor, established a larger ranch in this area about 1865, and his son, Percy L., carried on after his death. The slaughterhouse was built in 1916, while the San Pablo Reservoir was under construction, mainly to supply the camp kitchen. Now, Percy L., Jr. and his daughter are running the business.

Life for the Castros was, no doubt, very similar to that of the Moragas. Times were good and cattle prices were high, particularly in the last half of the 1840's. The land owners were rich in their expanses of land and in the number of their cattle and horses. Debts were seldom pressed and always could be paid off in cattle, hides and tallow—and usually were as money was never plentiful.[12] There were many rodeos, fiestas, wedding festivals, much music and dancing, as well as the various sports of the times. Indians did the garden work, raised the produce, and helped with the chores.

All the rancheros had a reputation of being the most excellent of riders, and they spent a great deal of time in the saddle. On special days they used elaborate saddles and outfits

9

Victor Castro was about forty years of age when this photograph was taken   LLS

which William Heath Davis said he had known to cost thousands of dollars.[13] The boundaries of their lands were described by springs, trees, creeks and mountains, and the land was so abundant that a boundary dispute was unheard of. Unfortunately for the early Californians, the Moragas and Castros included, this excellent life was not to last.

The Transition Period

The American conquest of California was completed in 1848. To add to the problems of the Californians, soon the news of the discovery of gold spread throughout the world. When settlers began to rush into the area in unprecedented numbers, "squatter troubles" began.[14] The settlers came and built on land where they found no clearly marked boundaries or surveyor's marks. After they had lived there and cultivated the seemingly unoccupied area, they felt that they had a right to that particular place.[15]

Still greater problems arose for the rancheros when the United States Congress passed an act to create the United States Land Commission in 1851. The commission was formed to investigate land ownership, and each grantee now had to prove his title to his land or it would be declared public domain.[16]

In the transition from institutions of Spanish origin to those of Anglo-Saxon, there was uncertainty and confusion, not only for the landowner, but also often for the United States Government. By the new standards, the titles were technically imperfect or carelessly defined. Land, which had been simply granted to those who wished it for the raising of cattle or for the cultivation of crops, was now put to much more complicated tests. Robert Cleland says of the Spanish-Californians: "Strangers to American laws and legal procedures, ignorant even of the language, they were required to submit to judicial processes in which they were wholly inexperienced, and to defend their rights under proceedings they could not understand."[17] Necessity forced the landowners to hire lawyers to represent them and to put their trust in these strangers' hands. Litigation was to prove costly beyond any expectation. To raise funds for taxes due and for their very sustenance, as well as for legal costs, they were forced to mortgage or sell their basic resource—the land. Cleland tells of the native rancheros being an easy prey to every ill produced by the questionable financial practices of the time: "Short-term mortgages (secured by property whose value was out of all proportion to the amount of the loan), unconscionable interest rates, and deficiency judgments levied upon whatever assets the defaulting debtor might possess, eventually took from even the wealthiest and most distinguished of the native California families, first their herds of cattle, then their broad leagues of land, and finally the friendly shelter of their simple adobe casas."[18] This was the fate that was to befall both the Castros and the Moragas.

Problems on the Moraga Grant

Troubles with squatters first began for Moraga on the land on which the redwoods grew. The middle section of the redwoods, between the lands of Moraga and Peralta, was public property, and here men had been cutting trees for some time. In 1849 a sawmill was built in the Moraga Redwoods, and, from then on lumbering started in this area as lumbermen ignored Moraga's claim to the land.[19]

Moraga sold 400 acres of the redwoods in 1853 to Elam Brown,[20] who by then owned the Acalanes Rancho.

On February 15, 1853, Moraga filed his claim for the grant with the United States Land Commission in accordance with the law. Moraga and Bernal's heirs employed a firm of lawyers, E. A. Lawrence, Charles B. Strode and William Carey Jones, to help pursue their claim. One-fifth of the land was deeded to these men for their fee or some 2,657 acres.[21] The claim was confirmed by the United States District Court on January 23, 1855, and was designated as 13,318.13 acres by the court on March 2, 1856. Before a patent could be issued, surveys to determine boundaries were ordered. A patent was not issued until 1878.[22]

Juan Bernal had died in 1847, and his widow remarried. The Bernal half of the grant was divided between the widow and four children. By 1861, Horace W. Carpentier, an attorney, claimed all of the Bernal interests which he had obtained in various ways—on tax sales, mortgage defaults, or by buying out any remaining heirs. The Bernal heirs relinquished their claims to Carpentier for small sums, Juan Bernal, a son, receiving $1,000. From this time, Carpentier seems to have been the legal owner of one-half of the Laguna de los Palos Colorados.[23]

Joaquin Moraga died in 1855. Within three years there remained in his estate only 2,626 acres to be assessed.[24] The selling of parts of the land had been necessary to help pay the taxes and the expenses of the estate. The court had ordered such sales to be made at public auction in 1857 on the court house steps in Martinez.[25] The auction was advertised in the Solano County Herald as the Contra Costa Gazette was not established until 1858. About a dozen parcels ranging from 6 to 900 acres were sold by the heirs to the estate.[26] As Francisco, one of Joaquin's sons, lived only two years after the death of his father, Jose was made the administrator of both estates. One of the buyers of 160 acres at this time was Jesse Williams who somehow managed to hold his property, now part of the present Rheem area, even when most of the grant ended in the hands of Carpentier.

Horace W. Carpentier

Horace Carpentier was a lawyer retained by many of the grantees to help them obtain a patent through the courts and, later, by owners to help them evict squatters from the land. He generally took land as his fee. He was well-known to the owners of the land grants near the bay area and was involved in transactions of property on many of their holdings. He seemed to have had an insatiable appetite for land and is generally spoken of by historians as an opportunist who took advantage of the confusion of the times and of the laws during the transition period. He became one of the largest single landholders in the vicinity east of San Francisco Bay.

Squatters, and a few renters, had begun to settle on the land of the Peraltas in 1849. Carpentier, along with Edson Adams and Andrew J. Moon, had started his ownership of land on the Peralta Grant in the present Oakland area. He was elected an assemblyman in 1853 in what has been called a questionable election; he then pressed for the incorporation of Oakland.[27] This event occurred on March 25, 1854. He became that city's first mayor. Soon, the Oakland residents found that he owned the whole of the waterfront through a transaction two years earlier in which he had agreed to build a school (later constructed near

4th and Clay Streets) and to erect some wharves in exchange for the property along the water.[28] There was eventually a long fight in the legislature over the waterfront property, and the end result was that Carpentier was declared the owner of about $8,000,000 of land in the area.[29] In the late 1870's he moved to New York permanently, and, from that time on, he transacted his business through his managers and agents. He died in February 1918, at the age of 94, leaving bequests of some $2,000,000 to Columbia and Barnard Colleges, $100,000 to the University of California, and bequests to other educational institutions.[30]

Carpentier's particular aim seems to have been the acquisition of the Laguna de los Palos Colorados. Claiming the Bernal half of the rancho by 1861, he then concentrated on acquiring the Moraga half of the property. He quickly bought up any land that was available through tax sales. It is said that he claimed an interest in all the land that had been already sold to settlers by Moraga, maintaining that a portion was his, due to an agreement with the Moragas. Some owners sold out to him as titles were still clouded with uncertainty; there was always a possibility the land would not be legally theirs. The final patent on the property had not yet been signed. By 1873 Carpentier claimed all of the Moraga ranch.

The Moragas did not give up the land and their adobe without a struggle. There were sieges and assaults against the Moragas, arrests for murder and feuds that lasted into the 1870's. The events make a story in themselves.[31] The family strongly resisted the efforts by Carpentier to evict them from their home.

Occasionally one of the heirs would settle his claim for cash. One sold out her interest in 1874 for $100 and another in 1876 for $100.[32]

The final patent on the property was signed by President Hayes, August 10, 1878, declaring the Moragas and the Bernals the original legal owners but, ironically, the final survey recorded on January 3, 1887, partitioning the land to the legal owners, showed not a Moraga or a Bernal.[33] Horace Carpentier owned the whole of the remaining Laguna de los Palos Colorados. The exception was six small parcels belonging to families who were able to prove title and who would not sell to him.

Carpentier was in New York during the final partitioning. An article in 1887 told of the death of his agent, John B. Watson of Moraga, who had been working for Carpentier since the 1850's, and the cause of his death was thought to be overwork![34]

The Moraga family were not evicted by Carpentier without some compensation. Not having any legal ground to stand on, after all of the transactions and court decisions, the Moragas settled on December 2, 1885, for $10,000 in gold coin.[35]

Problems on the Castro Sobrante

Few of the boundaries of the various ranchos had yet been finally surveyed by the Mexican government when the United States occupied the territory. Because the boundaries of El Sobrante depended on an interpretation of the terms of the grant, as well as the loosely defined boundaries of the adjoining ranchos, San Antonio, San Pablo, Pinole, Acalanes and Moraga, the land case became one of the most involved in California. It was not until 1883, forty-two years after the grant was made, that a patent signed by President Chester Arthur was issued to the legal owners. A final report of the referees in partition of El Sobrante was made as late as 1907.[36]

13

In 1852 Victor and Juan Jose Castro petitioned for title through their attorneys, John Wilson and H. W. Carpentier. Victor stated at the time of the petitioning that the government owed him for military services which he had performed, and for which he had never been paid, to the extent of $5,000 and that the land granted would not have brought anything near the sum owed at that time.[37] Both brothers also testified that "Victor had several years before the date of the grant settled on said land and built and resided in a house and cultivated fields thereon and both petitioners pastured their cattle, horses . . . upon it before the grant was made and have continued to do so ever since, and said Victor has constantly thereon resided and cultivated three different ranches."[38]

Governor Alvarado also filed a deposition in which he said that he had made the grant for the reasons stated by the Castros and, also, "that it was expected that the government of Mexico would in course of time send commissioners and surveyors to separate and measure the lands granted to individuals and establish the boundaries of each grant in accordance with the title papers."[39] It would have been very helpful to the grantees if this had occurred before the United States claimed the territory.

El Sobrante did not share the fate of the Moraga-Bernal grant and end up in the hands of one man. Although the Castros sold or lost most of the land, they managed to keep a very small portion of the grant. The major factors in determining the fate of El Sobrante were the sales as early as 1847 and 1852 of two separate leagues of land. The titles to these leagues remained valid despite many challenges.

The first league was sold in 1847 to the owners of the San Francisco merchandising firm of Ward and Smith.[40] This land was near the southernmost part of the grant and today forms part of the Orinda area. Another league, north of this, was sold in 1852 and was known from then on as the Kelly league after the name of the purchaser.[41]

In the 1850's the remaining Castro lands passed back and forth between various owners as the brothers heavily mortgaged or sold their holdings.[42] Also adding to the complexity of the transactions was the fact that the Castros had entered into an agreement with Horace Carpentier during the term of the land commission. If he prosecuted in their behalf to a final confirmation of the grant, the Castros agreed to give him one-eighth of their land.[43] The attorney, John Wilson, had received one-tenth of the land, less what had already been sold.[44]

All of the transactions in land were based on the grant ownership being confirmed at a future date. Owners who either purchased a portion, or received it in lieu of a fee or debt, would often convey their interest to another person, and, in turn, this person might again sell his interest. As a result of this trading, the transactions were many and complex. However, Carpentier never succeeded in owning the major portion of El Sobrante grant as in the case of the Moraga grant. At one time he filed a claim for ten leagues of land, but the claim was rejected by the courts in 1855.[45]

There were others who claimed they had legitimate title to portions of the land which they had purchased either directly or at tax sales or on which they had lent money in return for an interest in the land. Edson Adams and Andrew Moon were among these claimants; Moon, however, conveyed his interest to Adams.[46] Thus the confusion was to go on for many years, with confirmation of the grant delayed mainly due to the boundary survey

14

problems. In the present Orinda section on the Ward and Smith league, the title was more clearly defined than in other areas.

The "bloody 1870's" were very evident on the Castro Sobrante during the time that many suits of ejection were filed by the landowners against squatters, with resorts to firearms before the bitterness was over.[47] Particularly, after a survey in 1878, under the direction of the United States Surveyor General, there was a mad rush for land, each settler hoping that the location he chose would prove to be government land and not part of the Sobrante. The squatters paid little attention to survey lines or fences but fought for a claim to the land they had chosen as though it were a right to which they were entitled.

A survey map drawn in 1893 shows Victor Castro as the owner of 549 acres of El Sobrante and the total amount of land then located in the grant at 19,633 acres.[48]

Recivi de Don Guillermo Mc Smith
la cantidad de Quenientos Pesos
($ 500) en plata por una legua
de tierra que le bendi en la
Loma de Ocho Cientos Llezuros
Colinda Con los Vavechs de Don
Vicente Castro, el Pinol y San Pablo
lo cual entregara (con oro fino)
boluntad.

San Francisco Dicbre 14 1847   Juan Jose Castro

$ 500

Por abre que natica determine
hiyra me de Voluntad del Jerdo
M. Arruna
Nr 25 1848
Nin Abraum

The first land sold in El Sobrante grant was in present Orinda   LLS

III

The Ward and Smith League

The firm of Ward and Smith was the third merchandising store in San Francisco in 1846. Its location would now be east of Montgomery Street and north of Clay Street.

William Smith was a southerner nicknamed "Jim Crow Smith," and he had a reputation of being a very entertaining gentleman.[1] In August 1848 he married Susana Martinez Hinckley, the young widow of Captain William S. Hinckley. Susana was one of the daughters of Don Ignacio Martinez, the grantee of the Rancho Pinole. Smith became the business agent for the Martinez family and planned the original town of Martinez, laying out a townsite on 120 acres and naming the town after the owners.[2]

The Castros traded with the Ward and Smith store, as did many other bay area ranchers. Ward and Smith purchased the league of the Castro Sobrante in 1847 for $800. Juan Jose Castro later testified: "Smith paid me in 1847, $500 in goods, and the balance in 1848 he paid me in gold dust, $300."[3]

The Smith Ranch

Smith did not live on his ranch in the present Orinda area but had a "majordomo," Juan de dios Silvas, who resided here and grew crops on the land. In 1849, Smith's brother-in-law, Jose de Jesus Martinez, lived on the land as his agent.[4] The agents representing Smith lived in a small house which was located a little north of the present Orinda village, about 120 yards from the north bank of San Pablo Creek.[5] In all written transactions the house is designated as being located in the center of the league.

So, it was as early as 1847 that the Orinda location was occupied by someone living on the premises. The Moragas were living in the adobe, and the Castros lived near the northern end of their land at this time. Elam Brown purchased the Acalanes grant that same year.

Smith wrote a letter to his brother, John F. S. Smith, in 1849, urging him to come out from the states and settle on the ranch. John Smith came and, as a business arrangement, leased one-half of the Ward and Smith league which was Smith's, for $300 a year. He then built an improved house in the same location as the older one, enclosed a field of some ninety acres for crops, and pastured 60 horses and 400 head of cattle on the outside land. He spoke later of the marauding bears that he had to contend with. His rodeo ground was what is now the Sleepy Hollow area of Orinda. Altogether, he put in about $5,000 of improvements on the ranch.[6]

John Smith hired some American farmers at $75.00 per month and built some shanties for them to live in. After the rains came, he started to turn over the virgin soil for future crops. In his words: "I was as happy as a lord. My nearest neighbor, some three miles distant, on the only wagon road out to Martinez, was Squire Elam Brown, the Patriarch of his settlement."[7] John remained on the ranch for two years and, after that time, reconveyed his interest in the property to his brother, William, who was beginning to have serious financial adversities. He then moved to Martinez with his wife and children and was elected sheriff there in 1853.

Grover, Huertzel, and Lauterwasser

Because of the prevailing economic conditions, difficulties of Ward and Smith's business increased, and the firm found it financially necessary to sell the league of land to Mowry W. Smith and Lewis Brady.[8] The situation for William Smith became more desperate, partially because his extensive plans for the city of Martinez did not turn out as he had hoped. He committed suicide in 1853.

The land then passed through several hands during the next three years.[9] On January 1, 1857, Joseph Johnson sold the third interest that he now owned in the league to Frederick P. Lauterwasser for $2,000.[10] The property that Lauterwasser purchased included the old rodeo grounds, the Miner Road area, and the Orinda village location.

In 1857 Lauterwasser built his home near the entrance to the present Sleepy Hollow area.[11] It was a two-story affair. Edith Miner, whose family later owned the house, said that she understood the tall French windows across the front of the house had been shipped around the Horn, that many of the house beams were hand-hewn, and that the lumber had come from the sawmill in Lafayette, which in turn, had obtained the trees from Redwood Canyon.[12]

Lauterwasser was in the meat business in San Francisco and commuted to his ranch on weekends, leaving his wife and children on the ranch. He came by ferry to the foot of Broadway in Oakland and traveled the rest of the way by team.[13] He raised cattle on the ranch, and was assessed for 500 head as well as for 20 horses, some hogs and poultry.[14] The community of Orinda has kept his name in Lauterwasser Creek which runs along Miner Road from the hills in back of Sleepy Hollow to join San Pablo Creek.

The remaining two-thirds of the Ward and Smith league was purchased by Ira Grover who bought one-third interest, and by Laurentz Huertzel who purchased the remaining one-third early in 1859.[15] Huertzel lived in the old Smith house near San Pablo Creek, although he moved the buildings a little further north, and Grover utilized the remaining part of the league.[16] The trio—Grover, Huertzel and Lauterwasser—soon found it necessary to defend their right to the league where a large part of Orinda north of the crossroads is now located.

Edson Adams, the early Oakland settler, had been awarded, with Andrew Moon, in 1856, an interest in the Castro lands for $1,500 at a sheriff's sale. Three years earlier Victor Castro had mortgaged some property with the men.[17] Edson Adams was a large land owner along with Carpentier. Horace Carpentier had not yet given up his try for the Sobrante, always claiming an interest in the land already sold by the Castros prior to their agreement to give him one-eighth of their land. In 1860 Adams and Carpentier sued Grover, Huertzel and Lauterwasser to recover possession of their supposed rights in the Ward and Smith league.[18] The case was tried in 1861 after Grover, Huertzel and Lauterwasser petitioned to Judge Thomas A. Brown to examine the facts of their ownership of the Ward and Smith league and to bring a clear title for once and for all. Witnesses included Victor and Juan Jose Castro, Jose de Martinez, and John F. S. Smith.

During the trial Victor Castro testified as to the one-eighth interest given to Carpentier for his services. He stated: "In the first place my brother objected to giving his titles to Mr. Carpentier, but finally consented. The arrangement we then made was this: Mr. Carpentier was to present the titles and prosecute them to final confirmation by the United States authorities for which we were to give him one-eighth of the whole Rancho. Before making this arrangement, my brother distinctly informed Mr. Carpentier of the sale to Ward and Smith and others—and told him that the arrangement did not include the land thus sold. I also informed Mr. Carpentier at the same time myself of the sales made by my brother and also by myself."[19]

Judgment was brought against Adams and Carpentier in June of 1861. This decision should have been sufficient to end the matter, but Adams and Carpentier evidently were still trying to get this part of the Sobrante ranch two years later. At that time, Grover, Huertzel and Lauterwasser paid them $7,500 to get a document that signed over any right Adams and Carpentier felt they had in the Ward and Smith league for all time. This latest move finally ended any question on the ownership of this part of the grant.[20]

Although Carpentier sold any interests that he had in the Sobrante, Edson Adams' claim to a share of the grant held up over the years. After a long period of uncertain ownership of Sobrante land, a survey was made in 1893. A suit was filed by Edson F. Adams, et al. against Emily B. Hopkins, et al. in 1896. A final report of the referees in partition in 1909 showed a total of 19,893.24 acres in the Castro Sobrante.[21] The land was then divided into specific designated tracts, and 11,172.42 acres comprised this portion. The remaining 8,720.82 acres, valued around $72.00 per acre, was put in what was called the "Surplus Sobrante" for purposes of distribution. This acreage was divided among the various owners in common outside of the specific tracts according to their fractional interests, after land had been deducted for streets and roads. The Adams' heirs received over 5,000 acres in their share of the "Surplus Sobrante."

The Houston Tract

On January 1, 1859, Alexander H. Houston purchased for $1,800 about 450 acres of the Sobrante. One of the sellers was Horace Carpentier. This was a piece south of the Ward and Smith league bordering on the Moraga Rancho[22] and on public lands. The area today would include the land from the Orinda crossroads to the canyon opposite Camino Sobrante in the village. In the final survey of the property, only 208 acres would prove to be on the Sobrante. The rest was on public land.

As was common experience everywhere at the time, Houston found squatters on his land. James Bailey and Irene Conklin had built a hotel about 1858 on the new Telegraph Road, near the site of the present crossroads, not far from the bridge which crossed San Pablo Creek. There was a bar-room, dining-room, and hotel rooms.[23] As Bailey and Mrs. Conklin had no legal right to the land, they gave Houston a quit claim and deed of conveyance.[24] They were evidently allowed to stay and operate the hotel, as it was there for many years after this time. In deeds of the 1880's, Conklin's Tavern, as it was called, was still used in descriptions such as "off Telegraph Road, upper side of bridge by Conklin's Tavern."

Conklin's Tavern was the first restaurant of any kind in Orinda. It was probably built in anticipation of the traffic that would travel over the newly constructed Telegraph Road, through present Orinda and on to Lafayette.

The hotel achieved some publicity when, on Sunday evening, December 11, 1859, a murder was committed on the premises. Houston was trying to peacefully evict one of the squatters on his land by the name of Edward Norris. Norris had fenced in 70 acres and refused to give up possession. Houston's father-in-law, W. C. Pease, was left in charge of the property to try to settle the matter with Norris. When Pease went to Conklin's Tavern for supper, he overheard Norris and his friends speaking of him in an uncomplimentary fashion. Pease drew a pistol in anger, and Norris and Pease exchanged words. While Norris tried to disarm the other man, Pease fired and Norris fell dead. Although Pease was tried for manslaughter, he was acquitted in 1861.[25]

The same year Houston paid $190 to Charles and Elizabeth Silvero for their claim to 80 acres on the east side of Telegraph Road, southwest of the bridge by Conklin's, as well as for the dwelling house, corral and stable.[26] Some of the settlers gave up more easily than others.

Bryant Corners

Houston was dead by 1869, and his widow sold the property, now assessed at 600 acres, to Horatio Finch,[27] who in turn sold it to the San Francisco firm of T. H. Hatch & Co., on June 1, 1870.[28] Theodore Hatch was a shipping and commission merchant in San Francisco.

Hatch & Co. kept the property for seven years and then sold it to A. J. Bryant and six other men. The property agreement included the house and furniture, farm utensils, wagons, plows, hay, feed, and personal property, except for the library and small items. The amount agreed upon was $22,400. In the deal with Bryant were E. Ivers, J. D. Yost, S. Putnam, E. Woodward and R. Gaskell, all of whom took portions of the property which had been named "Maple Grove Homestead." A survey map, made by P. G. Rector in November 1876, shows the Conklin Hotel Grounds, a planned plaza, and the road to San Pablo.[29] The road was named Maple Grove Avenue.

The map shows four coal tunnels on the property ranging from 150 feet to 600 feet in length. Efforts were made to mine coal here but were soon discontinued.

Andrew Jackson Bryant was a well-known man and the mayor of San Francisco when he bought the property. He served the term from 1875 to 1877 and was re-elected for another two-year term from 1877 to 1879. Later he became manager for various insurance companies and was president of the California Light Company from 1882 until his death.

Bryant either improved the Hatch house or built a new one. The location, on a hill above San Pablo Creek, was probably about the center of the present freeway. Anita Miner Macey said about the Bryant house: "I remember very clearly visiting at Mayor Bryant's home with my parents. It was a lovely home, a white house set in the midst of a garden, wide lawn, flower beds and shrubs, a round summer house of white lath work with a pointed green roof, a glass greenhouse. . . . The high peaked roof of the house was trimmed with what I like to think was lace. Mayor Bryant drove over the old fish ranch grade, called the Summit Road in those days. . . . There are still a few fruit trees left from the orchard in the hollow just below the road and across the creek."[30]

Mayor Bryant's residence was in San Francisco, but he undoubtedly spent a good deal of

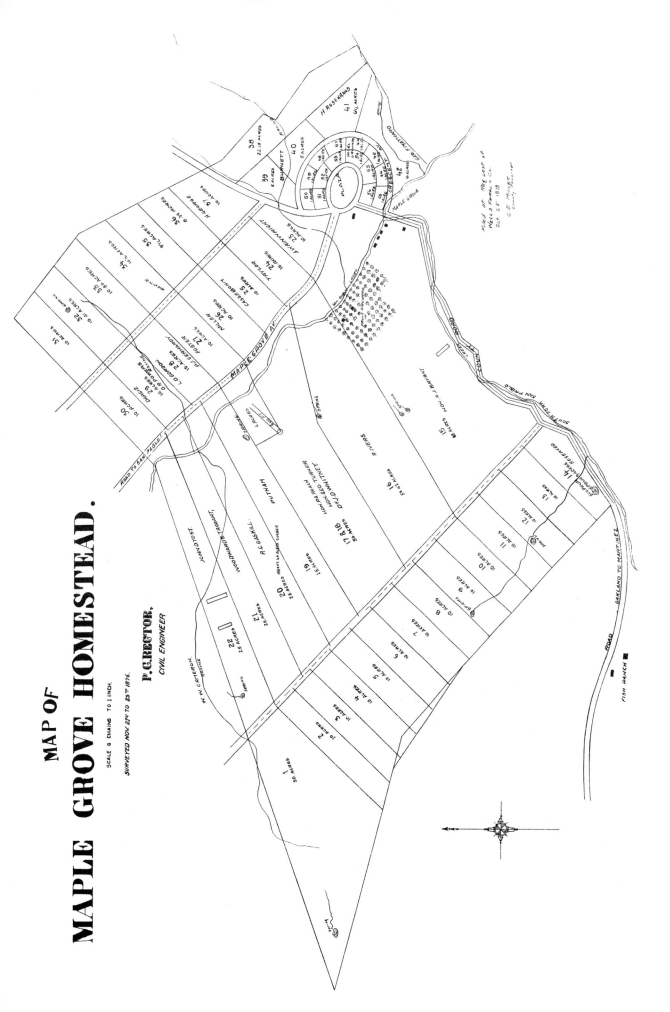

MAP OF
MAPLE GROVE HOMESTEAD.

SCALE 6 CHAINS TO 1 INCH.

SURVEYED NOV 21ST TO 25TH 1876.

P. G. RECTOR,
CIVIL ENGINEER

Filed at 7¼ past 1 o'clock at
Well's Fargo & Co.
Oct 25th 1878

C. E. Miller
County Recorder

Mayor Bryant's property included the hotel grounds around a plaza and four coal tunnels   CR

California and Nevada Railroad station was near present Highway 24-Moraga Way-Camino Pablo crossing   LLS

time at "Maple Grove"[31] in his summer and weekend home. Mrs. Frank Leslie, a visitor to San Francisco, describes Bryant as a genial gentleman with a gracious manner, as hospitable as a prince, and popular with his constituents. She wrote of her trip to Orinda, as his guest, "In one of these last days, Mayor Bryant invited us for a parting drive behind his elegant four-in-hand team. We went to Oakland, which rather disappointed us, being more city-like and less rurally beautiful than we had anticipated, but passing through the city we wound up into the hills, between high wooden slopes and constantly catching glimpses of the bay and the Golden Gate. We passed several ranches, and some green meadows completely perforated with the burrows of the gray and brown ground squirrels, who scampered about quite tame and undismayed.

"Live oak and chaparral were abundant, but everything looked brown and dusty until we reached the Mayor's own grounds, where care and irrigation will soon make a paradise around the pretty cottage which he has recently purchased as a summer home. Everything looked green and smiling, plenty of roses and other flowers, a rustic bridge, and a little summer house, all homelike and rural.

"We lunched in a pleasant company, and then walked up the hill behind the house to see the trout, artificially hatched in a pool and brook, manufactured for them, as nearly as possible on the model of their native New Hampshire streams; after this we visited the stables and horses, of which the Mayor is justly proud, sat in the cosy little house with Mrs. Bryant and her other guests, and then enjoyed one of the fastest of fast drives home in the purple twilight, and devoted the evening to the painful task of packing."[32]

Because Mayor Bryant was so widely known, although the California and Nevada Railroad did not reach the present crossroads until almost a decade after he sold the land to Samuel B. Welch in September 1884,[33] the station nearby was named Bryant Station. After 1893 the crossroads area was popularly referred to as Bryant's Corners, rather than Maple Grove.

Welch was the president of the firm of Cunningham, Curtiss and Welch, a large stationery, paper and book store in San Francisco. He was the owner when the final survey of the Sobrante was made in 1893 which showed only 70 acres in the "Welch Tract," 138 acres in the "Surplus Sobrante," and the rest on public lands. Title to all of these lands was legally confirmed.

In 1903 A. M. Souza purchased the Welch land. Three years later Souza sold it to the Syndicate Water Company which was then engaged in buying up lands in the area.[34]

Charles Hill

Between the Ward and Smith league, the Houston tract, Rancho Acalanes, and the Laguna de los Palos Colorados was another large piece of land. This land now can be found on both sides of the present freeway and includes the Charles Hill area. In the 1870's, when the boundaries of the grants were still questionable, it was difficult to tell public land from private land. A citizen who lived on lands which became or were designated as public lands, and who improved these lands, could file a claim. If he paid the taxes and his claim was to land not disputed by others, or later shown to be outside the grant line, he would eventually become the legal owner. Problems arose when claims were staked on land that would prove to belong to someone else, but just as often the claim would be on public land.

In 1874 Augustus Charles claimed 600 acres of land in the area mentioned above. Charles Hill is named after this early settler. The land was bordered on the north by the Ward and Smith league, east by the Acalanes grant, south by Taylor and Hough, and west by Hatch, and it was assessed at $2.50 per acre.[35]

South of Charles Hill, S. Hough and his son claimed 1,000 acres of land, where they lived, farmed and ranched for many years. The Houghs were well-known residents of the area, but they were forced to leave later when about three-fourths of their claim turned out to be on the Moraga grant, and the remainder on the Sobrante. The Charles claim later proved to be on the Castro Sobrante.

In 1877 Henry Pierce became the owner of the Charles land. Pierce also obtained the part of Hough's land which was in the Castro Sobrante.[36] However, when the final report of the referees in partition of the Rancho El Sobrante was made, in 1909, 843 acres of this area was declared in the "Surplus Sobrante" and was assigned to claimants Edson F. Adams, John Charles Adams and Julia Prather. This portion soon became part of the water company lands.

In 1935 Vernon Hardy purchased over 100 acres of the Charles land from Manuel Alves and Antonio Lemos who had bought it from the East Bay Water Company four years previous.[37] Hardy developed the first subdivision on Charles Hill known as Monte Vista.[38] The following year Las Vegas Road was connected with the Charles Hill Road.

IV

The Beginnings of Orinda

From 1870 on to the end of the century, there was a good deal of activity on the Castro Sobrante. In contrast to most of the Moraga Rancho which was gravitating to the ownership of one man, there were many sales on the Sobrante as owners of large parcels sold their holdings.

Richard Rowland

Huertzel, Grover and Lauterwasser, after ranging cattle on their land for eight years, had financial difficulties. They were forced to mortgage the land as early as 1865.[1] Huertzel was able to cancel his position in the mortgage in 1866 when he sold his share of the league, the most northern piece, to Richard Rowland, Andrew Walker and Martin Klinkerstrom.[2]

Richard Rowland and his family moved to Orinda and lived there until 1907 when their property was purchased by the Peoples Water Company.[3] Rowland was president of the wholesale grocery firm in San Francisco: Rowland, Walker and Klinkerstrom. His father was in the business before him. In 1852 the firm was commissioned to supply the Russian Grand Fleet. Klinkerstrom was the Russian consul in San Francisco, and, after he returned to his home country, the firm became known as Rowland and Walker.[4] It was located on Sansome Street in San Francisco.

The Rowland children, two boys and a girl, grew up in Orinda, and a grandson, Edward Rowland, now lives in Lafayette. Their Orinda home was located slightly north of the junction of San Pablo Highway, Bear Creek and Wildcat Creek Road and is now the site of the East Bay Municipal Utility District (EBMUD) corporation yard. At the time the Rowlands first lived there, the Bear Creek Road met the San Pablo Highway north of the present intersection. The Rowlands were among the first permanent settlers in Orinda. Their property includes about 450 acres.

The Grover and Lauterwasser mortgage was assigned the following year to Miller and Lux,[5] who, at the time, were engaged in buying country lands in California. Lauterwasser, personally, had another mortgage with Miller and Lux,[6] and the result was that by 1874 Miller and Lux owned both the Lauterwasser and Grover interest, amounting to 2,937 acres. Today this land comprises a large part of the developed area of Orinda lying on the north side of the freeway. The Huertzel third of the Ward and Smith league is largely owned by the EBMUD.

Alice Marsh Camron and William Camron

In 1875 William Walker Camron purchased 500 acres of the Miller and Lux property. Adjoining his land was the remaining piece of their holdings. He tried without success to obtain a right-of-way from them as he wanted to build a road that would connect his land

Elmer W. Barnes was conductor of the California and Nevada Railroad, 1895 photograph LLS

with the county road.[7] He then approached Miller and Lux again to try to interest them in subdividing the land into 160 acre parcels, but this attempt was also unsuccessful. They did, however, give him an option to buy the entire piece at $20 an acre.[8] Camron decided to buy the land, and in 1876 he paid $50,000 for the remaining Miller and Lux piece of approximately 2,455 acres, making his total holdings almost 3,000 acres.[9]

William Camron was the grandson, and not the son, as historians generally describe him, of the Reverend John Camron who had come to California in 1849. The Camron wagon train had included the Reverend and his only son, Thomas, as well as several of his eleven daughters. Thomas's wife had died previously, and he brought with him William, his six-year-old son, and his other children.[10]

The Camron name had originally been spelled Cameron, but the "e" had been dropped by Reverend Camron. After 1896, William again inserted the "e," but all records, deeds and letters until then use Camron.

The family mined for awhile and was evidently somewhat successful. They then came to Martinez where Reverend Camron built a home. Thomas settled on a farm at Danville with his son, William. Before long, on April 15, 1854, he was killed in an explosion of the steamer, *Secretary*, in San Pablo Bay. Thus, when William was eleven years old, he moved in with Judge Thomas A. Brown, his uncle, who took care of him from then on, since his step-mother had also died.[11] The cousins, young Elam Brown and William Camron, became close friends.

On September 5, 1871, William Camron married Alice Marsh at Grace Church in Martinez. Alice was the daughter of the pioneer California settler and land owner, John Marsh. She had inherited one-half of her father's estate, which included the Rancho Los Meganos. After the marriage, William managed her estate, eventually with disastrous results.

The year of the marriage, Los Meganos was sold.[12] In two years William became a director of the newly incorporated Bank of Martinez.[13] He built for his bride the twenty-room mansion on the shores of Lake Merritt that later became the Oakland Museum. The home was used as the museum for many years until the recent opening of a new museum building. The historic building is now standing unused.

The Camrons had two daughters, Amy, born in 1872; and Gracie, who was born in 1875 and lived for only two years. Amy became the collector of many of the Marsh family papers now at Bancroft Library.

Orinda is Named

When William Camron completed his purchase of the Miller and Lux acreage, he already had heavily invested in land and other projects in Contra Costa County and had a large investment in his Oakland home. He was most anxious to sell some of the property as he had over-purchased to assure himself of a way to get access to Telegraph Road. As soon as the purchase was completed, he spent $1,500 having a survey made by K. W. Taylor.[14] The resulting tract on a map dated 1876 was named Orinda Park.

The question is often asked, "Where did the name Orinda come from?" Alice Marsh Camron inherited from her famous father a few books that he had brought to California with him. Among these were two volumes of Johnson's *Lives of the Poets,* and the *Odes of*

Anacreon.[15] Alice became very interested in 17th century English poets and the classics. The books later went to her daughter, Amy, and are now at Bancroft Library. In Volume I of *Lives of the Poets* is a brief mention of the English poetess, Katherine Fowler Philips, who was known in her circle of friends as "Orinda." She was, in fact, known as the "Matchless Orinda" for what was considered her incomparable poetry.[16]

Katherine Philips became the center of a "Society of Friendship" which was in itself the subject of a poem. Philip Souers, Orinda's biographer, says: "For Orinda friendship had a peculiar meaning. It was a Platonic mingling of souls; it had about it a certain mysticism, which made it a kind of religion to be realized only by initiation into its esoteric knowledge."[17] The main theme of most of her poetry was friendship.

Among the poets of the 17th century, it was the fad to call themselves by classical names generally taken from a Latin or Greek character or name. It is a matter for conjecture as to why Katherine chose Orinda for herself, but she used it from the beginning of her writing period at a very early age. The word has various meanings,[18] but even Souers, her biographer, after the most intensive research, was unable to find her reason for choosing it, although many of the other poets' names are easy to trace.

The well-known poet, John Dryden, mentions Orinda in the famous "Ode to Mrs. Killegrew" after both of the ladies, who were close friends, had died of smallpox.[19] Another English poet of the times wrote directly to Orinda:[20]

> "The magic of Orinda's name
> Not only can their fierceness tame
> but, if that might word I once rehearse,
> They seem submissively to roar in Verse."

That the magic of the name appealed to the Camrons is evident as, in 1876, they used it for the name of their new subdivision. Perhaps the term, the Matchless Orinda, appealed to them as they looked over their new land. In the Camron scrapbooks at Bancroft Library are several newspaper clippings that dwell with the origins of Greek and unusual names and reveal their interest in classical sounding names. E. I. deLaveaga remembered hearing, as a child, his family saying that the name for the Camron estate had been taken from a book.[21] The lovely name has survived, but the "Park" was dropped after 1900.

Orinda Park Sales

William Camron was interested in improving the road situation so that his property would be more easily accessible. He surveyed a road to Berkeley (Wildcat Canyon), planning to build a turnpike road. However, money became tight for him at this time, and the road was not graded.[22] Meanwhile, the first subdivision in the area, Orinda Park, was beginning to be developed by Camron. There were several purchasers. Some were influenced by the prospects of an easier grade to Berkeley, some by the rumors of a railroad to be built to the area, and a few were real farmers.

Eugene Sullivan, who bought over 200 acres in 1879, was the first to purchase from Camron.[23] The same year Solomon E. Alden purchased 612 acres from Camron,[24] which included the Lauterwasser house and the present Sleepy Hollow and upper Miner Road area. In 1880 Camron sold about 350 acres to Herman and Alice Sandow.[25] The following year, William Minto, a well-known surveyor, purchased 73 acres,[26] adding another 100 acres in 1882.[27]

Camron's land was used during the summers of 1879 and 1880 as a summer camp for the Oakland Light Cavalry and the Oakland Guard,[28] and the name "Camp Camron" became rather familiar to bay area residents. There were also social gatherings held there. A now unknown but enthusiastic guest with the initials D.S.R. wrote a 14-stanza poem on June 27, 1880 titled "Camp Camron."[29] The first two stanzas went:

"It was summer, and the hillsides
    Day by day were growing brown,
When a band of merry campers
    Rattled out of Oakland town;
Rattled up the winding roadway,
    Past the Fish Ranch in the glen,
Down the wild San Pablo Canyon,
    Blessed of Heaven and loved of men.

Here, where birds and bees were busy,
    And the brook crept babbling by,
Snowy tents like white-winged cloudlets,
    Rose against the morning sky;
Rose amidst the bended foliage—
    Fragrant clover underneath,
And with shout and merry laughter
    Camp life opened on the heath."

Although some of the Orinda land was selling, Camron was involved in other speculations that had not turned out to his advantage, and he lost the beautiful Oakland home that he had built near the lake. Eventually, he also lost all of his wife's inheritance from her father's estate.

At 2 p.m. on June 11, 1881, he held a sale of the stock on his ranch in Orinda. Included were "finely bred horses, brood mares, work horses, pure blood and graded cattle, also vehicles and farming equipment." Neighbors and residents of Contra Costa County attended the sale, and Camron realized $14,943.[30]

The marriage of Alice Marsh and William Camron ended in divorce about 1895, after he deserted her and their daughter, Amy. The daughter of John Marsh, her funds gone, moved to San Francisco where she kept a lodging house.[31] She later moved to Santa Barbara with Amy who remained there and never married.

Jose and Miguel deLaveaga

Camron sold the remaining property that he owned in Orinda Park to Edward (Elisha) Dubois of Spanish Town, in 1883, for $20,000.[32] The property had been resurveyed the previous year by William Minto for Camron and General Theodore Wagner, who now lived on the Sandow property.[33] All of the numbered lots in the Orinda Park tract went to Dubois except for two that had been previously sold along with the larger sections. Dubois held the property for four years. In 1887 Jose and Miguel deLaveaga purchased the property consisting of 1,178.04 acres from a third party, Philip Barth, for the sum of $50,880.[34] Barth had evidently acted as owner-agent as there is a deed recording his purchase of the property from Dubois on the same day as the sale to deLaveaga. The deLaveaga family became largely responsible for the development of modern Orinda.

The California and Nevada Railroad

There was another incentive for buyers to purchase parcels of land in the Castro Sobrante and the Moraga Grant. This was the prospect of a narrow-gauge railroad coming into the area, bringing with it the easier access that was so badly needed. In 1880 a franchise was granted to the California and Mt. Diablo Railroad which organized and made a survey.[35] A line was planned in the optimism of the times, with a rosy vision of the development of the land through which it would pass and the amount of freight it would carry. The name was changed later to the California and Nevada Railroad. The route was to start in Emeryville, then to pass through Berkeley and on to San Pablo, curving eastward and winding up the east side of San Pablo Creek through the present El Sobrante area to Orinda Park, then to Lafayette, Walnut Creek, Livermore, on to Nevada, and possibly even Utah. A brochure printed in 1881 spoke optimistically of the prospect of freight, the tourist attraction of Mt. Diablo, and the prospective profits of lines running into the mining area of Nevada.[36]

It was 1885 when the first train left Emeryville for Berkeley which was as far as the track was then completed.[37] The following year there was a test run to San Pablo, and, by the next year, it was completed to Oak Grove. By 1890 trains were running to the Orinda Park station on the Symmons ranch near Wagner's,[38] but service was most unreliable and dependent on the weather. From the beginning to the end of this struggling, wood-burning, narrow-gauge railroad, it was plagued by earth slides and washouts caused by heavy rains. In the summer months stages met the train to carry passengers on to Walnut Creek,[39] but in the winter, when the rails sagged and the supports of the many wooden trestles were washed out, service ended and could not be restored until the necessary repairs and reconstruction were done. Finally, in 1891, two trains ran daily to Orinda Park from Emery Station when conditions permitted.[40]

The railroad did fulfill its aim of carrying freight, mostly hay, grain and farm produce to Oakland and supplies on the return trip for the farmers. However, it is remembered mostly for the many picnickers it brought out to the various recreation areas that developed. The San Pablo Creek provided marvelous picnic spots and swimming holes. There was one at Thode Oak Grove, another at the Clancy Ranch, a picnic area at the Symmons Ranch at Orinda Park, and one near the railroad station called Bryant, when the line did reach that far. Still another picnic area was Laurel Glen Resort on the Castro Ranch which had a dance platform and recreation area run by a Frenchman named Chapeute, popularly known as Sharkey.[41]

Another stop was at Olinda, a town planned by Victor Castro in 1888,[42] with a name so similar to Orinda that it is sometimes confused. Olinda did not survive to the present day,

Map Showing the

CALIFORNIA AND **NEVADA**

RAILROAD

and its Extensions and Connections.

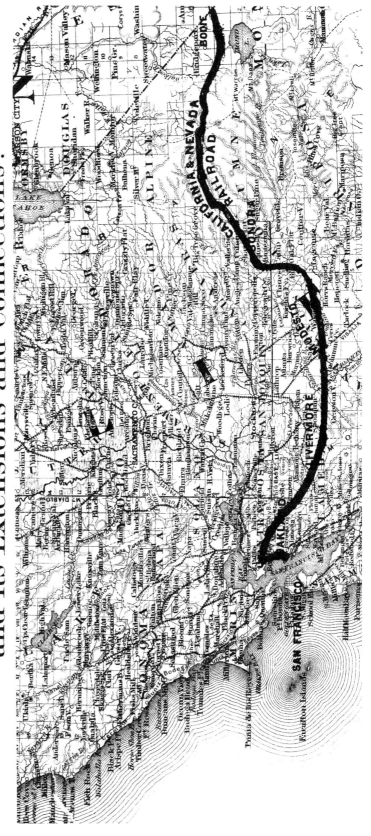

Section of a map (1882) showing the planned route as far as Bodie   LLS

and, although Castro laid out a townsite with city blocks, there was little development beside the Barrett family place and a general store. Even Barrett deserted the place by 1890. By this time the railroad was in serious financial trouble.

Grant and Williamson and the Railroad

The final partitioning of the Moraga Rancho, in 1886, showed Horace Carpentier to own almost the whole rancho or about 12,000 acres. By the late 1870's he had left California as an extremely wealthy man and was living in New York.[43]

After the death of John B. Watson, his ranch manager, in 1887, J. Arthur Burton came to California to manage the ranch for Carpentier, carrying on business with the owner through correspondence. Among Burton's relatives were the Grant Brothers who were railroad contractors. They became interested in the California and Nevada Railroad and land in the area of the Moraga Rancho. In 1889, one of the brothers, Angus A. Grant, and James A. Williamson, bought the Moraga Ranch from Carpentier on a purchase contract.[44] Williamson had been a Land Commissioner and president of a railroad.[45] Burton stayed on to manage the ranch for them, and Grant and Williamson turned their energies to the possible completion of the California and Nevada Railroad and, also, to land development.

Grant and Williamson formed the Pacific Construction and Improvement Company which leased the railroad, planning to complete the line through Charles Hill, as originally planned, with a branch to be extended toward Moraga.[46] The branch would rejoin the main railroad in Lafayette. A tunnel had been bored in 1882 through Charles Hill by a crew of Chinese laborers, but it had never been maintained.[47] In anticipation of the arrival of the railroad, grounds for a depot at Walnut Creek were donated by the Botillo family in 1891, and a construction train and a gravel train arrived on the site.[48] When the tracks were in good condition trains ran to the present Orinda crossroads,[49] and a track was graded five miles further in 1893, as far as the Glorietta area. An article from Moraga printed in the Contra Costa Gazette on May 6, 1893, reported: "Track laying will commence this week." There is no evidence that tracks were ever laid beyond Bryant Station at the Orinda crossroads although the grading was done. A good wagon road was completed by the contractors from the terminus of the railroad to Willow Springs, according to another article on April 15, 1893.

The station at the Orinda crossroads was named Bryant Station after the former local resident. The building stood opposite, slightly south, from the present Orinda theatre. A small restaurant was opened at the terminus. Close by was a willow grove and a dance platform near the creek-bed. There were two more stations in the area, Orinda Park on the Symmons Ranch and deLaveaga Station near Miner Road on the present golf course. This last old station building is still used as a garden house by the deLaveaga family who moved it closer to their home when the golf course was built.[50]

The track went over two large trestles in this area. One was near Miner Road and cut across the present golf course, hitting the hill by La Plaza Road. The track then went over the other trestle beyond which it ran above the present Orinda Grammar School and on through the old pine grove ending finally at Bryant Station. Children take a short-cut across part of the old flat road-bed when they come from Pine Grove School down toward

California and Nevada train in Orinda (1894) LLS   University of California about 1904 LAV

the Orinda School. This is one of the few places where the old grade can still be recognized.

The California and Nevada did not surmount its financial troubles. Some reorganization took place in 1893, but the Grants were still in the deal. In two years the railroad was leased to F. M. (Borax) Smith who had elaborate plans for its development. They failed to materialize. However, the transaction furnished Smith with the all-important right-of-way to the Emeryville waterfront, so he could build the trestle and pier which gave him the fastest and most direct train-ferry service to San Francisco, the "Key Route."[51] In addition, the Santa Fe, into whose hands the California and Nevada Railroad passed in 1899 with Angus Grant as receiver,[52] obtained their important trackage rights from Oakland to Richmond.

One last hope was given to the community when an article appeared stating that over $100,000 would be expended immediately by the Santa Fe in improving the old line.[53] In August daily trains were still running to Bryant, the fare being 50 cents to Orinda Park, deLaveaga or Bryant Station, or 75 cents for the round trip. Before long, however, the railroad was abandoned. It continued to deteriorate until, today, practically no trace of it, or its many trestles, can be found.

Although the line to Orinda was abandoned, the tracks from Oakland to Richmond were utilized. On March 5, 1902, the Oakland and Eastside Railroad was incorporated as a subsidiary of the Santa Fe.[54]

These tracks which are now standard gauge are still in use and run from McDonald Avenue in Richmond to the Santa Fe Oakland Depot. They are all that remain of the original California and Nevada right-of-way.

It is thought-provoking to note that the station of the new modern Bay Area Rapid Transit is located only about one quarter of a mile from where the station of the now defunct California and Nevada Railroad terminus was over seventy-five years ago.

Glorietta

Angus Grant and James Williamson bought the Moraga Rancho for $434,000 from Horace Carpentier in June of 1889. This sum was to be paid in $50,000 installments over a period of five years, with the first to be paid in February, 1890, with eight per cent interest per annum.[55] Before they left the area, they had put an investment of around $750,000 into the railroad and land development.[56] They formed the Moraga Land Association, with A. A. Grant, President, and J. A. Burton, Secretary, which undertook to divide the land into farms of from 5 to 80 acres, and they reserved two sites for towns. Brochures were issued extolling the virtues of the area and the beauty of the land.

Landholders in William Camron's Orinda Park had already put substantial investments in their properties. They shared the enthusiasm of General Wagner in the prospective development. He wrote on September 23, 1892, "Being a resident of this county in the near vicinity . . . I feel a deep interest in the matter, for nothing is more discouraging than to stand comparatively alone in any enterprise, and most of all, in building a pleasant home. . . . One of the great drawbacks of California in the past has been in fact that so many tracts of land were owned by a few men, who would not sell portions of them. . . . I therefore look upon those who bring about that result in the nature of public benefactors."[57]

The first subdivision offered to the public was called Glorietta. This was the area which

The "old yellow house" on Moraga Way was built by Captain Jenkins in 1894

Casa Vieja was built by Judge Gartlan the same year, 1894

now was made more accessible by the new railroad. The Contra Costa Gazette wrote of the unsurpassed beauty of the site of the newly planned town, the romantic sound of its name, and the pleasant country surrounding it.[58]

The following year, Grant made a trip to his Chicago office for the Moraga Land Company to try to interest farmers from the east in coming out to help develop the area.[59] Despite all of the efforts to sell the land, there were very few buyers. There were several tenant farmers on the land, many of whom had been there for years, but the only purchasers, in 1894, were James Gartlan, an Oakland attorney, and Alexander Jenkins, a captain of a ship. Jenkins bought Lot 74 of Plat B of the Moraga Land Association in July 1894, two months after the Gartlan purchase. It consisted of 2-1/5 acres.[60]

Before long, in the Gazette there appeared the following notation: "A real commodius cottage is being erected in Glorietta on the north side of Camino Pablo,"[61] perhaps referring to the Jenkins house. The house is now at 209 Moraga Highway, still standing and known as the "old yellow house." It is almost opposite the nursery location, a mile or so from the business district of Orinda. It was occupied from 1918 until 1966 by the Charles Nelson family who still own it. When Nelson bought the house, the old wagon road to Moraga was narrower and further toward the hill than the present road. There was a picket fence in front of the house, and a woodcased water well with a hand pump on the property. Later, Mr. Nelson dug a well twenty-seven feet deep underneath the house which provided excellent water.[62] The house is still the same color as it was in 1894, and it is one of the oldest existing homes in this area. The fact that the house is the color of old railroad stations has caused speculation. The house was by the graded trackbed of the California and Nevada Railroad, but, at the time it was built, the owners of the railroad had not given up the idea of completing the road. The company had been reorganized the previous year. The house has doors and windows similar to those of the old railroad stations. However, no record has yet been found of a station having been built there. Captain Jenkins may have used paint that belonged to the railroad, or there may be some facts that have not been uncovered.

There were more sales of lots made in 1898 by the Moraga Land Company,[63] but the development did not occur as hoped for. Grant and Williamson were discouraged by the failure of the railroad to be extended by Borax Smith, who now owned it, and by the failure of their land speculation. Within two years they gave up their holdings and departed for Los Angeles, taking a financial loss.[64] On September 30, 1899, Horace Carpentier was the highest bidder for the property at public auction, paying $450,000 for it,[65] close to the price for which he had sold it. His attorney, George Leviston, handled the transaction. Once again Carpentier was the owner of the Laguna de los Palos Colorados, except for the few lots that the Moraga Land Company had sold.

One of the sales made in 1898 by the Moraga Land Company was to James V. Feeley. The Bello family, whose father worked for Feeley's neighbor, Judge Gartlan, remembered Feeley as the man who taught them catechism at the school. Feeley sold the property, Lot 117, to George Sanborn of San Francisco in 1905. The Sanborn family lived there for many years, and their old house is still located on Sanborn Road.[66]

In 1902 James Gartlan was able to get a clear title to his property on the Moraga Rancho

36

from Carpentier.[67] Gartlan had purchased 10 acres, Lot 124, in May 1894, from The Moraga Land Company, but for some reason the purchase had never been recorded. Gartlan either built the Casa Vieja which still stands on Casa Vieja Road or improved an old house already on the property. Mr. Ezra Nelson remembers that when his family purchased the Jenkins house, in 1918, it was generally considered that Casa Vieja was the older place. The Gartlan property was fed by one of the excellent springs on the Moraga Ranch, and water from it is still being used.[68] When Gartlan was legally clearing his right to use the spring, it was stated in the brief that water issuing from the spring had been used for this property for a long time prior to his legal action in 1902.[69] The water issued out of a tunnel and came by a two-inch pipe to the land. The water tunnel is still in existence.

Gartlan maintained his practice in Oakland and came out to his country place on weekends and in summer. He later rode on the Sacramento Northern Railway when it was completed and often walked to his house from the station at Moraga. He was a bachelor and left his property to his secretary at his death. Casa Vieja was vacant from around 1920 to 1940, according to Mr. Harrison Sigworth, the present owner. George Brockhurst built a new road into the property with a Fresno grader, but the line of the old roadbed is still visible. The remains of a stone floor show the old site of a barn now gone.

This gathering was in front of Theodore Wagner's home   LLS

V

The People and Life in Early Orinda

Before 1921 a chain of farms stretched from Moraga to San Pablo, and the only semblance of a village between these settlements was at Orinda Park at the present junction of the Wildcat Canyon Road, San Pablo Road and Bear Creek Road. Here was located the Orinda School, a blacksmith shop and the Orinda Park Hotel. Nearby were the beautiful estates of Theodore Wagner, William Minto and Miguel deLaveaga, as well as the homes and farms of other settlers. North of the Rowland property, Jacob and Mary Baden had settled in 1874 on 500 acres of land, and they remained there until 1904.

The typical farmer had a few cows to supply his family with milk and butter, but some had sizable herds and sold their products to Shuey's Dairy Company in Oakland.[1] Hay, the chief crop, was carted by four and six-horse teams to Berkeley and Oakland livery stables and feed stores.[2]

The choice of the roads was the new Wagner Road (Wildcat Canyon) full of turns and grades or the older Summit Road (Fish Ranch). The Summit Road was used by the big teams. Cattle generally were driven to market over the hills via Wildcat Canyon and down Spruce Street in Berkeley or up Brookside Road, past the Fish Ranch, then via the Summit Road over the hills. It took two hours for a good team of horses to pull a buggy to Oakland and twice as long for teams to haul loads over either road.

Theodore Wagner

Some of the people who purchased sizable amounts of acreage in Orinda Park were enthusiastic about the future of the community, and they invested a good deal of money in their homes and in the development of their property. One of the most colorful characters who did this was General Theodore Wagner, a widower and an attorney who had come to California in 1873 to specialize in land cases. He was admitted to the Supreme Court of California in 1875 and was appointed United States Surveyor-General of California on May 22, 1878. The title of General remained with him after he left this post. He had originally come to Visalia; then he moved to San Francisco; in 1882 he moved to the home he had built in Orinda.[3]

General Wagner married Ida Sandow, daughter of Herman Sandow, who owned 365 acres of the Orinda Park Tract.[4] Sandow gave 241 acres to Ida a few years later. The Wagner family first camped on the property, which they named Oak View Ranch, then built a home there in 1882.[5] They are reported to have spent around $140,000 on their estate.[6] Ida's brother, George Sandow, later became the owner of a 73-acre section, now Fairway Acres, and Lot 23, a portion of 53 acres.

Ida Wagner raised her husband's two daughters and, also, had a son, George, and an adopted relative, Willie Sauer, whom she raised as a son; there were four children then to enjoy the beautiful home and ranch. In 1882 Wagner donated a site for a school,[7] and the Orinda Park School was built. Carrie and Lulu Wagner both attended the new school, which was at the junction of the newly planned Wagner Road to Berkeley and the road from San Pablo. History has turned a full cycle, as in the case of the railroad, as the new Wagner School is now located a short distance from the old site of the school built in 1883.

Theodore and Ida Wagner's estate was almost a complete unit within itself. Even a brick-kiln had been built on the property to save the long haul from Berkeley during the construction of the buildings.[8] There was a carbide gas plant, drying plant, store house, mushroom cellars, a complete dairy and barns, a conservatory, and the first telephone in Orinda.[9]

As the property has remained in possession of the EBMUD, the interested can still visualize the location of the house from old foundations, see the old stone bench and wall that a garden path leads to, and make out the remnants of the vineyards and the large apple, peach, plum, cherry and walnut orchard. And high on the hill is a large grove of old olive trees. There are still some fence posts visible along the line of the old cypress hedge which enclosed about ten acres of the estate and which once marked the entrance and the road to the bridge that crossed the creek. An old pear orchard remains on the hill above the highway.

With this investment, Wagner was certainly glad to see Grant and Williamson plan in 1889 for the completion of the railroad and the development of part of the Moraga Ranch.

The hospitality of General and Mrs. Wagner was known all over the county. They had reputations for being excellent hosts, and one annual occasion was the Independence Day Celebration. On the Fourth a bandstand was set up along with many picnic tables. Chinese cooks prepared the food for days, and on this day, as well as Admission Day, all the localites and friends came to share in the delights. Patriotic oratory, music, barrels of lemonade and iced ginger beer, decanters of Wagner's own fine wines, ice cream and all of the trimmings were offered along with the spectacular fireworks. Down the stream a short walk was a beautiful fish pond.[10] Wagner School, through its nature area program, has cleared many of the old sites.

Wagner maintained his law practice after retiring as Surveyor-General and was a partner of Eli Chase with offices in Martinez. Chase had been District Attorney for Contra Costa County. Wagner was well thought of in the county, and, in 1886, he was invited to give the speech at the annual County Fair, which was a big event. An excerpt from the speech gives a glimpse into the times in which he lived. He said, "Today is the 36th anniversary of the birth of this glorious state. Just imagine what this county was 36 years ago today. The land was here and it was just as productive then as now, but what was the county then: There were no roads, and but a few wheeled vehicles and those only ox carts with solid homemade wheels. When we look at the display in the pavilion today, the transformation seems wonderful and reflects credit on the men who brought it about. . . . But while we have accomplished much, a great deal more remains to be done; there are many drawbacks and complaints. There is a very general impression that the producer does not get his fair share of the reward of his toil and the need of concert of action among farmers became apparent. This finally resulted in the organization of the Patrons of Husbandry whose lodges or different branches are called Granges. Farmers . . . are at a disadvantage over those that

Orinda Park,
Contra Costa County, Cal.
June 28th 1890

To **Albert Stone & family**

You are respectfully invited to attend a
Natal-Day Celebration at Wagner's Ranch,
Orinda Park, Contra Costa County, Cal., on

—July Fourth, 1890—

The exercises will commence at 11 o'clock A. M. with
a National Salute, after which a Prayer will be offered, then the Declaration of Independence will be
read, after which Singing of National Hymns, and
then an appropriate Poem will be recited.

After partaking of Luncheon an Address will be delivered, and from thence the time will be filled out
with patriotic Songs and Music until evening, when
a Display of Fireworks will close the Exercises.

Theo. Wagner and Wife.

This yearly social occasion in Orinda Park was attended by many prominent guests   LLS

live in communities, in towns and localities within reach of daily mails, daily newspapers and the telegraph, while in most cases the farmer only has his weekly paper. This isolation, if not counteracted, is what makes our children often bashful and awkward; it is a mistake to suppose that hard work does it."[11]

The Wagners took many first prizes at the fair with their produce. Here was where the farmers exhibited their products; and their wives brought the jellies, jams, preserved fruits, plants and handiwork. The Oak View Ranch premium butter was regularly advertised for sale at Blum Bros. in the Contra Costa Gazette.[12] An article in 1887 tells that General Theo Wagner had "a splendid exhibit of apples, pears, quinces, grapes, dried fruits, prunes, raisins, nuts, butter . . . one of the most attractive features of the pavilion exhibit at the county fair."[13]

On July 10, 1887, a tragic fire burned the Wagner home to the ground. The fire started from a defective chimney in a kitchen stove. Although a servant girl alerted Mrs. Wagner and the children as soon as she saw the smoke, and men came running from the fields, only the parlor could be entered. A piano, organ and some furniture was saved, but the money value of the loss in no way covered the valuable surveyor instruments, silverware, the costly library and most of the beautiful furnishings in the house, many of which had been made to order.[14] Within a month, Wagner had let a contract to rebuild the house on a somewhat reduced scale.[15]

Orinda Park Hotel

Wagner also built a hotel on his property at the junction of the roads from Martinez, San Pablo and Berkeley. The old foundations can still be seen on the northeast corner of the junction. According to Carmel Martinez, a descendant of the pioneer Martinez family, the hotel was first built in 1885 but, evidently, was not a success, probably due to the fact that a liquor license could not be obtained.[16] The hotel was rebuilt in 1889,[17] the year the railroad reached Orinda Park, and was leased by August and Catherine Kuehne who ran it. By summer of that year it was open for business.[18] The following ad ran in the newspapers:

ORINDA PARK HOTEL
August Kuehne, Manager
is now open.
Rooms limited. Camping ground available.
Postoffice on premises.
Beautiful scenery unsurpassed.
Distance from Oakland by Walnut Creek road—11 miles
and from Berkeley by new Wagner Road—8 miles.

Hunters and fishermen used the hotel during the seasons, and there were plenty of boarders during harvest season. Visitors could drive out from Oakland over the Fish Ranch Road, have a fine meal for fifty cents, return home by Wildcat Road, or spend the night.[19]

When the hotel was closed, the community used it for their parties and dances. The building was torn down about 1913.

The failure of the railroad, the slow development of the Moraga Ranch, and the large mortgages on their investment, which may have had more enthusiasm than good judgment

The foundation was commenced on August 15th 1887 and the building is to be finished complete on Thanksgiving day, 1887.

Our family consists at this time of the following

Theodore Wagner,
Ida Wagner,
Carrie Wagner,
Louise Wagner,
George J. Wagner,
Willie Sauer.

Placed in the cornerstone—a document, bottle of wine and packages of seeds LLS

Jeff Harris's milkroute in 1904 took him past this entrance to Miner Road LLS

behind it, were discouraging to the Wagners. By 1891 the property and the hotel were owned by Moses Hopkins (a brother of Mark Hopkins) who held the mortgage.[20] For ten years, Hopkins had been buying up mortgages and large tracts of watershed land, particularly in this area of the Castro Sobrante. Although Hopkins died in 1892 at 72 years of age, his lands eventually all went into the Contra Costa Water Company holdings, which, in 1907, became the Peoples Water Company, later absorbed by the East Bay Water Company. The manager of the water company used the old Wagner house for his residence.

Theodore Wagner moved to Berkeley in 1895 where he built a beautiful home, and his sons attended the University of California. He later moved to Glen Ellen, to Casa Wagner, which adjoined Jack London's property.[21]

When the old Orinda home was torn down, William Borland built a cottage on part of the foundations and leased a large tract of land from the water company on which he ran cattle.[22] This cottage was razed in 1950 when the water company sold the building.

Wagner's touch was still close when, in an old cornerstone, was found a sealed bottle containing a document in General Wagner's handwriting, a bottle of wine from the old winery, and three packages of seeds.[23]

The Sullivan Family

Eugene Sullivan first came to Orinda in the 1870's, and, for a time, he leased and farmed some land adjoining that of his brother, Patrick, who was already located in the area of Wildcat Creek near the present Tilden Park.[24] In 1879 he purchased the 250-acre piece from William Camron[25] that today stretches from the end of the county-maintained portion of El Toyonal to the Wildcat Canyon Road. Part of the property was later shared with the O'Brien family who also ranched there. The roads join through the Sullivan property but are not as yet accessible from the El Toyonal side in the winter. Gates were opened in 1937 so the public could use the road when weather permitted.

Patrick Sullivan failed to return home from a trip to Oakland on March 28, 1881, and his family found his shot-riddled body near the road and his wagon. Patrick had accused a neighbor, Robert Lyle, of stealing pigs from his ranch. Because of the ensuing feud, footprints in the area of the shooting, and the fact that his shotgun had been recently fired using shot the size of those found in Sullivan's body, Lyle was accused of murder. A trial was set, but, despite the evidence, he was discharged the following month.[26] Patrick Sullivan left a wife and seven or eight children.

Many of the families of old Orinda left for three reasons: The children left the ranches for the city, to be followed by the older folks; the water company bought up as much land as it could; and many of the ranches were lost in mortgages.[27]

Eugene Sullivan and his family did not leave but stayed until the present day. They worked hard at their ranch, and, although they built a large home and barns, they did not invest as Wagner had with the hopeful expectations of community development but lived only as farmers.

In 1913, one of the sons, James, who attended the Orinda Park School in the 1890's, married Florence McNeil, who had come in 1907 to teach in the same school. The couple lived in Richmond, briefly, but soon lived on the Orinda ranch which they operated until only a few years ago. Jim Sullivan was for a time a builder, and he constructed the Orinda Country Club as well as other buildings and homes that Edward deLaveaga planned in the 1920's. From 1932 to 1938, Florence and Jim Sullivan operated the Orinda Creamery which was one of the first milk companies to deliver to the area. The completion of the low-level tunnel brought large creameries into competition with the Sullivan dairy.

Soon after 1900, Jeff Harris had operated the Varsity Creamery on San Pablo Road near Bear Creek. There also had been a dairy on the north corner of the deLaveaga property on San Pablo Road, operated by the Azeveda family and later leased by the Fleitz family, but it was torn down in 1924 when the EBMUD pipeline from the Mokelumne was planned to come through the location.

Florence Sullivan now lives in Walnut Creek. She has maintained her interest in Orinda and its past and is blessed with an excellent memory. She wrote[28] long ago of the trip bringing her to teach at the Orinda Park School. When she first saw Orinda, the old had begun to decline and the new had not yet started.

MEMORIES OF ORINDA
Florence Sullivan

"It had rained and rained incessantly during the latter part of February and most of March in 1907. The roads were washed away in many places and one passed a multitude of tiny rivulets as his horse carefully picked his way along deep ruts of mud, struggling desperately at times to extricate the wheel from a particularly stubborn mud hole. This was my introduction to the Contra Costa hills. We started from the S.P. Station in Berkeley, thence out Spruce Street, past the reservoir and on around, turn after turn of the road. What a vista of new life was opening up before me: green rolling hills, a mass of budding leaves and occasionally a tiny spot indicating a farm with its attendant houses. This was living! Far from the noise of the city where you could pause long enough to wonder what it was all about anyway.

"Finally we reached a spot which Mr. Ed Rowland, driver of the wagon, told me was called Cape Horn, so called because of the wind that always blew there and the sharp turn. We left Wildcat Creek behind us and now journeyed on, looking down below us to San Pablo Creek and more tiny ranches. The road was washed out ahead of us, so we opened a gate and drove over the hills, part of the time on the trail and then again over an open field. It was steep and the horses slipped, the brakes squeaked and I gasped. Maybe this wasn't going to be such a good country after all. But eventually the valley was reached and we stopped before an interesting farm house with a wide veranda, the Rowland home. Here some of our passengers remained but it seemed to me I was to go on and on.

"I was tired by this time. About two hours had elapsed, and one can satisfy oneself in that time, no matter how hungry you are for the great outdoors, if you have been holding your breath with anxiety for much of the time. On we went past the school where I was to hold forth. It was a tiny one-room affair with the usual steps, small door, two ante-rooms and blackboard lined interior. To our left was the old hotel. This was something to investigate when I had an opportunity. The chimneys leaning at different angles, the windows boarded up, the eves sagging, weeds everywhere but green and most attractive and seeming to in-

From the Sullivan Ranch and Dairy was a view of Briones Dam site   FS

vite one to come closer. Mr. Rowland told me that this hotel had not been a success and that its builders had had to give up the operating of it and close the doors. I began to think the place I was coming to was undergoing a sort of decay. Prosperity didn't seem to be lurking anywhere, and I found myself wondering where I was going to live.

"A little ways past the hotel I could see the roof of what looked to be quite a mansion hidden among foliage and large oaks. This, I was told, was the home built by General Wagner. He had spent a fortune on the place, had planted pears, peaches, apples, olives and even persimmons; in fact, it was difficult to name any tree that had not been given a try to see what it could do.

"The grounds around the home had been laid out with infinite care, a hedge here, an ivy grown oak there. As you wandered you came to an enclosure hidden by a fence of cypress and box wood. A platform had been built and here the band would play on a Sunday afternoon while the delighted neighbors would bathe in the glory of the music and surrounding grounds. Now you would see a young couple stray off. Were you to follow them you would be amazed at the new surprise revealed just beyond the hedge. It was a gigantic fish pond, all of cement and surrounded by many varieties of flowers and shrubs. A bench here, a cozy seat there, almost anywhere your eyes strayed you would spot Dan Cupid busy with his darts. A fountain sprang up from the center of the pond, shooting forth a tiny spray of water, the birds fluttering near, and in the branches above the many songs could be heard.

"But this was what had been—not what I was to see—for all that glory was past and now the well-kept walks were still beautiful but neglected by human hands. Nature had been busy both beautifying and destroying. The fine old house was sagging and in bad repair. General Wagner was no longer there, and it all seemed neglected and alone.

"On we went while I listened to this story. Finally we turned to our left, over a bridge and stopped at a very attractive little house with high steps leading up to it. A tall bewhiskered man and a smiling little woman greeted us and I learned my new friends were Mr. and Mrs. Falkenburg, a lovable German couple who were willing, in spite of many warnings, to house the new school maam. By this time I was most grateful for their hospitality. It was nearly dark and something did smell so good. My trunk was placed in my little room and, after a delicious meal and a visit with the Falkenburgs, I was glad to climb into bed and in no time was fast asleep.

"The next day was Sunday. I learned the way to walk to school, had the precious key in my possession and hastened over to get acquainted with my new realm and plan my first day. It was great fun. When I opened the door, I immediately sensed that something was amiss. One window was open, books were scattered about, a little ink had been spilled, the desk had been ransacked and the blackboards were covered with the messages of the intruders. I must stop this, I thought. Throwing open the windows, I started a general reorganizing. In a short time all evidence of vandalism was forgotten and everything was in readiness for the first day. There was the bell, a big hand affair, the clock was swinging its pendulum, the erasers and chalk were ready, the legal cap paper in a neat pile. It didn't take much for the register told me I need only expect about seven or eight pupils. After carefully closing windows and locking the door, I went back home well satisfied with the whole, big beautiful world.

48

"Many were the stories I heard of the people of Orinda. In the Wagner place were living Mr. and Mrs. Smith; nearby was Mr. Patterson; in a cottage surrounded by roses lived Mrs. Helene Chester and her two boys, Sydney and Cyril; across the road and up the hill lived Dr. Bateman, in the old Minto place. He had two tiny girls.

"I learned that if you took the next road to the left, you passed the picturesque chapel, a little white building which had been erected by Mrs. M. A. deLaveaga. On further you came to the road leading up to the beautiful deLaveaga home where young Mr. and Mrs. Edward I. deLaveaga lived. Continuing on this road by the Lauterwasser Creek, you came to the Symmons house (on the left). Here lived Mr. and Mrs. Symmons, and their son, Jack, who raised beautiful horses.

"On further we passed several bridges and trees which almost met in the road, and upon the branches hung deep strands of moss. At the end of the road lived George Brockhurst, a bachelor. All in between were Portuguese families. The general occupation of the people seemed to center around cows and raising hay. I found that the community center was the old hotel where the dances were held in what had been the dining room. The music was generally an accordion and a violin or else a banjo and a piano. There was to be a dance soon and I began to thrill at the thought of it.

"It was nine o'clock! I reached for the bell, walked out on the platform and rang vigorously. In stomped the children. Just six. There were Sydney Chester, John, Joseph and Julia Bettencourt, and two small Portuguese, brother and sister."

The Miner Family

Memories and landmarks were also left in Orinda by the Miner family. Solomon Alden, of Oakland, onetime owner of the Oakland home which later became Children's Hospital of the East Bay, purchased 612 acres from Camron as an investment in 1879.[29] This was the Sleepy Hollow and Upper Miner Road section where Smith had his rodeo grounds years before and where Lauterwasser had built his home.

Alden's nephew, James Ogden Miner, brought his family to live on the ranch in the fall of the same year. He improved the old Lauterwasser home and raised hay and blooded horses. The Miner family named the farm "Brookbank." James built the road along Lauterwasser Creek which is now called Miner Road.

When Solomon Alden died in 1884, his niece, Ann E. Miner, inherited the 612 acres and, in 1887, she sold the land to James.[30] Occasionally, he would lease small sections to other farmers,[31] but, for the most part, he continued to operate the whole farm.

James Miner died in 1909, at the age of 72, and, in two years, his wife, Anna, and his daughters, Gertrude A. Cotton, Edith Miner and Anita F. Macy, signed the land back to Ann Miner in consideration of the mortgage indebtedness to her.[32] The family loved and remembered their life here, but, like others, they found it was hard to make farming and horse raising a prosperous business in Orinda.

George Brockhurst

After James died, his sister, Ann Miner, rented the farm to George Brockhurst, and, in 1917, Brockhurst purchased about 200 acres of the 612-acre piece.[33] He and his wife lived in the

James Miner farmed and raised horses where Sleepy Hollow School was later built   RB, AB

Mr. and Mrs. James Miner in the parlor of their Orinda ranch home in the 1880's   RB

old Miner house. This was the first sale of the land since 1879 outside of the Miner family. Brockhurst farmed the land until he sold in 1924,[34] when he moved to a home on El Toyonal.

Henry Brockhurst, George's father, had settled in 1883 on land which is now mostly inundated by the waters of the San Pablo Dam.[35] Here George and his brother, Ben, were raised. Both of them spent all of their lives in the area—George in Orinda and Ben in Walnut Creek. Both were prominent in Contra Costa County. George was only twelve years old when the family came to Orinda, living until 1963 to the age of 92.[36] He remembered the struggling California and Nevada Railroad, went to the old Mount Pleasant School, and danced in the old hotel.

George was known unofficially as the "mayor" of Orinda, being a backbone of the community with his participation in community affairs. He later took care of Orinda roads with his teams of horses and, at one time, had a large barn near the creek in back of the present location of the Orinda Store. For twenty-one years he served as a trustee of the Orinda School District before retiring in 1939. His story of trips to Berkeley through the old, unlighted high-level tunnel told the adventure of living in Orinda during the early 1900's. He recalled, "I was driving a six-horse team through the tunnel, and all of a sudden my lead-span got around to the side of the wagon and the whole team was in a dickens of a snarl. I had no light and was at my wits end. But finally, I left the team and walked back to the mouth of the tunnel, and as luck would have it, met a fellow who had a candle. With that dim and flickering light, I untangled my team and got safely through."[37] At that, the tunnel was an improvement to the steeper grade over the Summit that earlier teams had to face.

More about the Miners

When Ann Miner died in 1925, she left the remainder of the property, some 400 acres, to Gertrude Miner Cotton.[38] This area has been designated on some maps and spoken of as the Cotton Tract.

The three Miner girls compiled a scrapbook of their memories of life in Orinda in the 1880's and 1890's.[39] Here are a few excerpts from the book: "There were busy years. Lots to do. Much hard work. Roads to be built, barns for the horses, barns for the hay, bridges, fences and pastures to be fenced for the stock, mostly horses.

"Dad brought with him his lovely stallion, Don Victor, and continued to raise fancy riding and driving horses. Whenever the time came to sell a team, he hated to part with them, and the $500 in $20 gold pieces that he brought into the house never compensated....

"The Isabella grapes Dad planted grew to cover a large arbor by the side of the house.... A small family orchard out in front did nicely for years, and the garden through Mother's supervision saw climbing roses about the house, a large syringa bush, a glory in the spring, also the row of lilac bushes and the many roses and annuals.

"Dad had three hay wagons made to order, longer than the usual wagon used. Each of ours held two and a half tons! The hay was sold in Oakland and hauled there in six-horse team wagons. Other farmers were hauling hay, too, and if you chose to drive to Oakland you'd find yourself behind a long slow-moving hay wagon which you managed to pass only to find another one—there were twenty to twenty-three of them every summer morning and—deep dust! Our linen dusters were really needed!

"It was a game with us to follow the creek. We knew just when the gold and silver-backed ferns grew, where to find the best bank of maiden-hair and when and where to find the many, many lovely wild flowers. We poured over the pages of Buck and Parsons and learned to name so many of them.

"When we first needed teaching, the Orinda School District had not yet been organized so we three girls had a governess. Then Gertrude went to Oakland to stay with relatives and attend school there and later Edith spent some years at Fields Seminary. When it was Anita's turn the little school house on the hill near the Wagner place was a reality and she went there for a time. At first, big sister, home now from school, drove her in a cart. Five gates to open on the way! Then, she went alone on horseback. Next in a cart taking along Maggie, the cook's little girl, and picking up on the road to school, Willie and Josie Minto. Others came to school on horseback or in carts and before the school bell rang all horses were unsaddled, unhitched and tethered for the day. Competent little country kids! And Miss Parkhurst was a good teacher, too.

"What food we did not raise we bought in Oakland. Mail came from Oakland. Later, quite thrilling, by Rural Free Delivery from Berkeley. We only had to ride about a mile to the mail box on San Pablo Road.

"No phone, no electric light, no refrigerator except as you cooled your icebox with ice from town. A wood stove to cook on. A fireplace in the front room, and, oh yes, on your wood stove you heated your sadirons and ironed your starched and embroidered undies and your long skirts and changed your iron so often to keep it at correct heat. You washed with a wash board and boiled your clothes in a big tin boiler.

"There were many guests at the ranch which father and mother enjoyed. Friends came to hunt and fish. There were quail, cottontail and doves in season, trout in the creek. In the winter, at high water, salmon came up San Pablo Creek and we had many a 10 or 12 pound fish that the men got with a pitchfork for a spear."

In later years the Miner girls moved away from Orinda, but Miner Road still follows the same course up Lauterwasser Creek as when James Miner built it in 1879 for an entrance to his home.

William Minto

Another prominent Orinda resident was William Minto who owned the 170 acres[40] now, the area of Acacia Road, Haciendas Circle and Bobolink, as well as the Claremont Avenue property on the west side of Camino Pablo. Minto's home was located between Claremont Avenue and Sol Brae and had lovely grounds with a guest house and a stable.

Minto was a prominent surveyor and had been, at one time, an assistant to Wagner. With Wagner and Camron, he resurveyed the Orinda Park Tract in the spring of 1882, the new road planned to Berkeley, and the Oak View Ranch area.[41] Another big job that Minto had locally was to make a survey of the Rancho El Sobrante in 1878. Within four years this survey was set aside in an involved decision of the Secretary of the Interior, and another was ordered to be made.[42] El Sobrante was one of the most complicated grants in all of California, its boundaries based on those of the adjoining ranchos.

There was always some activity near the present Oakland-Walnut Creek and Orinda-Moraga crossing. From the days of Conklin's Hotel and Tavern, there seems to have been an eating establishment there, sporadically. The railroad opened a restaurant for a time. There were some cabins and picnic spots in the vicinity of the Willows restaurant, and near here, also, was Edward S. Gerow's blacksmith shop. Gerow settled in Orinda in 1880[43] and operated his shop into the 1900's. (He was seventy-four years old in 1904 and still was on the voting list in Orinda). Two of his daughters married into local families and spent most of their lives in the area. Adelaide Gerow married Charles Allen, step-grandson of Elam Brown of Lafayette, who had purchased the Acalanes grant. She remembered that her father had stayed until the Sacramento Northern Railway replaced the stage to Oakland.[44] Adelaide was one of the eight pupils in the first class at Orinda Park School in 1882.

Esther Gerow married James E. Symmons in 1905. His family had arrived in Orinda in 1883 to operate the James Eva ranch near Bear Creek Road where the Orinda railroad station was located.[45] Esther and James lived on the George Sandow property until 1917,[46] when they moved to Walnut Creek. This property of 70 acres is now known as Fairway Acres section of Orinda. Their home was located above Miner Road near Oak Arbor, where the Franklin Kales later built a beautiful Spanish-type home, now owned by the Woodburn Lambs. Here they farmed and raised blooded horses, according to Florence Sullivan.

There was quite a commotion, in 1896, when John Symmons applied for a liquor license to be used in connection with the picnic grounds on the ranch, used mostly by railroad passengers. A protest was mailed to Martinez signed by nearly all of the voters in the district, and the license was refused. Mr. Symmons also agreed that it was probably best to run a temperance grounds at Orinda Park, and the matter was amicably settled.[47] Both the ranch and Wagner's Hotel were too close to the Orinda Park School to get liquor licenses.

The Fortiers and The Reynolds

Both of the Gerow girls lived long lives and shared many of their memories to enrich our glimpse into the past. Mrs. Symmons remembered the Pierre A. Fortier family who, in 1892, lived in Mayor Bryant's old home. The Fortiers planned to purchase the estate from S. B. Welch[48] who owned it at that time. They did not stay long, but they had an interesting idea for their place. They dammed the creek against the advice of the local residents and planned to use the water for a spectacle factory, but, instead, their home was almost washed away.[49] They both became ill shortly thereafter, and within three years gave up their plans and moved to San Francisco, cancelling their agreement to purchase the property.[50]

The E. G. Reynolds family had a ranch on the Moraga Rancho for many years located in Indian Valley. When the Fortiers left, the Reynolds family rented the Welch place and lived in the old Bryant home. One of the daughters, Alma Reynolds, attended the local school with Olivette Moraga and the other local children.

For a time there was another blacksmith shop in Orinda besides the reliable Ed Gerow's on Telegraph Road at the crossroads. Joe Roland was a bachelor and was no relation to the Rowland family. His shop was on the hill not far from the location of the Orinda Park School, near the intersection of the present San Pablo Dam Road, and the Wildcat Canyon Road. He had a reputation for intemperance, and the shop was not always found open. For a short time the local post office was here.[51]

In May 1899 Roland had some callers in the middle of the night. Henry Welch dropped in about 3 a.m., asked for some money which he did not receive, then left and returned in a little while with some wine. James Clancy also arrived, and the three men sat around drinking. An altercation started during which Welch supposedly pulled a knife, and Clancy shot and killed him in self-defense.[52] A jury composed of Edward Rowland, then the constable of Orinda Park, Rafael Martinez, Rudolph Ehlers, George Brockhurst, Alexander Fleitz, D. C. Moore and T. W. Martinez decided that Clancy should be tried for murder. A trial was held and much testimony given on both sides of the case, but, in the final result, Clancy was found not guilty because of justified self-defense.[53]

Oldtimers and Romance

Another family who had settled on a quarter section of land on Bear Creek, as early as 1856, participated in Orinda Park activities. Nicholas Brenzel was one of the very earliest farmers on land which is now under the water of the Briones Dam. Brenzel was murdered by his partner on May 21, 1859, at his Orinda home. Mrs. Brenzel, left with five children, married Jacob I. Ehlers about 1862. Seven children were born to the Ehlers who later farmed over 250 acres. It was not until 1909 that this family moved to Berkeley.[54]

The Rowland family had been living for some years on the old Huertzel property when the Sullivans, Brockhursts, Currans, Lasserots, Badens, Symmons, Grays, Gerows, Mintos, Miners, Hopkins, Sandows, Wagners, deLaveagas and others arrived to settle in Orinda. Further on down toward San Pablo, on land now inundated by waters of the San Pablo Dam, were the Wohlfroms, Clancys, Muirs, Warneckes and other families who often participated in local events.

The population was not large, but there was no lack of romance among the young people who met at the dances, picnics and family gatherings. Sarah Gray, a daughter of John Gray who had purchased land across the creek from the Rowlands, studied nursing in San Francisco. She and her sister boarded there during the week, but they returned on weekends riding on the California and Nevada line when it ran. She remembered that the roof of the small passenger coach of the train leaked so badly that she and her sister raised umbrellas to keep from getting shower baths while traveling.[55] Sarah married August Warnecke, Jr. from the ranch now at the bottom of the reservoir.

August Warnecke's sister, Charlotte, married Joseph Wohlfrom from the adjoining ranch. There were still more Warneckes to add to the romance. Dora Warnecke, another sister, became George Sandow's second wife after the death of his first wife. Their wedding was held at the Warnecke home, and the reception took place at the Orinda Park Hotel.

Orinda Park Social Club.

Admit Mr. ....and Ladies,

Saturday Evening, ...189......

Compliments of ....

ADMISSION, 50 CENTS.

This card admitted members to parties in the old hotel—abandoned when this was taken   FS

The party rode to the Orinda Park Station on the train from the Warneckes, and then a team of Colonel Thornton's horses met to haul them up the hill to the hotel from the depot; however, the team balked, and the bridal party had to walk most of the way.[56]

Mary Ehlers married William Curran, and Rudolf Harding Ehlers married Emma Brockhurst. With George Sandow's sister, Ida, married to General Wagner, Esther Gerow married to James Symmons, and Florence McNeil married to James Sullivan, it is certain that many of the community festivities consisted of weddings. In 1904 there was another wedding of a member of a famous old-time family when Woodward J. Martinez married the girl who had come to teach at the Orinda Park School, Fanny Tyrell.

Martinez Family

The Martinez family was not immediately on the Castro Sobrante, but on the border and considered a part of the Orinda life.[57] Jose Martinez, son of the pioneer, Don Ignacio Martinez, had purchased 1,670 acres of the Briones grant in 1860 for his son, Rafael, who lived there most of his life. The location of the Hacienda Santa Domingo in Bear Valley which was home to three generations of the family has been changed by the construction of the Briones Dam. Rafael's two sons, Rafael, Jr. and Woodward, grew up at the Hacienda. The family attended the Santa Maria Church in Orinda after it was built in 1892.

Woodward's daughter, Carmel, has researched and recorded much of the Martinez family history. Fanny Tyrell, her mother, taught in the Orinda Park School about 1902–3 before her marriage to Woodward, who had previously attended the same school. Woodward was Orinda's first mail carrier for rural free delivery in Orinda in 1903.

A 300-acre section of the Martinez property was purchased by Edward Hampton in 1927. In 1933 Hampton deeded 70.62 acres to Contra Costa County to be used and maintained as a public park. The property was used by the Mt. Diablo Council of Boy Scouts for hikes and overnight camping trips for many years until the advent of the Briones Dam, and it is well-remembered by many young men of Orinda. Hampton, who died in 1935, was buried according to his wishes on a high knoll overlooking his ranch home. He had dug a huge hole, constructed a crypt and had the ground consecrated by a Catholic Priest. His friend, R. D. Fearey, another resident along Bear Creek, was his confidant in his secret plan and saw that it was carried out.[58]

Social Activities

Parties were often held in the local schoolhouses, Orinda Park, and Moraga which was about a mile and one-half southwest from the crossroads. A typical social notice ran in the Contra Costa Gazette, December 5, 1885: "A party was held at the newly rebuilt Orinda Park School-house last Saturday. It rained, and the party lasted until 6 a.m. Sunday. Refreshments were served by Misses Rowland and Wagner, and Mrs. Minto." Parties were very apt to last until dawn, particularly in the rainy season. It was much more fun to be at a party than to face the difficult combination of darkness, horses and buggies, when the roads were muddy from the rain and chuckholes could not be seen. Transportation presented enough problems even in the daylight when the rains were heavy.

Another article two years later included many of the residents from both sides of the

Mr. Rowley, E. I. deLaveaga, and James Sullivan (1920's) FS   deLaveaga home (1915) FS

Telegraph Road: "The first social gathering in the vicinity after the winter season was held in the Orinda Park Schoolhouse, Friday evening, May 15, 1887. Edward Rowland and Dell Miller were sponsors. Dancing at 9 o'clock and supper at 12. At daylight all departed." Those present included General and Mrs. Wagner, the Grays, Symmons, Mrs. Warnecke and Mrs. Arreagada, the Misses Buckley, Clancy, Rowland, Warnecke, Wagner, Thompson, Muir, Norman, Brockhurst, Arreagada, Devlin, Lawless, Heinforde and the Messrs. Rowland, Miller, Clancy, Warnecke, Wilson, Thompson, Hunsacker, Moore, Smith, Trainer, McHale, Rivers, Ehlers, Brensel, Scanlon, Buckley, Van Duyn, Arreagada, Wagner, Amend, Reilly, Symmons, Devlin, Brockhurst and Morgan.[59]

Parties held in the Moraga schoolhouse often included settlers who had been living on the Moraga ranch for years, as well as residents from Telegraph Road. In November 1888 a party included the Arreagadas, Ninos, Mulhollands, Welchs, Buckleys, Kings, Williams, Dunns, Huesteds, Van Duyns, Rowlands, Lamps, Houghs, Daleys, Pachecos.[60]

There were parties at the Orinda Park Hotel and in people's homes as well. Old Decemcember, whose identity is lost to us now, wrote the local social news for the Gazette, and here is what he says about New Year's Eve in 1896 and a party given by William Attebury and his sisters, Ruth and Lydia. "Long before it was finished (supper), the Happy New Year shout, the firing of guns and the ringing of bells was o'er. The folks took to dancing after supper, and the sweet mourning tones of the organ, even while sounding the lively waltz seemed to have a lingering regret for the old year. The ladies took advantage of the leap year and chose their partners."[61]

Every Sunday during the summer, Orinda went to the horse races on the long straight stretch between the Symmons and the Gray ranches.[62] This is the area where Contra Costa cattleman, Frank Dutra, has for many years had the headquarters of his Orinda cattle ranch.

Another activity was a hunting club with headquarters at the Sullivan ranch. Dogs were trained to hunt out coyotes, coons and wildcats.[63] Then there were baseball games on the Symmons ranch. To quote a local scribe, "The weekly fieldday of the Orinda Park Athletic Club was held at the baseball grounds last Sunday. Not only was the baseball a grand success, but also the horse-racing, foot-racing, and boxing. The first event of the day was a championship game between the Orinda Parks and Bear Valleys."[64] Varied sporting events were also available at the University of California which some of the young people of the area attended.

Rafael Martinez, Jr. was the first president of the Orinda Park Social Club which was formed mainly for the young people. According to Mrs. Delight deLaveaga there were two distinct sets in Orinda: the more adventurous "Periwinkles," and those who belonged to the Orinda Park Social Club, whose membership was strictly invitational and its smart white cards mandatory. Once a month the Club gave a dance at the Orinda Park Hotel after it had been abandoned as a hotel. The members danced to the Smith Brothers' Orchestra, consisting of a violin and a guitar, then had coffee and cake for refreshments. A drink of beer was enough to ostracize anyone from the Club. The "Periwinkles" who were not adverse to a drink of beer called this group the "Bontons." The Club had its Ladies Auxiliary, a group of young women who met in the afternoon at different homes and drank tea, did a little sewing, and talked about any girl who went out with a "Periwinkle."[65]

Edward I. deLaveaga LAV

VI

From Old to New Orinda

The deLaveaga Family

Among the families who came to Orinda in the 1880's, only a few stayed until the 1920's, but one who did was responsible for much of the development and the character of the community as it is today. This was the deLaveaga family whose men were endowed with a pioneer spirit and great vision.

Five generations ago, Jose Vicente deLaveaga journeyed from Spain to Mexico where he became interested in silver mines and banking.[1] On a return trip from Mazatlan to Spain in 1857, he decided to visit San Francisco[2] and became so impressed with the booming city that he decided to remain. He was prominent in the banking business in San Francisco until 1870.[3]

One of his sons, Miguel, met and married Marie LeBreton, daughter of a prosperous San Francisco family, the Edward LeBretons. Miguel became a very successful business man who acquired a great deal of land in the city, as well as a large ranch near Hollister and property in Branciforte (Santa Cruz).

The deLaveagas undoubtedly knew Mayor Bryant of San Francisco and probably visited him at his home here in Orinda in 1878. Earlier, they may have known some of the Moragas and visited at the adobe. Perhaps they were acquainted with General Wagner whose estate in Orinda was a showplace in the 1880's and who had lived in San Francisco. Whatever the introduction to Orinda, in September 1887, Miguel and his brother, Jose, purchased 1,178.04 acres of the Ward and Smith League of the Castro Sobrante that Camron had owned and subdivided in Orinda Park.

Miguel and Jose then divided the property between them, Miguel taking the western half of lot 14 and lots 15–21 or 264.26 acres. Jose received 273.46 acres of the eastern half of lot 14 and lots 8–13, and a parcel of 134 acres. The remainder of the property was held in both of their names. The brothers retained rights of way across each other's property.[4]

Miguel and his wife wanted their children to have the advantages of country life, and in 1888 they erected a large and beautiful home on the hill above Miner Road, not far from the present ninth fairway of the Orinda Country Club. The estate was called Bien Venida which is also the name of the long private driveway and present road. Miguel contracted with H. M. Waterbury, who was then foreman of the Wagner ranch, to build the original road.[5]

Bien Venida means "welcome," and the name was well chosen as the deLaveagas became renowned for their hospitality in the early California tradition. The beautiful home was destroyed in a tragic fire in 1915, but was duplicated from the original plans and rebuilt the same year.[6] The estate included the usual barns and ranch buildings, spacious gardens, arbors and a rose walk, a lawn tennis court, and, nearby, a beautiful natural swimming pool, constructed with its separate bathhouse. Today, several other beautiful homes are located on a portion of the property. The deLaveaga home is enjoyed by the fourth and fifth generations of the family. Recently the estate was the scene of an 1890's day sponsored by the Orinda Art Center. Still Bien Venida!

Miguel's wife, Marie LeBreton, built the beautiful chapel, Santa Maria, in Orinda, which stood, until a few years ago, near Miner Road. about 100 yards from San Pablo Dam Road. Two homes are now where the chapel was. There will be more about the church and its history later. Marie deLaveaga died soon after the dedication of the chapel, and Miguel, thereafter, spent much of his time with his children at Bien Venida.

Edward I. deLaveaga

A year before he died, in 1914, Miguel came to make Orinda the permanent family residence. He made the prophetic remark, "Some day the land in Orinda will become too valuable to hold. We will give it away and sell the climate."[7] His son, Edward, who was born in 1884, stayed to make Orinda his home for life. Edward carried out the vision of his father and made his own plans for Orinda a reality. He loved the area and intimately knew the terrain—the flowers and birds, the springs and streams. He fished for trout and steelhead in the San Pablo Creek before the advent of the dam. As a horseman, he played polo and jumped hurdles that were set up on his estate.

Edward, known as E. I. deLaveaga, and called E. I. by his friends, raised his children at Bien Venida where he had spent his summers since childhood and had lived permanently since 1913. His son, Edward L. (Ned), now lives in the old home with his wife, Alysone, and their four children. Another son, Richard, is in business in Orinda, as is Ned, and a daughter, Lucia (Mrs. Harrel Ward), also lives nearby.

DeLaveaga was an excellent huntsman and, at one time, went on an assignment for the Oakland Museum to gather trophies for their collection. His companions included the curator of the museum and James Sullivan whose father, Eugene, had settled here in 1879.

Edward I. deLaveaga married Delight Woodbury of a pioneer Oakland family in 1906. Both of them contributed much of their time and talents to the life of the community, participating in charitable, church, civic and school affairs. Mrs. deLaveaga remembered her early trips to Orinda: "In summer all the roads were dusty, and *thick* dust, too; and in winter they were muddy, *thick* mud, too; but somehow, like all things difficult to achieve, Orinda seemed the more beautiful when reached. Often the trip was made walking or on horseback, and finally in 1907 by automobile. Only I must admit one might start out in 1907 for Orinda by automobile, but one arrived there by horse and buggy. Somewhere in the middle of the road the automobile might elect to sit down like a balky mule and refuse to move. But an S.O.S. brought the horse and buggy after hours of waiting, and we reached our goal, Orinda."[8]

Lake Orinda

In 1921 deLaveaga began to prepare his property for subdividing. He built a small lake on the hilly property on the west side of the highway and put in winding roads—Ardilla, El Toyonal, Canon Drive, Vallecito Lane, La Madronal and El Rincon. The lake was called

M. C. Sorensen family in front of Mitchell & Austin office in the village MCS

Picnics were held at the present location of Orinda Park Pool MCS

Lake Orinda which was the name of the first deLaveaga subdivision and, later, became as it is today—the Orinda Park Pool. To supply the prospective homes with water, an elaborate system of springs, wells, water pumps, tanks, valves, siphons, cut-offs, and trails was developed. The springs were given charming names such as: Fern, South Fork, Twin, Middle Fork, Quail, Toyonal, Coal, Rabbit and Current Springs.[9] Every drop of water that could be found was used, and Lake Orinda was a catch-basin.

By October 1922 one-third of the lots had been sold. Some of the very early purchasers included Ed. McVay, O. F. Heagher, R. A. Simpson, F. A. Kauffman, H. Barbeau, M. Truesdell, H. Arnold, O. L. Jones, H. C. Wood, L. Bouchard, F. Page, Frank Enos and A. W. Elkinton.[10]

Orinda Park Terrace

By 1923 the area of Lake Orinda had expanded toward the summit of the hills, and the entire subdivision was called Orinda Park Terrace. Roads such as Mira Monte, Camino Diablo, Chapparal Place and others yet unnamed were added.

More springs were developed to extend the water service, some at an elevation of 1,500 feet. Again deLaveaga used names which were intriguing and meaningful: Coyote, Canon, Bluejay, Saddle, Eagle, Laurel, Prospect, Rock, Basin, Bear, Fall and Saddle Springs.[11] Every lot buyer received water and owned one share of the water company.

Before he was finished subdividing in Orinda, deLaveaga formed three separate mutual water companies.[12] The local company for Orinda Park Terrace sold its assets for $1.00 when the Orinda Water District formed in 1932, which then purchased water from EBMUD.[13] Lack of water had been one of the main drawbacks to the few previous subdivision attempts that had been made. Before 1922 most settlers had been located near the main creeks or streams.

Orinda Park Pool

By 1924 the bottom of Lake Orinda had been cemented, the grounds had been converted into a picnic area, and a bathhouse built. The place was used for prospective customers to swim and picnic, as well as for the new residents who were now on the property. Not only could people from the city come to look over the new prospective subdivision in Orinda, but also could they have a pleasant day in the country. Nearby was the subdivision office, and, on the highway that ran through the area, which would soon be the Orinda Village, a large sign with an arrow pointed the way up the hill to Lake Orinda.

The pool became rather neglected after the financial depression of 1929. Then, in 1931, the grounds were leased to Joseph Wear. A small building was erected, the grounds were fenced, and he opened the pool to the public. Wear also built a dance platform.[14] Sometimes during good weather, on Sundays and holidays, the crowds of people who came would be very large. After a few summers homeowners began to be distressed by the numbers of strangers who came to enjoy the day and evening, increasing the noise from the pool area with its music and traffic.

In 1937, Warren Harrold, A. W. Elkinton and other neighbors, serving as a special committee of the Orinda Improvement Association, met with Ned and Dick deLaveaga who represented the owners of the pool.[15] As a result of this meeting, the non-profit organization, Orinda Park Pool, Inc., was founded. The pool was leased for a three-year period. In the spring of 1938 the pool was opened as a private club with the grand opening on Saturday, May 14.[16] Dues were $20.00 per family per year or $10.00 for a single person. Mrs. E. A. Dawson was secretary of the organization.

With the successful operation of the Orinda Park Pool, a longer lease was soon signed. Improvements were constantly made over the years until the area became the center for swimming and social activities that it is today.

After the success of sales of property in Orinda Park Terrace, E. I. deLaveaga began to plan further the development of Orinda. As early as 1923 were plans drawn for a village, Lake Cascade, the Orinda Country Club and the golf course, as well as for a new 418-acre subdivision on the northeast side of the highway to be known as Hacienda del Orinda. He reserved seventeen acres out of this for his own estate.[17] There was one stumbling block that needed to be taken care of before plans for this area could be completed. Part of the property was not in his possession.

The Marshall Family

Miguel deLaveaga's brother, Jose, who owned approximately one-half of the original deLaveaga property, had died in 1896 and left his share to his heirs, members of the Cebrian family. His daughter, Maria, had married John Cebrian. In 1920 the Cebrians sold 273 acres of the property on the northeast side of the highway to Antonio J. Marshall and his wife, Mary.[18] Marshall had been farming the Cebrian land in the area of the present Orinda Country Club for a few years before this and had built a modest home and barns there. Their cow-barn stood on the exact site of the present Clubhouse building, and their home was approximately where the club swimming pool is now located. Pumpkins in season grew in the rich valley land now at the bottom of Lake Cascade. Sheep, hogs and cattle ranged over the remaining land. Marshall stored extra hay from his harvested crops in a Moraga barn. The cows supplied milk which was separated from the cream by hand and then taken to Moraga Mercantile (Moraga Barn) to go by train (Sacramento Northern) to Oakland. At the Moraga Mercantile, Helen Hetfield, whose father had purchased the building in 1915, wrote the bills of lading for the various farmers.[19]

The Marshall family also had a wood business and woodchoppers would come from Oakland bringing their own tents which they set up to live in while they worked at cutting the wood. Hogs and calves were butchered and then taken to Oakland where they were inspected before being sold.[20]

Albert Marshall, the older son, was born on the old Brady Ranch in Grizzly Canyon near Moraga in 1916. He remembers the family telling that Dr. Leach came in his horse and buggy from Walnut Creek to attend all of the family births. Eva, the daughter, was born in the home at the site of the Orinda Country Club. Tony was born after they moved to near the San Pablo Dam Road.

Frank Enos

Marshall first sold a small piece of land to Frank and Ruth Enos in 1921.[21] They had operated the Canary Cottage, a small restaurant and gas station stop located on the east side of the old tunnel, well-known to travelers between Alameda and Contra Costa County.

65

Above The White Swan and firehouse (1923)   RE   *Below* Orinda village in 1926   WH

Frank Enos and his wife decided to build a new and similar place in Orinda on the property they purchased from Marshall, which was located just past the bridge built in 1920 at the north end of the Orinda Village. The San Pablo Dam Road as well as the road to Moraga were scheduled for improvements, and, with the planned subdivisions and prospective traffic, Enos decided a place on the type of the Canary Cottage would be most welcome. Mrs. Enos later said, "There was nothing there in those days." The building, "The White Swan," on the banks of the San Pablo Creek, was completed in late 1921 or early 1922. It was the first structure in the village other than an old barn further up. It served as a refreshment stand, a small store, and had an adjoining gas station. Today, the building is still there, no longer white, and now known as the Casa Verana, a name which deLaveaga later gave it after it had been enlarged and remodelled.[22] During Casa Verana's lifetime, it has been "The White Swan" and, with an addition in 1924, a bunkhouse and boarding house for the men working on the golf course, an office, a nursery school, a church meeting place, and today houses various offices and businesses.

In 1922 Enos bought a site almost opposite the store. It was slightly north—across the highway.[23] Here they built a home which, also, is still standing. From there they could see the store and gas station, hear the honk of a horn, and cross the road to assist any passerby. The small store with its few staples and stamps was the only place an Orinda resident could purchase anything he might have forgotten on a major shopping trip to Berkeley or Oakland.

The Orinda Village

In 1922 E. I. deLaveaga bought almost ten acres from Antonio Marshall.[24] This was land near The White Swan. In November of that same year, he purchased from Marshall the remaining land that he needed for the subdivision, Lake Cascade and the Orinda Country Club and golf course.[25] Now there was nothing to impede his plans.

The second structure to be completed in the village was the fire house, built in 1924, across the highway from The White Swan, on the other side of the bridge. This building has since been enlarged, the fire department having moved, and today it houses offices for owner, Kenneth Courtright, and renters, realtor Frances Lax and the Orinda Furniture Store.

Upper Orinda center in 1920's EP   *Lower* Shops replaced the riding academy DB

DeLaveaga had plans for a village which included a riding academy, garage, hotel, chapel, theatre, village store and other stores.[26] The Orinda Store, built in late 1924, opened for business January 1925.[27] It is at present the oldest store of any kind remaining in Orinda. DeLaveaga ran the general merchandise store himself for the first few years, mainly for the convenience of the new Orindans, and he lost money in the process. Mr. Dumphy managed the store for deLaveaga. In the rear was the headquarters for the Orinda Properties Company, which handled all the details of building homes for the deLaveaga subdivisions. Also available through this company were such services as watchman, caretaker, gardener, architect, builder and repairman. At the store were the postoffice, a candy and soda fountain, supplies of various kinds, and two shelves of books, forming the beginning of a community library.

About 1929 the store was purchased by E. M. Jones who was popularly known as Jonesy. He kept the store until 1938 when it was sold to Jarvis Clark, who also had a grocery store in Berkeley. Jarvis Clark turned over the management of this store to his son, Guthrie.

In October 1939 a lightning and thunder storm caused some destruction by fire as a bolt hit the store causing some $25,000 in damage. One of the services the store offered was a beauty parlor, run by Marie Bennett, who rented space in the rear. Marie had opened the first beauty shop in Orinda there. After the fire, she moved to a larger shop in the new Vashell Building at the crossroads. Marie was, also, an early real estate saleswoman in Orinda.

In August of 1941 Ewart J. Phair and George B. Gibson purchased the store. The well-known butcher at the store was C. P. McVicker (Mac) who stayed on for the new owners. Mac was an excellent photographer who often won prizes for his art and took many pictures of local events.

Ewart Phair bought out Gibson and has continued in ownership to the present time. He has made the Orinda store into a village specialty shop known throughout the bay area. In it a gift shop and dress shop are available along with many gourmet foods and an excellent wine cellar.

All of deLaveaga's plans for the Orinda Village were carried out with the exception of the chapel, hotel and theatre. The second fire house building on Avenida de Orinda is on the approximate location of the planned hotel. Supposedly, the very thick and substantial foundations were meant for the hotel or the chapel, neither of which was ever completed. The depression of 1929 forced changes in some of the original plans for the village.

The riding stables were installed in 1925, and there for many years, Miss Graham (Mrs. P. R. Donaldson) operated a riding academy. P. R. Donaldson also had an active role in Orinda life, at one time being Fire Chief and, from 1935–1962, a sheriff. During the Second World War, some of the local women took target practicing from Sheriff Donaldson. The retired sheriff still lives in Orinda and may be seen daily either sitting in his car or passing the time of day at the Phillips gas station in Orinda. Here he watches the activities at the crossroads, the changes in the landscape, and, no doubt, occasionally thinks back to the differences of the 1920's.

The local Orinda Garage is still in the same location as it was in the 1920's next to the Riding Academy. The Orinda Nursery was built in 1926 and operated by Scanlon and

Antonio Marshall had a cowbarn where the Orinda Country Clubhouse now stands (1917–1922) AM
Building the eighteenth fairway of the golf course LAV

Klemmer. Professor Vaughn purchased the nursery in 1927, and, in the 1930's, Arthur J. Memmesheimer operated the business. In 1940 it was purchased by a Mr. Wolters.

In 1928 other stores were built in the village between the Orinda Store and the Nursery and, later, on the other side of the Nursery, which was itself soon replaced with more stores as the present character of the village came into existence. The old Riding Academy space became shops, too, at a later time, but now these shops have been torn down, and the space is used by the Richfield Oil Company.

The only structure known in the area of the village before the advent of The White Swan was an old barn and corral near the creek located at the end of the present Avenida de Orinda. This building belonged to George Brockhurst and was used by him when he farmed the Sleepy Hollow area. In a wet winter the corral would often go under water as the San Pablo Creek became a raging torrent—a problem suffered several times by the fire house later built here. The creek now runs underground in a culvert. Before the riding academy was built the old barn was used for a community stables, run by a Mr. Warren. Here, residents could rent horses at $1.00 for the first hour and fifty cents thereafter.[28]

The Orinda Country Club

By 1924, E. I. deLaveaga had completed another step in his plans; Lake Cascade had been formed by the construction of a dam across an 18½-acre valley into which Cascade Creek emptied. The dam was originally 400 feet long, 200 feet wide and an average of 35 feet high. When full, it was supposed to contain 62,740,000 gallons of water. By May 13, 1924, the lake contained over 28,000,000 gallons.[29] Some of the water from the lake was carefully filtered and used by the homeowners. Provision was made to raise the dam another ten feet in the future. All of the water problems and engineering were carefully planned as is evidenced by the fact that it was not until 1965 that the dam was strengthened for the first time to meet new standards.

Tourists from Berkeley and Oakland drove out to see the new Lake Cascade, but, in 1924, they found themselves turned back by the quarantine that was placed by the county on all of the cattle still in the area; a plague of hoof and mouth disease had hit Contra Costa County cattle. That year many cattle had to be destroyed and buried, and stock losses in the county amounted to $426,844.

Hacienda Homes, Inc. was formed by deLaveaga to take care of the business of the subdivision. An office was opened in Casa Verana. This organization is still in existence. Another Mutual Water Company was formed as in the former subdivision, and each lot owner became a stockholder owning one share. One of the purposes of Hacienda Homes, Inc. was to carry out the provisions of the deeds under which the lots were originally sold, which included care of the roads in the subdivision.

In 1941 the corporation was taken over by the Orinda Improvement Association in trust for the lot owners. The seven directors of Hacienda Homes, Inc. were re-elected by the Orinda Improvement Association. After a period of twenty-five years, Hacienda Homes, Inc. became a non-profit corporation no longer connected with the Orinda Improvement Association.

A distinct entity from Hacienda Homes, Inc. was the Orinda Country Club with a sep-

71

The eighth hole at Orinda Country Club. First foursome to play the course included
Archie Andrews, Mike Hadden, F. J. Reagan and F. W. Beard   JH

arate Board of Directors and a separate set of by-laws. The Club was to own and maintain the clubhouse, golf course, swimming pool and adjoining ground, a total of about 159 acres. It was also to own a two-thirds interest in the water company so that water from the lake could be used for the golf course.

The clubhouse was started in 1924 at an estimated cost of $80,000, but, when completed and furnished, the cost was $214,000.[30] Hamilton Murdock was the club architect. The Orinda Country Club opened its doors in September, 1925.

An eighteen-hole golf course, laid out by William Watson, an internationally famous golf course architect, was also built. When the club opened, a few holes were still to be completed. The finished course was 6,315 yards long, and there were four par fives, ten par fours and four par threes, with a total par of 72.

Each hole was named in the deLaveaga fashion, with a touch of the romantic, by the Greens Committee in the summer of 1927. The first hole was appropriately called "Inspiration" with its magnificent view. The second hole was "Bonita," the beautiful; the third was "Orchard," from the old pear orchard on the property; the fourth was "Meteor" from the structure of the rocks above the green; the fifth was "Mousetrap," a tricky dog-leg where most were well-satisfied with a par four. "Long Tom," the sixth, was named after the Scotish tradition for the longest hole, and "Sobrante," the seventh, parallels the street of the same name. The eighth, "Dead Horse," was called so after Dead Horse Gulch which ran through there. "Horseshoe" was the name for the ninth, nearby the old deLaveaga stable. The tenth was named "Delight," Mrs. E. I. deLaveaga's name, and the eleventh was "Graveyard," the site of the old Indian burial ground where skeletons were unearthed during the construction. Number twelve was named after the architect, "Willie Watson." Thirteen was "Mokelumne" after the water tunnel outlet nearby; fourteen was named "San Pablo," alongside the San Pablo Creek. Fifteen was called "Despair"—173 yards surrounded with trouble; sixteen was "Gibraltar," by the rock wall; seventeen was "Rincon," Spanish for cozy corner. The magnificent long eighteenth, leading up to Cascade Falls and the swimming pool was called "Cascade."

In April, 1928, the Orinda Country Club was host to its first big golf tournament, sponsored by the Northern California Golf Association. Lawson Little, then seventeen years old, won the tournament.[31] Ralph Longo was the club professional, a position which he held until 1942 when the popular Pat Patten took the job. In over forty years there have only been two head golf professionals at the Orinda Country Club.

In addition to the clubhouse and golf course, a swimming pool was located below the lake and the clubhouse. Water fell from a spillway over a rock falls into a small pool, which in turn spilled into a large swimming pool as it does today. The upper pool was a replica of the famous "Blue Hole" situated on the Mokelumne River. A bath house was constructed of Spanish-type architecture which has since been remodeled. The bath house and swimming pool were, in fact, completed in 1924 before the clubhouse was constructed.

The club was indebted to Haciendas Homes, Inc. This indebtedness was secured by a Deed of Trust upon the real and personal property and also by an unsecured note. Provision was originally made for 350 regular members, 50 life members and 500 social members. At this time, a person had to be a property owner in Orinda to apply for and purchase a mem-

73

Orinda Country Club, Lake Cascade, Casa Azul and a few other early homes can be seen in this partial view of Haciendas del Orinda (1926) WH

bership in the Orinda Country Club. Twenty-eight life memberships were sold after the incorporation of the club, and then this class of membership was closed as it was found that more would not be economically feasible.

The first manager of the Orinda Country Club was Edwin Cooper. Other managers over the years have been Mary Gallagher, in the early 1930's; then Joe Varni; next Clarke Matthews, 1946–1948; Frank Branstetter, 1948–1950; Clarke Matthews again in 1950 until 1970. Alec Churchward is manager at the present time.

Haciendas del Orinda

The large subdivision of Haciendas del Orinda[32] was now a reality with every convenience planned for the homeowners. A tract office was built at Mira Loma and Camino Sobrante to handle sales and inquiries. One of the first couples to purchase a lot in Haciendas del Orinda was Ernest and June Hadden who built a home in 1925. Mr. and Mrs. Hadden still live in the same home in Orinda today and are the only local residents who are life members of the Orinda Country Club. Mr. Hadden is still an active golfer, and he remembers playing in one of the first foursomes on the course with Archie Andrews, Hal Beard and Sonny Regan. The Haddens remember the old well on their property and their one share of stock in the small water company before the advent of the East Bay Municipal Utility District.[33] June Hadden was one of the founder members of the Orinda Garden Club.

Early Village Realtors

The first sales manager of the Lake Orinda subdivision, in 1921, was Robert Brent Mitchell with the California Subdivision Company. In a few years, as James L'Hommedieu, a civil and subdivision engineer who became deLaveaga's close associate, was further developing and selling Orinda properties, Robert Mitchell became the sales manager for L'Hommedieu. He remained in this capacity for five years, and then, with Harold Austin, he opened the office of Mitchell and Austin. This firm became the agent for selling Hacienda Homes, Inc. properties. Their main office was in Oakland, but they soon built a small Spanish-type building that, until recently, was used as a real estate office between the forks of Camino Sobrante as it starts up the hill from the Orinda village. Zoe Woolsey had an office there for many years. The landmark structure has recently been torn down. Mitchell and Austin's second office was in Casa Verana; they next moved to an office in the village. Throughout the 1920's and 1930's they were responsible for selling a great deal of Orinda property, and, during the period before the completion of the low-level tunnel, they were extremely active in Orinda real estate.

Two large homes built during the 1920's were Casa Azul, built by Chester Williams near Camino Lenada, and the Frank R. Fageol home, overlooking the golf course, now owned by Glen Cramer. Many of the early homes have red-tiled roofs reflecting the Spanish background of the area.

Mason McDuffie also had an office in the village in the 1930's, and, several years before that, Warren Harrold had been selling property in Orinda. Warren Harrold was the first real estate agent to actually live in Orinda. He was very active in community affairs for many years and was one of the first presidents of the Orinda Improvement Association. He

Sorensen's well near San Pablo Creek was lined with bricks from the old hotel MCS

lived in Orinda until 1968 when, because of illness, he found it necessary to sell his building and move closer to his daughter. Since the death of his wife, he had lived in an apartment above the remodeled old fire house, which was part of his office building.

Another early realtor was Hayden H. Bridwell, who handled most of the deLaveaga property sales on the north side of the highway. His office, Bridwell Realty, was opened in 1941. Mr. Bridwell is still in the real estate business in Orinda.

Development is Slowed

It is obvious that the problems deLaveaga had to meet to bring a community into being were colossal. But these challenges he seemed well-equipped to handle. Many had already built their homes. The village was partly developed. The Orinda Country Club was in operation as well as the golf course.

Then came a reversal, such as had affected Orinda in the 1890's, only this time on a larger scale. The prosperity of the 1920's ended in the financial collapse of 1929, which was the beginning of the great depression.

As the country plunged from prosperity to adversity, buyers of property in Orinda defaulted on their purchase contracts, and land sales came almost to a halt. E. I. deLaveaga lost his personal fortune with which he had backed his plans. Although he was unable to make payments on his bank loan, the bank in these troubled times did not foreclose but, because of deLaveaga's reputation, asked him to continue to sell the Hacienda Homes, Inc. properties. In the 1940's, deLaveaga paid off the principal of the loan to the American Trust Company (Wells Fargo Bank).[34]

Between 1929 and 1937, sales were at a much slower pace and Orinda stayed much as it was in 1929, but then the new Caldecott tunnel was built through the hills, and only a look around today is necessary to see the development since that time. The groundwork had been laid, and the community grew with a rapidity typical of many suburbs, making it a problem to keep up with itself.

E. I. deLaveaga was a genius at planning and was strong-willed about carrying out his plans. He knew the property so well, over hills and valleys, that it was difficult at times for him to work with others who might not see things as he did. He had a colorful personality and occasionally got into heated arguments with his oldest and closest associates. Oldtimers remember that both Jim Sullivan and George Brockhurst, who worked with him for years, had scraps with him over how to do this or that. There has been no one in the past history of Orinda who has contributed as much to the character and development of the community as deLaveaga.

The last of the subdivisions emanating from the deLaveaga holdings was Ranchitos deLaveaga, situated around Lomas Cantadas on the west side of the highway in upper Orinda. It adjoins East Bay Municipal Utility Company and Tilden Regional Park land not far from Grizzly Peak Boulevard.

In 1933 E. I. deLaveaga and his wife separated, and, later, he married Elizabeth Patterson. She helped design homes in the new subdivision. Their home was at 56 Camino del Diablo.

DeLaveaga died on December 31, 1958. Mrs. Delight deLaveaga died in 1960 and, at the time, was living in the old home.

Richfield Oil Company delivered the gasoline to Marshall's place (1920's)   AM

VII

Other Settlements North of the Crossroads

Between the time that William Camron developed his land into Orinda Park and the time that E. I. deLaveaga started his subdivisions, there were a few people who moved into the area, and one attempt at subdividing was made. Later, several other small subdivisions were planned by those who purchased some of this land.

Orinda Villa Park Land Company

In 1914 an effort was made to develop residential sites on the 173 acres that William Minto had purchased from Camron. Minto had lost the place for taxes in 1901, and William C. Spencer purchased it for $11,115 at public auction.[1] In three years Spencer sold the piece to Frank and Marie Bateman who held it for almost ten years,[2] and, in 1913, they sold the acreage, including the old Minto house, to W. J. Mortimer.[3]

Mortimer formed the Orinda Villa Park Land Company. He filed a subdivision map in 1914 which was approved by Elam Brown, grandson of the pioneer, at that time county surveyor.[4] "No cold fog" and "every acre a money maker" were advertised by the sellers.[5] There were some purchasers, but the major stumbling block to any large development was water, and homes were, for the most part, located by necessity near streams or springs upon which they were dependent.

The Residents of the Twenties

Although most of the residents who settled on Orinda Villa Park and along the San Pablo Dam road have moved away, for a time this area was a busy part of Orinda. On property since taken over by the water company were the Frank Teiches, Helene Chester and her sons, M. C. Sorensens, and the Vinther, Alquist, Dutton and Wheeler families. The Marshall family also had moved there when deLaveaga purchased their property.

The Alexander Fleitz family ran a dairy on the deLaveaga property just adjoining Orinda Villa Park. Here there was a barn, milkhouse, a house and other farm buildings. The Fleitz family had settled on a 100-acre ranch in Bear Valley in the 1880's but had been moved twice, slightly southward, by the encroaching water companies which eventually took the land of most of the residents on the east side of the highway. Their first move had been to the Eva property where the Symmons family had farmed, and which later became the Dutra Ranch. The children of the Fleitz family and of the others nearby all went to the Orinda Park School.[6] Mary Fleitz Borel now lives in San Ramon.

The location of the old dairy was approximately at the north end of the present golf course. Before the Fleitz family came, it was operated by the Ezevedo family whose children were registered at the school as early as 1900. When the main water tunnel brought

Mokelumne water to the Orinda Filter Plant, it went right through the location of the old dairy.[7]

Cattle have been grazing for many years on much of the water company land. From about 1920, Pete Bruno held a lease on a large section of this land in Orinda, and about 1940, Frank Dutra took it over to run a cattle ranch. Dutra leased almost 17,000 acres which included much of the vacant land on both sides of the highway from Charles Hill Road to the tunnel.

The Orinda ranch included about 7,000 acres although it is less than that now. The ranch headquarters is still on Bear Creek Road, not far from where the Orinda Park Railroad Station stood on the old Symmons Ranch.

Dutra's trucks may be seen occasionally on the local highway transporting cattle during the seasons. Although the Briones Dam has changed this area greatly in recent years, cattle still graze on nearby hills.

Orindans who came in 1917 and stayed for many years were the T. C. Kendalls. Kendall came as an inspector of the San Pablo Dam, as construction was started that year. He worked for the water company for 42 years. Mrs. Grace Kendall taught at the Orinda Park School around 1918 to 1921. Later she was the first official postmaster when the postoffice became a separate entity in 1945. She was clerk of the school board during the 1920's and participated in other community affairs.

When the Kendalls first came to Orinda, they moved temporarily into the old Wagner house which was still standing, staying with Guy Palmer who was then manager of the water company. The Kendalls soon moved to a cottage on the old Rowland ranch where they lived from 1918 to 1923. The water company then built a house for them on the same ranch where they lived for many years. The house is still used by EBMUD at their maintenance yard. Many Orinda neighborhood gatherings and parties of the 1920's and 1930's took place there.[8]

The Sorensens came to Orinda in 1919, and some of the trees they planted are still visible on the property by the Filter Plant. They raised chickens on their ranch. Water was obtained from a well near the creek; it was lined with bricks taken from the ruins of the old Orinda Hotel.[9]

When the Sorensens celebrated their tenth wedding anniversary in 1924, the guest list included families in a typical Orinda gathering: Ogdens (he was the damkeeper), Kendalls, Brockhursts, Vinthers, Rowlands, Teiches, McVays, Marshalls, Fleitzs, Miss Woodin (the new teacher at the Orinda Park School), Miss Ostrid Iverson (who had been teacher for two years), Miss Ricketts (the girl who delivered the mail from Berkeley each day), Mr. Starr, her fiance, and Mrs. Wheeler.

After 1900, the character of the land had changed in the area of the present San Pablo Dam. The large farms located there began to disappear when the Peoples Water Company started to buy up valuable watershed lands. This transition from farming land continued until the major water problems for the East Bay were solved. In the 1920s there was some unhappiness along the northeast side of the highway in Orinda as EBMUD took many of the small homes, paying what the residents felt was a low price. With the District being in the position of belonging to the public, no individual could present much of a case for himself.[10] Land was needed for vital water projects, and a small but active part of Orinda was eliminated.

Across from the site of the old dairy is the E. A. Dawson house. The Dawsons moved from Oak Springs, in 1925, and still live in this location on Camino Pablo, as the San Pablo Dam Road is now called in this area. The location is at the north end of the deLaveaga property. Mrs. Dawson was librarian of the community for many years, served in the post office, and in various other community jobs. She remembers much of the development of Orinda. Mr. Dawson was manager of the Orinda Water Company, formed by deLaveaga to handle water for his properties. Later, he worked for EBMUD, going along with the Orinda Water Company into the larger system in 1934.[11]

North of the dairy were the Marshalls who had moved from the Country Club site about 1923. On the highway they had a small store and snack shop and a gas station selling the first Richfield products in Orinda. They also had a coal business, rented cabins for vacationers, and had a swimming pool surrounded by a large lawn and picnic grounds which people from Oakland came out to use. At the gas station, the Marshalls sold and delivered gravel that came from the creek for which they needed two and four-horse teams. Marshall also worked on the golf course, so it is easy to visualize how busy this family was. After their land was taken, they moved to Santa Cruz where all of the children are in business today.[12]

Orinda Oaks, Orinda Court, Garden of Eden

When Frank Teiche had to move from the northeast side of the highway, he purchased Lot 2, formerly John Hoyt's, of the old Orinda Park Tract, adjoining Orinda Villa Park Company land. The land had been farmed around 1885 by Ormund S. Owens' family. A son, Charles S. Owens, remembered fishing in the San Pablo Creek when he was a boy and hunting for quail and rabbits. He recalled, "In those days fishing was very good in the San Pablo Creek, where one caught trout, and also salmon three feet long."

The Teiches sold forty-five acres of land to J. D. Murphy in 1924, and that year Murphy filed a subdivision map for Orinda Oaks. The property is northwest of San Pablo Dam Road, north of Claremont Avenue, and includes California and Stanton. In 1939 Mrs. Murphy redeveloped the area with new roads, built to county specifications, and utilities were installed.

In 1925 Frank Teiche planned the small subdivision, Orinda Court. Mrs. Teiche lives today in a house on North Lane.[13]

A small section of Orinda Park Terrace was resubdivided in 1927 as the Garden of Eden Tract. The streets were Rio Vista, Cresta Blanca, Los Conejos and La Bolsita.

Snug Harbor

Harry and Johanna Oakley purchased Lots 29, 30 and 31 of Mortimer's Orinda Villa Park Land Company in 1924.[14] For several years they had camped on the property, but, in 1924, erected a more permanent house at the end of Kittiwake Road. It is located there today, having been remodeled by the new owners. Before water service was installed the Oakleys obtained their water from a spring. Oakley was a Captain on the Richmond-San Rafael

Lake Cascade (1926)   WH

Ferry. He was active in the Orinda Association and many early community affairs. Captain Oakley was always ready to lend a helping hand to a new resident inexperienced in the ways of the countryside.

The Oakleys subdivided their property in 1946, calling the subdivision "Snug Harbor."[15] The main roads were Bobolink, Oriole and Kittiwake, bounded by Los Altos Road and Manzanita Drive.

Lind-O-Rinda Estates

Adjoining the Oakley's property is a tract that was developed by the Sidney K. Rosenthals on land which they purchased in the Orinda Villa Park Tract in 1924. This property had on it a cottage built by a minister, some years before, on a foundation of old railroad ties from the defunct California and Nevada Railroad line at the bottom of the hill. School teacher Florence Sullivan rented the cottage for awhile. In 1951 the Rosenthals put in a new foundation, and the cottage is today a charming small home.

They spent only summers in the cottage during the first few years but soon moved in permanently. From October on, the skies were anxiously watched for rain, as their only water supply was from a well which went dry about then.[16]

In 1945 a subdivision map was filed by the Rosenthals for Lind-O-Rinda Estates, an area of about twenty acres.[17] The roads Vista del Mar and Del Mar Court are included in this property. By now there was a new bridge over the creek on old Bridge Road. Bridge Road no longer exists but was the name of the main road in the Mortimer subdivision.

Dissension with Pacific Gas & Electric Company

In 1949 Rosenthal carried on an extensive personal fight with the Pacific Gas and Electric Company over the large towers which they erected on his property. This was the beginning of several such episodes between members of the community and the P.G.&E. over towers, some of which crossed the golf course and also obstructed treasured views. In 1953, an aroused Orinda Protective Committee, representing the citizens, successfully resisted a plan of the company to erect a proposed new set of towers through the center of the valley.[18] Members of this committee included Orinda citizens Joseph Rupley, Lindsey Spight and George Hauerken.

In 1969 another group opposed a line of towers through a section of the Briones Dam area and met with the company in discussion groups. Joining the opposition were the Orinda Association and the Sierra Club who were also seeking to change the route.

Fairway Acres, Orinda Estates and Orinda Vista

In 1927 Franklin Kales purchased the Sandow holding of around seventy acres off Miner Road. A year later he planned the subdivision, Fairway Acres, in which Oak Arbor and Haciendas Road are the main streets.[19]

Kales built a beautiful home in 1928, not far from where Esther Symmons and her family had lived for many years on the Sandow property. The old cottage, which had been unoccupied for several years, was torn down.

Mrs. R. F. Fageol and Mrs. Amy Long Sutton purchased twenty acres of another piece of

Sandow property, off of the San Pablo Dam Road, and, in 1940, the area was developed into Orinda Estates. The two main streets here were called Acacia Drive and Hacienda Circle.

The area of Orinda Vista, previously owned by Edward Jensen, was subdivided by Sidney and Evelyn Harding in 1941 around Monte Vista Road.[20]

The Dutch Merchant Marine

The old Minto home on the Orinda Villa Land property had been purchased by the J. P. Miller family. It no longer stands, and a few homes near Sol Brae and the rear of Stanton Court take its place. Before the old home was destroyed, there was a flurry of excitement in the community over an incident that took place in 1942.

During the Second World War, the Dutch government wanted to buy the home and grounds in order to offer refuge for the duration of the war to members of the crews of the Dutch Merchant Marine which was then working under the United States Navy. The existing house was to provide a dining room, living room and a kitchen to care for forty men, with sleeping accommodations for the manager and his wife and for five sick men. In addition, there were plans to build a dormitory for twenty-four European crew members and a complete house in Javanese style with a kitchen, dining room, living room and sleeping quarters for twenty-four Javanese, as well as a small building for extra personnel.

Immediately, there was considerable apprehension among neighbors and some of the residents of Orinda who were particularly concerned about Javanèse natives living near them. Other residents regretted the unfriendliness shown by the community and the "un-Christian spirit and the narrow provincialism." Lieutenant Commander M. S. Wytema wrote: "It will not be a public place but a strictly exclusive one where only guests with the approval of the Liaison Officer are admitted. It is hardly possible that the institution and the behavior of the men will be a disgrace to the neighborhood or to its good name.

"The natives of the Netherlands are most gentle and quiet and my twelve years in Java enable me to say that these men will never cause any disturbance whatsoever. Their building is at 200 yards distance from the main house, about 300 yards from the San Pablo Dam Road, and is entirely hidden behind trees."[21]

Opposition, however, did not lessen, and the Dutch government withdrew its plans for a retreat for the members of the Dutch Merchant Marine and did not purchase the old Minto estate.

Sleepy Hollow

Smith's old rodeo grounds became the present Sleepy Hollow. Lauterwasser had chosen a site by the creek near the entrance to the valley for his home which the Miner family later enlarged. The land was used for ranch and farm land until George Brockhurst sold the 200-acre section he had purchased to Jacob F. Kaar in 1924.[22] Within two years the Sleepy Hollow Syndicate was formed in which John Morton Allen had a major interest.[23]

The Syndicate built the first stone gates at the entrance and named the valley after the Legend of Sleepy Hollow. The gates have since been replaced. Allen visualized the influx of population into the Orinda area in years to come and predicted that the property would become very valuable.

A dance platform was built near the gates by the creek where picnics and dances were held for several years. It was occasionally rented by clubs and lodges.[24] On one occasion the fire department held a benefit dance there for the purpose of raising funds to purchase new equipment.

Another 500 acres of land were purchased from EBMUD in 1930 to add to the holdings.[25] In 1934 the Syndicate incorporated with directors: Jacob F. Kaar, John M. Allen, George F. Gould, M. C. McGowan and George Brockhurst.

Three miles of roads were laid out on 300 acres of the Sleepy Hollow property. All of the street names were taken from the Washington Irving story. "If ever I should wish for a retreat whither I might steal from the world and its distractions, and dream quietly away the remnant of a troubled life, I know of none more promising than this little valley," was the quotation from Irving that was used in the little hand-done bulletin advertising the new community. It continued: "To undertake a more fitting description of the 'Sleepy Hollow' of Washington Irving would indeed trangress [sic] the bounds of modesty. By the above token we have discovered and christened our country homesite community: 'Sleepy Hollow.' "[26]

Poets and writers seem to have inspired our Orinda settlers!

Allen's original idea was to subdivide the property into one to three acre parcels, divided according to the topography of the land. He became ill in 1936, and his original plans were not carried out.[27]

In 1935 Richard Rheem purchased nine acres of the property that included the old Miner home and barn and, shortly thereafter, obtained sixteen more acres. Two years later, Rheem purchased the entire holding which amounted to 705 acres.[28] He demolished the old Miner home that had been standing since Lauterwasser erected it in 1859. In its place he built a beautiful home and developed an estate that included a caretaker's house, now a private residence. The Rheems lived in this smaller house while the larger home was under construction.

In 1945 Rheem decided to subdivide the property through Clyde O. Sweet. The transaction involved the transfer of 650 acres. A map of Unit No. 1 for the subdivision was filed December 22, 1945.[29] Since then Sleepy Hollow has developed into the community it is today.

In a few years Rheem sold his home to the Joseph Longs. The Longs have enlarged the beautiful gardens, offering a vista to be enjoyed by anyone driving by on Lombardy Lane.

Gertrude Miner Cotton

Gertrude Miner Cotton, the eldest Miner girl, had inherited about 400 acres of the old Miner property which included all of the original ranch outside of the Sleepy Hollow section. She gradually sold off all of the land, mainly in the years 1932 through 1939. Warren Harrold, early resident and real estate salesman, handled practically all of the transactions in the Cotton Tract as it was known.

In the early 1930's, several of the purchasers, including Richard Breuner, Alden Macomber, Earl Norton and A. W. Bowron, planned to extend Miner Road from where it ended at Brookbank. They contracted with George Brockhurst who did the grading. Water was brought into the area from the entrance to Sleepy Hollow where Allen had brought it earlier.[30] Mr. and Mrs. Breuner still live on their property off of Miner Road. The site is where the Miner family originally had a large vegetable garden.

Further up Miner Road, as more residents purchased property and built, the Canyon Ranch area was formed. In 1941 James and Nellie Dieterich subdivided Orinda Uplands, the furthermost part of the Miner property. Here are the roads Diablo View, Canyon View, Tamalpais and Briones.[31]

Orinda Downs, Orindawoods

Two new and partially undeveloped areas are planned at present. Orinda Downs, east of Sleepy Hollow, was started in 1969, but growth has been somewhat slowed by the recent tight money situation.

Projected Orindawoods, planned on the old Pine Grove property as a cluster development with open space, has been approved by the Board of Supervisors of Contra Costa County. It will contain standard homes with half-acre lots as well as townhouses and condominiums. Developers have stated that 10,000 trees will be part of the landscaping.

VIII

Development at the Crossroads and South

Land on the Moraga Ranch that is included in the Orinda School District remained basically undeveloped in the early 1900's. Still owned by Carpentier, an absentee landlord by then living in the east, the main property which he had obtained in the original grant was almost intact. Other than a few landowners who had purchased during the brief era of Grant and Williamson and various farmers who leased land, there was little change until about 1912.

The Moraga Company

In January 1909 the Oakland, Antioch and Eastern Railroad was started between San Francisco, Oakland and Sacramento. The line was completed in 1913. Later, reorganized into the Sacramento Northern Electric Railway, it had local stations at Canyon, Moraga, St. Mary's College and Burton.

During this period, combines of men looking for land investments began to show some interest in the Moraga Ranch. In 1912, Arthur H. Breed, representing a group that included James Irvine, went to New York to talk to the elderly Carpentier. The price for the ranch was $1,000,000 which these men felt was too high. Charles A. Hooper, representing another group, purchased the ranch at this price the same year. The land was transferred into the name of C. A. Hooper & Co. in August 1912. A month later, Hooper sold to the James Irvine group, under contract, approximately 7,300 acres of the ranch. The Irvine group formed the Moraga Company, and each company managed its share of the land. This arrangement, after several years, proved to be unsatisfactory, and, in 1923, the Moraga Company, of which Irvine was a 50 per cent stockholder, purchased the remaining 4,000 acres from Hooper & Co. Including both purchases, the price paid for the ranch was more than the $1,000,000 originally asked.[1]

James Irvine, who had large land holdings in California, was extremely interested in agriculture, and he kept close watch on every small detail of the planting of crops and their growth. Many fruit trees were planted on the ranch, including large pear orchards and the walnut trees still to be seen in various locations. Beans were planted between the rows of the young pear trees. Tomatoes and other crops were grown in substantial quantities.

The Moraga Ranch was an operating ranch for years under the supervision of William U. Barnes. Barnes had worked on the Burton ranch and came to manage Moraga Ranch about 1921. Burton, Carpentier's original ranch manager, had remained with Grant & Williamson and then again Carpentier; but he did not see eye to eye with James Irvine and left the job.[2] He continued, however, to manage the land by Redwood Canyon until he died in 1925.[3] From then on, working with Breed and Irvine for many years, Bill Barnes, known as Emperor Barnes, was the ranch superintendent for the entire property.

Sacramento Northern train ran in front of the Moraga Barn where Helen Hetfield wrote bills of lading for farmers AF

The Moraga Company inherited the leases of families on the ranch, some of whom had been farming the land for many years. Company policy was that they could continue to rent the land, the result being that in some families a third generation farmed the same land.[4]

Any attempted development of the property in the subdivision field was in the area of the town of Moraga, and little change occurred in the Orinda section of the ranch after the early effort of the Grant brothers until the 1920s. The Moraga school in the Glorietta section still held classes for the children of local families. Cattle were still being driven to market through the old tunnel, via Brookside road, after they had been held for the night in corrals at the base of the road where the McDonnell Nursery is presently located. They continued in this manner until hoof and mouth disease in the state caused legislation that required the cattle to be shipped by train or truck.[5]

The Crossroads

Other than Ma Conklin's Hotel, Gerow's Blacksmith Shop and the California and Nevada Railroad Stationhouse, which included a restaurant of sorts for a time and may have had rooms and operated as a small hotel on occasion,[6] there had been no business at the intersection of the Tunnel Road and the Moraga-Orinda roads. In the 1800's, when these businesses were located there, the roads were little more than wide dirt trails following the easiest possible grade.

All of these establishments had gone by 1921, when, one day, Alfred Elkinton drove over the gravel road from Berkeley and turned left at the Orinda turnoff. He stopped to watch the Fish and Game representative, who was sitting on the running-board of his Model T Ford skinning four wildcats and who had come in response to a plea from Jim Sullivan, whose chickens the wildcats had been getting.[7] But just before crossing the bridge and taking the turn to Orinda, he did pass one building.

The Willows

A restaurant has been in business at the site of The Willows since 1917. In the early 1890's there was an open air dance platform and a picnic area nearby that train passengers and other groups enjoyed.

Mrs. Eve Nelson, who with her husband, Milt, operated The Willows during part of the 1940's and 1950's, researched some of the history of the restaurant. She wrote: "Other than a wigwam, the earliest structure to occupy the present site of The Willows . . . was placed there in the early nineties by an engineer on the California and Nevada Railroad. . . . His name was Brady. . . . On one of his daily 'hay hauls' he brought along a flat car loaded with two shacks that he had somehow wangled from the company. Knocking an end out of each, he placed them where The Willows now stands and with the use of a few nails and tarpaper fashioned a summer cabin for himself and his family."[8] After Ed Brady retired from the railroad, he opened a meat market in Lafayette. He advertised, "There are no flies on Brady's meats."[9]

The Willows was built on the Baker Ranch and was opened by Jack Willey who managed it under the name of the Contra Costa Country Club. In two years, Mrs. Anna Baker, known as "Ma Baker," whose husband had recently died, moved into the building from

89

Upper Orinda Willows (1952) AB   *Lower* Driving from the tunnel into Orinda (1920's) WH

her adjoining ranch. She named it Oak Villa Inn, operated a small restaurant, and leased the building to groups. Mrs. Cyril Chester, an early Orinda resident, remembers renting the place for $15.00 in 1919 to give an evening dance. Mrs. Baker was still the proprietor when Mrs. E. A. Dawson went to a dance there in 1925, but the following year another manager took it over.[10] Oscar Young, a pianist who played at The Willows in 1950 also played there in 1926. As he recalled, the name was again The Contra Costa County Club.[11]

The Dolio family, who had lived and farmed near Tunnel Road since 1914, purchased the building in 1928. Martin Dolio, a son, has owned it since 1947 and leases it to various tenants.

Again, according to Mrs. Nelson: "One story is told of a gala opening. The manager had spent considerable . . . both within and without. A night for the grand opening was set. Engraved invitations were sent out to personages for an exclusive evening with Bacchus and the gods of chance. But when the tuxedos gentry and fine ladies arrived at the appointed hour, the sheriff's padlock barred the road to revelry and the manager lost his shirt and his lease."[12]

The establishment went through its ups and downs—sometimes open, sometimes closed —under a varied succession of proprietors, as roadhouse, private club, and hash-house, before an excellent restaurant, The Willows, was opened in 1938. Managers have been Dominick, with the well-known chef, Armando, Milt Nelson, Mike Lynn, Mrs. Lynn, and Bob Hecocks.

The Willows was remodeled by the Nelsons in 1948 after a fire struck the building. The name for the establishment came from the group of willow trees near the creek and the fact that one tree grew through the floor and extended through the roof of the building.

Early Crossroads Businesses

Before 1928 oldtimers remember that Bert Morrill had a gas station on the Lafayette side of the old bridge near The Willows.[13]

When Frank Enos left the Canary Cottage at the east end of the old tunnel in 1922, August Reuter took it over.[14] Gus operated the roadside stand until 1927 when he moved to Orinda, following in the footsteps of the former owner who had opened The White Swan in the Orinda village. The following year Gus opened The Crossroads Restaurant, where he served beer, wine and sandwiches and ran the first Standard gas station.[15]

In 1931 route No. 24 became a state highway as more and more traffic began to pass through Orinda and the nearby communities. The following year, the Standard station was moved near the center of the crossroads, and Gus moved his restaurant to the west side of the highway.

In 1936 the state made some improvements on the Tunnel road, making more of a right angle and clearer open vision at the crossroads,[16] in anticipation of the traffic which was expected to follow the opening of the new low-level tunnel the following year. A reflectorized stop sign was now installed for westbound traffic. This was the first traffic control necessary at the crossroads.

At this time a new market was built by Harry Craviotto next to Gus Reuter's restaurant.

Moving day to make room for an on-ramp to the highway (1951) BRAD

Selling groceries, produce and meats, the market, called Craviotto's, now boosted Orinda's total to two such stores.

The Standard station was moved a short distance to the corner, next to Gus Reuter's Crossroads Restaurant. Eleven years later a Shell station was built across the Orinda road on the northeast corner.

In December 1941 Gus Reuter was honored at a stag dinner at the Orinda Country Club by many of his friends on his twentieth anniversary in the area. Within a few years he retired. Ruth and Don Thompson purchased the Crossroads restaurant in 1945 and remodeled it, making it one of the fine restaurants of Orinda. The Thompsons had owned The Curve in Lafayette in 1936, but Don had gone into the war on active duty from 1942–45. Later they became the owners of the Cape Cod Restaurant in Lafayette and Newell House in Walnut Creek. Since Don's death, Ruth has operated both establishments.

In April 1943 Craviotto's Market was sold to the Bradley family and became Bradley's Cash Market. The store remained at this location until 1951, and, as the lease was up, and major road changes were planned for the highway, the Bradley family gave the building to Clyde Coggins and Ray E. Wadsworth who moved it to some property near Brookwood Road "at the little bridge near The Willows."[17] Here the Bradleys operated for two more years, until August 2, 1953, when the Division of Highways took over the property. One of the delights of the market was a partly open-air vegetable stand alongside of the building.

Ray Wadsworth, who owned the property on Brookwood Road, was one of the early realtors in the crossroads area. He was in business by 1937 and had an office in Orinda until he died recently.

By 1940, Orinda, backed by state and county officials, was strongly supporting plans for channelization of the Tunnel Road at the intersection, with two safety islands planned for cars turning left. The following year an electric signal was installed at the crossroads for the first time. In 1943, as the highway between Orinda and Lafayette was widened to four lanes, there was some channelization to improve traffic control. In 1953 and 1954, plans were completed and work started on major improvements including an underpass beneath Mt. Diablo Boulevard, a six-lane divided freeway and cloverleaf interchanges serving the highway. When the work started, the crossroads had traffic exceeding 31,000 vehicles a day, with 3,000 cars an hour crossing the intersection during peak periods.[18]

Moraga Highway now became Moraga Way, the old highway known as Bryant Way, and the freeway, for a one-mile section, became a six-lane divided road. The gas stations, Standard and Shell, were forced to leave. Standard moved further up toward the village, and Shell followed at a later date—December 1958.

The Crossroads establishment was eliminated, and the Thompsons opened the Cape Cod Restaurant in Lafayette. There was now no business on the village side of the highway at the crossroads. In 1969 road changes necessary for the planned rapid transit system were completed.

Moraga Oaks, Moraga Uplands and Oak Springs

Southeast of the crossroads, The Moraga Company also started selling land for homes in the late 1920s. On May 2, 1922, a subdivision map was filed for the Moraga Oaks area

93

Highway 24, Camino Pablo and Moraga Way intersection (1927)   IM

Donald Badgley children played in Orinda snowfall (1937) on Camino Encinas near Moraga Way   EB

which was planned around Camino Encinas, the main road. The subdivision was replanned by A. H. and H. Horace Breed in 1929 and 1930.[19]

In June 1922, the Moraga Company subdivided Moraga Uplands which stretched from Sanborn's property south past Glorietta Road.

In 1924, 1925 and 1926, subdivision maps were filed on the Oak Springs area, adjoining Moraga Oaks, and building sites were sold. Coy Filmer acquired the subdivision the following year. A swimming pool was constructed on the property on land reserved for general recreational use of the residents. The clubhouse adjacent to the pool was built in 1945 and has, subsequently, been greatly improved by, among other things, modern filtering and heating equipment. Many of the residents accomplished the improvements by physical work and by money raised from picnics and other functions. The recreation areas are administered by Oak Springs Home Association, the creation and authority of which are authorized by restrictions in the deeds to the lots in the subdivision.[20]

Fred T. Wood

In 1936 Fred T. Wood, realizing the potential for growth near the crossroads, established an office on the southeast side of the highway. He formed the Fred T. Wood, Inc. and began construction of homes in his first subdivision, Moraga Estates. Within eight months this area had sold so well that a second subdivision was started, Moraga Woodlands. Fred Wood soon developed sites in the area of Davis Road, Southwood Drive, Overhill Road, Oakwood Road, Estates Drive, Orchard Road, Brookside and along Moraga Highway. He continued to sell home sites in Orinda for over twenty years, eventually developing several other subdivisions including Orinda Hills, 1953; Sunset Village, 1946; Moraga del Rey, 1946–48; Lost Valley, 1947; and in 1948, San Miguel Terrace.[21]

In 1939 Fred Wood constructed a building for Paul Vashell to house stores and apartments. Vashell was an electrician who, later, was active in the Orinda Lion's Club, the Chamber of Commerce and other community affairs. After his death in the 1960s, Mrs. Vashell sold the building.

The Vashell building provided a home for a restaurant called the Wild Duck, run by Camilla Gibbs and Irene Blackman who lived in an apartment overhead. The restaurant did not serve liquor. Many of the citizens of Orinda had often waged opposition to additional applications for liquor licenses of restaurants at the crossroads. The temperate Wild Duck, however, did not survive more than a couple of years.

Cianciarulo Building

Property across Moraga Highway from Fred Wood's office was purchased by Anthony Cianciarulo in 1937. He leased it to the Associated Oil Company (Phillips) who constructed a gas station there in 1938, which is still operating in the same location, having moved back from the road slightly to accommodate road improvements. Cianciarulo purchased the property to the rear of this, in 1938, and erected the Cianciarulo building for which A. T. Beckett was the contractor. The building was completed in 1939, and the Casa Orinda restaurant, owned by Jack Snow, opened its doors.[22] Originally on the highway, this street is now Bryant Way.

Highway 24, Camino Pablo and Moraga Way intersection (May, 1947). Note the Pine Grove   RLC

Wallace Realty Company

On the same side of the road, in December 1938, Ed Wallace moved into the little red-roofed realty building that was a landmark in Orinda for many years. The building remained through all of the changes at the crossroads, until the Bay Area Rapid Transit necessitated its destruction in December 1967.

Originally on Highway 24, its address changed to Bryant Way with the road changes in 1955, but the location was the same.

The Wallace family, which includes Ken and Clark, both well-known in local affairs, now have an office in Moraga. Ed Wallace was responsible for many of the transactions of land around the crossroads, and, later, on the Moraga Ranch, and was the agent for many of the subdivision land sales. One large sale was to Donald Rheem in 1936. In 1953 the firm sold 5,000 acres of the ranch to the Utah Construction Company which heralded the beginning of the intensive development of the area south of Glorietta to Moraga.

Moraga Hills Building

In 1941 Fred Wood built the Moraga Hills building on the corner next to his office to provide stores and offices for the now rapidly growing community.

The first tenants were Gray Minor's Hardware Store, a dress shop, coffee shop, and, right on the corner, a drug store owned by Frank A. Delos, which was moved in 1957 to its present location across the road. Also, there was Henry Hodap (Heini), the first local barber, known to a generation of Orindans. He had started cutting hair in the back of the Orinda Store while waiting for the completion of the new building.

Casa Orinda

In April 1942 Casa Orinda moved to the new building from its old location in the Cianciarulo building. This is the oldest restaurant location in Orinda, excepting The Willows. It is still owned by the Snow family. Their vacated spot became, consecutively, Rambeau's Hacienda and the Orinda Roost, which opened in 1949.

Jack Snow, the present proprietor of the Casa Orinda, is well known for his excellent gun collection which is on display at the restaurant. He also owns some bridles, given to him by Barnes, manager of the Moraga Ranch, that reputedly belonged to the Moraga family.[23]

In 1965 a tragedy occurred that shocked the community when Tommy Snow, one of the owners, was murdered on his way home at night, by an unknown assailant, still at large.

McDonnell's Nursery

The property on which McDonnell's Nursery is located was purchased shortly after 1930 by Mrs. J. D. Murphy who had subdivided Orinda Oaks. Galen C. Darr's family purchased the site from her in 1935. Known until very recently as the Moraga Nursery, the business by Brookside Road was started, the same year, to help supply plants needed by homeowners in Orinda. This is the only business outside of the crossroads area south of the freeway until Moraga or Rheem is reached. It was established before zoning ordinances went into effect.

On at least two different occasions before the ordinances, citizens fought successfully to keep business from the Glorietta area.

Back of this property was another area that had been owned since 1891 by John P. Rose (also known as John Carrick). This was purchased by Clarence Betz, a local business man, about 1940. The old home on the property was refurbished by Betz.

Still further up Brookside Road is the Domingos Ranch. In 1882 Jose Domingos settled on this property, eventually buying the land of two neighboring families. The children of the family went to the nearby school. The Domingos farmed, had some cattle and a small dairy, and for years worked hard to live off the land.[24] The family still own a large section of property here.

Orinda Theatre

In December 1941 the Orinda Theatre, built by Donald Rheem, opened its doors with Ben Randall as manager. After the theatre was opened, the Orinda Sweet Shop held forth next door serving lunches, dinners, sandwiches and soft drinks, but by 1950 the space was converted to shops. Randall also managed the Orinda Camera Shop and later the Rheem Theatre. A popular man, he was honored at a dinner in 1961, attended by more than 200 citizens, for his many services to the community. His untimely death came just four days later.

Wells Fargo Bank

Next to the theatre, Orinda's first bank, the American Trust Company (Wells Fargo Bank) building was completed, and the bank opened for business on February 10, 1947. The structure was designed by Cantin and Cantin, who also had planned the theatre. John L. Stoffel was the first manager.

Donald L. Rheem

In 1949 Donald Rheem built the Rheem building at the crossroads, and, from then on, new businesses and buildings have made the area grow to the busy place it is today.

Rheem also was responsible for developing a large section of land, not all of which is in the Orinda School District. Rheem first built a large home and later acquired 1,800 acres of land. He initiated a home development program in 1948. The first residential subdivision was Rheem Highlands, 1948; second, Rheem Glen, 1951; then Rheem View Acres in 1953. That year he also had zoned for business about 100 acres, and in 1954 the erection of Rheem center started with construction of Clark's Market (Safeway).

Within two years, a service station and building to house a bakery, hardware and a dime store were built. In 1957 additional stores and the Rheem Theatre were added.

In 1955 Donald Rheem began the development of Rheem Valley Estates. A year later, another unit was started on Donald Drive. In 1956 a post office was built.[25] Rheem Valley settlement has been continuous since that time and many homes and apartments have been erected.

Other Subdivisions on Moraga Ranch

From late 1930 other sizable areas southeast of the freeway have been developed in the Orinda School District. The Moraga Company subdivided Moraga Manor, Moraga Glorietta and Moraga Park after 1939. From then on the company sold land to private developers rather than attempt to subdivide.

Moraga Meadows was planned in 1945, and various sections were developed by Abe Doty, A. J. McCosker, Albert Lockwood, Mason Case, Ralph Church and Miles Hudson. Tarabrook was planned by Abe Doty in 1947; Orinda Hills in 1953—Fred Wood and Miles Hudson; after 1950, Woodland Terrace—C. M. Teigland; Warford Estates—Bernard Muth; Broadview Tract—Bob Platt; Moraga Gardens—Mason Case; and Glorietta Gardens—Miles Hudson.

Utah Construction Company

In December 1953 the Utah Construction Company purchased the remaining land holding of The Moraga Company consisting of 5,000 acres.[26] Beginning in 1957, Utah developed in Orinda the subdivisions Inland Valley, Ardith Drive and Ranchitos de Moraga, and Lincoln Estates, with Abe Lincoln.

Various builders have developed tracts of land south of Orinda, and Moraga's growth has boomed as a result. In 1957 Moraga's population was only 2,000, but by 1967 it had reached 8,000 and was growing at a rapid rate. At present the area is faced with inadequate access roads for the amount of traffic, but there are plans for new roads in the near future.

Some local residents at Bear Creek Falls; William Buckley home; deLaveaga carriage on Summit Road   LLS, LAV

IX

Roads

Orinda is so closely dependent on the roads leading in and out of the area that they must be considered in the story of community development. The slow period of settlement, and later, the rapid growth, relate directly to the facility of access to the area. As of January 1970, about 78,000 cars passed each day through the Caldecott Tunnels.

The First Roads

The first paths generally followed the course of the streams. Settlers found their way into Orinda up San Pablo Creek canyon much as the road traverses today. Local Indians probably used this way to trade with coastal villages. Another trail that led in and out of the area followed Bear Creek canyon into the Briones valley. A rider could branch from this path to Lafayette, to Martinez or to the Pinole area. The early wagon road to Martinez from Orinda followed what is now known as Miner Road, then on up the creekbed to join the road from Lafayette to Martinez.

John F. S. Smith mentioned the wagon road to Martinez in 1850 when he spoke of his life on his ranch in the present Sleepy Hollow area and on San Pablo Creek.[1] The road Smith spoke of included two public highways. Although the first roads were little more than trails, as early as July 20, 1850, the county was partitioned into road districts, and a few main roads were declared public highways. Number five was the road from the Moraga redwoods to the road leading from Martinez to San Jose. Number six was the road usually traveled from the rancho of Vicente Castro by the ranch of Elam Brown, intersecting the road from the Moraga redwoods to Martinez near the house of Jonah Bernell.[2]

Orders were given for all able-bodied males between the ages of eighteen and forty-five to be called upon to work on these thoroughfares for five days each year or to have a substitute do the work for them, when the supervisors or overseers of the districts needed them.[3]

The road from the redwoods back of Moraga had been in existence before this time as lumber was brought out of the area this way to Lafayette. The section from Moraga to Lafayette was known as the Jonas Hill Road. In 1853 a shortcut was built from the woods to Martinez through Pleasant Hill rather than the longer Walnut Creek route.[4] Several other routes were built from the redwoods into the Oakland area within a few years.[5] One of these, the Thorn Toll Road, built in 1854, could be traveled free of charge only in 1887, the franchise finally having expired.[6]

By 1861 road districts in the county had been increased, and the San Pablo Creek route was now included in district number seventeen. The description of the district included the local resident in the Sleepy Hollow area: "Commencing at the south side of the Cerrito; running thence east to a sugar loaf on the top of the mountain; thence north in a straight line to the house of Lauterwasser, formerly known as Smith's Ranch, thence in a southwesterly direction, following San Pablo Creek to the bay and around to the point of beginning."[7]

Telegraph Road

One of the first roads to lead north from Oakland was the county road which later became San Pablo Avenue. Only a trail led from the Rancho de San Antonio of the Peraltas and wound precipitously over the hills, on down toward present Orinda, Lafayette and on to Martinez.

On July 4, 1858, the stringing of a telegraph line was started along its approximate route. The line reached as far as Genoa, Nevada, by the fall of the year. The road was from then on called Telegraph Road. It followed the present Telegraph Avenue route from Oakland to where Claremont Avenue connects with Telegraph, ran along what is now Claremont Avenue, then over the hills, following the approximate path of the present Fish Ranch Road, down the West Branch of the San Pablo Creek and what is now Brookwood Road, and on into Lafayette.

No sooner was there an improved road than settlers sprang up along the way. Between the Castro, Moraga, and Peralta grants, there was some land thought to be public. By 1860 several people laid claims to this land along Telegraph Road.[8] Hough and his sons claimed 1,000 acres near Telegraph Road, Alex Houston owned about 450 acres which included Conklin's Tavern, John Frese had a residence near Telegraph Road, as well as Benjamin M. and J. H. Grinnell, two Grunon brothers, John Holland, James Port and some others. One of the very earliest settlers was Ben Jennings. All of these residents did not remain, but the family of William N. Buckley who claimed 320 acres near the Alameda County line lived there for over sixty years. William was thirty-eight years old when he built his first home near Telegraph Road, and his son, Henry, was a one-year-old. Before the family left, Henry was over sixty-five, having lived all of his life at this location. The old house was torn down in 1935 to make way for the east portal of the Caldecott Tunnel.

In May 1860 a petition was presented to the Board of Supervisors, asking for the road to be declared a public highway.[9]

That the road was passable for stages is evident by the fact that J. W. Morris, proprietor of a stage that had offices at the J. Bamber & Co. Express on Park Street in Oakland and at the Morgan House in Martinez, began to use the new route. Morris commented: "On about the 26th day of September, 1859, I commenced running a two-horse stage from Oakland to Pachecoville and Martinez over a route but newly established, and over which there was but little travel, and the road was in bad condition to such an extent that the great aggregate of travel from the San Ramon valley to the city of San Francisco was by way of Martinez, but by great dint of exertion and indefatigable attention to my duties as a stage driver, I succeeded in developing the superior advantage of this route. The line has been established at great expense of both money and labor as part of the country which the stage passed is mountainous and constantly requires a great expenditure of money to keep it in good condition." The Morris stages had a stop in Lafayette.[10]

Morris enlarged his stage to four-horse coaches, one traveling from each end of the line, and kept it running for several years during good weather. He advertised: "Leaving Oakland on arrival of the first boat from San Francisco; returning will leave Martinez on arrival of the first boat from Benicia, connecting with the 2 o'clock boat from San Francisco. Travelling over a romantic and delightful country, making the trip through in six hours, affording passengers a safe, speedy and pleasant journey."[11]

The Pony Express rider used this route over Telegraph Road, passing through Orinda when the early westbound trips missed the Sacramento-San Francisco boat and used the Benicia ferry instead. On one trip in April, 1860, Thomas J. Bedford of Benicia, who was in charge, arranged for the ferry boat, *Carquinez*, to be at her berth in Benicia at an early hour. The horse and rider were met and not a moment was lost in getting the boat to Martinez. As it touched land, the horse sprang from the deck and dashed up the wharf as horse and rider went "flying on their way to Oakland." The Express left Martinez at 7:33 a.m. and arrived in Oakland at 9:32, making the trip in one hour and fifty-nine minutes.[12]

Discussing the road, an article in the Contra Costa Gazette of March 30, 1861 says: ". . . then there still remains the route by Benicia and Martinez, through Pacheco and Lafayette to Oakland, which is now in good condition to travel. On this route wharves are already built on both sides of the bay, ferry boats are actually running, and the Pony Express has often passed over this line without inconvenience or hindrance."

Bayard Taylor describes a harrowing trip over the new road in late 1859 with a two-horse buggy that took two hours and fifty-two minutes from Martinez to the Oakland boat when he was in a terrible rush to get to San Francisco.[13]

By April of 1861 there was a bill before the legislature authorizing the construction of a tunnel through the mountains lying between Alameda and Contra Costa County.[14] The project was conceived by Contra Costa residents who hoped to avoid the heavy grade over the hill. Although a joint stockholder company called the San Antonio and Alamo Turnpike Company was proposed as early as 1860, plans for the tunnel did not materially progress in the next ten years.[15]

On the Contra Costa side of the hills, a trail split off from Telegraph Road, taking almost the same route as the proposed Gateway Boulevard will follow. This was locally known as Adobe Road,[16] and one branch came down at the present Brookside Road. The other branch went on through the canyon in back of the Moraga adobe for which the road was named. Later, when the Fish Ranch was on Telegraph Road, the road that came down by Brookside was spoken of as the road from the Fish Ranch because it branched off at the ranch site. The line of the old dirt roads can still be seen in many sections.

Telegraph Road was later called the Summit Road. At the top of the grade was the Summit House at an elevation of 1,315 feet. This was a welcome stop for the dusty, tired traveler in summer or the rain-soaked one in winter. It was managed by Milton J. Rook in 1861 who was the proprietor for at least the next six years. The Miner girls remembered the stop on their way home from town in the 1880's: "As we entered the Summit Road there was a little saloon stuck into the side of the big hill close to the road called the Last Chance. . . . From the Last Chance there was the long, slow climb to the summit. There stood the Summit House, a reminder of the days when the stages ran to Mt. Diablo and changed horses there. It was a tall, gaunt, grey house."[17]

Telegraph Road on the Contra Costa side for a time in the 1890's was called Golden Gate

Way and, later, Tunnel Road. It became State Highway 24, now a major freeway. After the 1904 tunnel was opened, the part above the tunnel was renamed Fish Ranch Road.

Kennedy Tunnel

Although the initial proposal to build a tunnel through the hills had failed, the matter was not dropped from the minds of the Contra Costa County citizens. In 1871 a franchise was granted to a group who planned to construct a tunnel, but this plan as well failed to materialize. A road was planned from the head of Broadway to the foothills and, turning right, past the residence of J. Ross Brown, was to have had a tunnel that would pierce the summit for a distance of 500 feet. However, within a few years, work actually started on the tunnel, as another group formed the Oakland and Contra Costa Tunnel Company and took up the franchise to build a toll road. The new road started at Claremont Avenue adjoining the south property line of Thornburg's Sanitarium on the Martin Dunn Ranch, now the Hotel Claremont, and passed through ranches of Edson Adams, Kohler, John R. Glascock, Anthony Chabot (Lake Temescal), then the ranch of William Gwinn, which was leased by William Kennedy. The bore on the Oakland side started at this last ranch, and the road was known as Kennedy Toll Road. On the Contra Costa side of the bore was the John Buckley Ranch.[18]

The tunnel was pierced to about 100 feet on the Contra Costa side and to about 200 feet on the Alameda County side,[19] when the project had to be abandoned for lack of funds. So ended the first effort to tunnel through the hills.

Contra Costa Tunnel

The road over the summit continued to be difficult and dangerous. On a June day in 1882, Hugh Carroll, whose family were early settlers on the Moraga Ranch, drove up the dusty road from Oakland toward his home. He was almost to the top near the water tank when his wagon was run into by another wagon that came hurtling down the grade with its horses out of control. Carroll's passengers included his sister-in-law, a young niece and a nephew. The Carroll wagon with its occupants was hurled over the edge of the road. The boy was dead by the time they managed to return to Oakland, and the young girl was badly hurt.[20]

Earlier that year a citizens' meeting had been held, with William Camron of Orinda on the committee, to again look into the construction of a tunnel. Residents felt strongly that the development of Contra Costa County was held back by the lack of a good road into the area.

However, despite danger and need, it was not until 1893 that definite action was taken, and the Board of Supervisors was petitioned to survey the land from Buckley's ranch to the mouth of the "Kennedy Tunnel," three-fourths of a mile long. The petition mentioned that Kennedy had constructed a road from a point on old Telegraph Road up beyond the water company reservoir to the mouth of a tunnel which had been abandoned. It said that the present hard grade over the mountain range through the canyon with its steep banks left no room to swing the road to get an easy grade. The turns were sharp and the road dangerous to four or six horses loaded.[21]

Note old tunnel entrance above west portal construction of Broadway (Caldecott) Tunnel   CDH

Interest in improving conditions of the drive over the hills was spasmodic. But in 1895, the Merchants' Exchange Club of Oakland, one of the forerunners of the Oakland Chamber of Commerce, started a real campaign to facilitate the building of a new tunnel. The club which had formed in 1877 and disbanded in 1880, was reforming and looking for a worthwhile project to which it could devote its energies.[22] Now, in both Alameda and Contra Costa County, citizens became enthusiastic over the prospects.

J. H. Sohst became Chairman of the Tunnel Committee and said at that time: "One of the reasons why I have taken such interest in the diggings of a tunnel is that in 1863 I started to take a ride to Lafayette, Contra Costa County, but did not get there because in going down the grade on the other side of the summit, I was thrown out of my buggy. After gathering myself up and being convinced there were no broken bones about me, I changed my course. I went down the creek to San Pablo and from there home. Many a story can be told how people lost their lives and others their limbs, to say nothing about damaged vehicles, ruined horses and destroyed goods on that road to Contra Costa."[23]

On the Contra Costa side, a barbecue was held on May 23, 1897, at the William Buckley Ranch on the road to the site of the new bore. Representatives from both counties were there, and subscriptions toward the new project from some of the Contra Costa men included $200 from J. M. Stow, $40 from J. O. Miner, $100 from E. J. Hutchinson, $100 from W. B. Roberts and $100 from A. Hemme, all well-known men from the county.[24]

A problem developed when three-fifths of the planned tunnel was found to be in Contra Costa County and only two-fifths in Alameda County. Contra Costa Supervisors were not too promising for the future of the project until the Merchants Exchange obligated itself to raise one-fifth of the money required to build the tunnel,[25] thus leaving each county to supply two-fifths.

After eight years of planning and fund raising, the formal opening of the Contra Costa Tunnel was held on November 4, 1903. The new tunnel was 1,100 feet in length and 320 feet lower than the top of the Summit Road. Timber-lined, dark and a narrow two lanes, with a slight bend in the middle where the bores from either side did not quite meet, the tunnel was welcomed by the citizens as a major step in connecting the counties. Officials and guests of the Merchants Exchange were present at the opening, and a newspaper account of the occasion reads in part: "Upon reaching the tunnel the party disembarked from the various conveyances and inspected the interior of the tunnel which has been splendidly timbered and is evidently a very satisfactory piece of engineering and constructive work. At this point the visitors were met by Supervisor de Martini of Contra Costa County and several people from the neighborhood. . . . After walking through the tunnel and inspecting the construction and also the approaching from the Contra Costa side which is from a point several hundred yards to the southeast of Buckley's place on the old Fish Ranch Road, the members returned to the Alameda County side and drove down the grade some distance where a luncheon had been provided for the guests. An express wagon, loaded with sandwiches, hot coffee, fruit, and cakes, together with a supply of Theodore Gier's best brands, had been sent forward to this point where refreshments were thoroughly enjoyed in the open air.

"There were no formal exercises but several toasts were proposed by Wilber Walker of

AUCTION! AUCTION! AUCTION!

THURSDAY, DECEMBER 30th, 1897,

AT 10 A. M.

Weather permitting; if not, first fine day following at same hour.

— AT —

FISH RANCH

CONTRA COSTA COUNTY,

THE PROPERTY OF THE

Estate of late J. H. OLIVE,

CONSISTING OF

Fine Bred Trotting Stock ; also, a number of first-class Business, Saddle and Work Horses.

Fine chestnut Stallion, 7 years old ; sired by *Dexter Prince*, dam *Corette;* record, 2.19 ; gentle, sound and kind, and very promising.

Some 40 head Horned Stock, consisting of calves, yearlings, two-year olds, and new milch cows.

Express wagons (side spring), four-spring wagons, buggies, road cart, breaking cart, pole cart, track sulky and farm wagons.

Also, all kinds of Farming Implements, such as plows, harrows, disk cultivators, mowing machines, horse rakers, sleds, drags and various other articles.

Harness, both double and single, work and driving halters, blankets, surcingles, boots, etc., etc.

Per Order of Administratrix,

R. M. EATON.

LLS

the Merchants' Exchange who proposed the sentiment: 'Here's to the Contra Costa tunnel —may it be the first child of a large family of progress.' "[26]

The future would see Walker's toast become a reality but not for awhile.

Fish Ranch

Almost everyone who has traveled over Fish Ranch Road has wondered about its unusual name. Bounded on the east by James Taylor's land, on the south and west by Buckley's claim, and lying south of Telegraph Road was the Oakland Trout Company which claimed 175 acres of land. It was there by 1872 and was managed by George Winslow, his wife, Martha, and their son, George, Jr. From early days the ranch was a stage stop and had a wayside inn to refresh the travelers. It soon was popularly called the Fish Ranch.

The Winslows had a daughter, Elizabeth, who met and married John Hanford Olive when the family lived in Merced before coming to the property on Telegraph Road. Olive came to California in 1854 with Captain Young's party, and then worked for the California Stage Company out of Sacramento. The Olives' daughter, Ella, was born at Knight's Ferry in 1859.[27] John Olive remained in the stage business except for a brief farming stint and purchased an interest in the Dooley and Company line in 1876. In April of the following year, George Winslow wrote to his son-in-law and told him he was getting too old to carry on alone on the trout farm and asked him to come and help. The Olives left the valley in 1877 and came to live with the Winslows. Winslow died in 1879, and Olive was in full charge.[28] That same year, Ella Olive married Gabriel Moraga, a grandson of the grantee of the near-by Moraga Rancho.

Mrs. Olive was an excellent cook, and Fish Ranch became a favorite spot for visitors. Besides the main house, there was a saloon. There was also a row of guest cottages in the bottom of the canyon near the stream by the big alder trees. Olive provided cattle corrals, and a fine stable, and engaged in horse trading. He was said to be a great judge of horse flesh, and had a reputation for being honest in his dealings. He owned a fine stallion named Nikanor. The carriage horses of many Oaklanders were pastured and boarded at the ranch.

Mrs. Winslow lived with the Olives until her death in 1895 at the age of 85. Her will left the ranch to John Olive who helped to pursue title to the land on which she had filed a claim in the 1860's. Olive himself died two years after Mrs. Winslow, and it was not until after his death that President McKinley signed the final papers on the Winslow homestead.[29]

The Olives had two daughters, Ella and Rose. Rose was married to Albert Eaton who helped with management of the ranch. After Olive died, the land was leased out by the widow and the girls for several years, and Ella and Gabriel Moraga leased the tavern. Often Ella ran it with a hired man and her children as Gabriel managed a cattle ranch near Alamo for the superintendent of the Contra Costa Water Company. The Moragas lived at Fish Ranch a good part of the time after they were evicted from the adobe in 1886. Part of the time they lived in Bollinger Canyon near the cattle ranch. Finally, in 1903, Olive's widow and daughters sold the Fish Ranch property to Otis Engs, who, in turn, sold it in 1906 to the Syndicate Water Company.[30] The tavern was kept open until 1915 when the tunnel road was closed to travel for almost a year.

Ella and Gabriel Moraga had eight children, including Olivette, who attended the Mo-

Above Tunnel Inn (1910)   LLS   *Below* Enlarged by 1917 and called Canary Cottage   RE

raga School, and Eugene, who has visited here and spoken to the Moraga Historical Society. Another member of the Moraga family, Gumincinda, married John Avila, and they lived and raised their children on the Fish Ranch property for many years. Their daughter, Rose, also attended Moraga School in the late 1880's and later recalled her classmates and her life on the ranch.[31]

The Fish Ranch was well-known for so many years that it seemed only proper to use its name for the road over the hills when the first tunnel was opened. The new road was called Tunnel Road. The freeway goes over the site of some of the old ranch buildings not far from the present Gateway Boulevard exit.

Canary Cottage

Another place with an unusual name that was known to all who came to Contra Costa County through the old single-bore tunnel was the Canary Cottage. Located on Henry Buckley's property near the east portal of the tunnel by a wide sweep in the road, it offered sandwiches and snacks and boasted a gas pump as well. Teamsters with loads of hay and motorists negotiating the curvy road and the narrow, dark tunnel stopped here for a welcome break in the often arduous trip.

When automobiles first traveled the old road, drivers would stop for water at an old wooden horse trough that stood here. Some enterprising individual took advantage of this well-patronized stop and sold sandwiches and cold drinks from an open stand. The business grew at the roadside stop, and the stand sprouted a roof. The first gas station was a fifty-gallon gas buggy to service those motorists stranded by lack of gasoline. As this flourished, the owner removed an old steel service station building from Oakland and erected it on a spot next to the restaurant.[32] The Shell Oil Company delivered the gasoline.

In 1917, when Basil A. Perry and his wife took it over, it was named the Tunnel Inn. Mrs. Perry ran the establishment while Mr. Perry operated a jitney on Grove Street. Each day he delivered the ice cream and perishables that his wife needed.

Mr. Perry had at one time worked on the Moraga Ranch after coming to California from the Azores in 1900 and then had driven a four-horse stage between Piedmont, Walnut Creek and Danville from 1907 until 1909. He was thus well-acquainted with the watering stop on the road. The Perrys found it hard to run a jitney business and the Inn, so they sold the restaurant and gas station to Frank Enos in 1918. Mr. Perry went on to become one of the founders and vice-president of Peerless Stages.[33]

After Frank Enos became the owner, he got the Shell Oil Company to paint the building yellow one day when they were repainting the traditional yellow gas pumps. He then changed the name to the Canary Cottage. He hired Miss Ruth Edwards of Oakland to come out to the Cottage to work for him. She lived with Henry and Ann Buckley, brother and sister from the old-time Buckley family who had lived down the road since 1860. Within a year Frank and Ruth were married and managed Canary Cottage together.

By this time the tunnel boasted electric lights, but the bulbs which hung from the ceiling were often burned out. Frank made a deal with the power company and tended the lights in the tunnel in exchange for lights at the Canary Cottage. He would hop on somebody's hay wagon as it went through the tunnel, and, while the obliging teamster stopped under a burned-out light, he would replace the bulb.

Enos was also able to get an appointment as a deputy of Contra Costa County, and a telephone was installed for him at the Canary Cottage.[34]

During the early 1920's, Frank and Ruth Enos built The White Swan (Casa Verana building) in Orinda. They gave up the establishment at the entrance to the tunnel to move to Orinda where they operated their new business as mentioned earlier.

Gus Reuter followed Frank Enos as owner at the Canary Cottage, but in 1927 he also moved to Orinda where he established his business.

Wild Cat Canyon Road

When William Camron purchased 3,000 acres of land in 1875 and planned Orinda Park subdivision, he immediately wanted a road with an easier grade to Berkeley. His first purchaser, Eugene Sullivan, actually surveyed the road for him, and Camron planned to build it, but his financial problems kept him from fulfilling his desire.

Before long, another settler on the Camron property, Theodore Wagner, took over the task. On July 29, 1882, the following article appeared in the Contra Costa Gazette:

TOLL ROAD NOTICE

Notice is hereby given that I will apply to the Board of Supervisors, Contra Costa County at meeting of said Board to be held in the County Court House at Martinez and to the Board of Supervisors of Alameda County at a meeting of said Board on 8-28-1882 10 A.M. . . . for authority to take the necessary land and to construct and maintain in said counties a graded wagon road . . . and to collect thereon for 50 years; said road to begin at a point near my house on the public road leading up San Pablo Creek, in said Contra Costa County thence by the most practical route along or near the line of the road surveyed on petittion of E. Sullivan et als.

Theodore Wagner

The road was important to Wagner who was beginning to develop his elaborate estate. At this time the completion of the Kennedy Tunnel looked doubtful, and the only direct way to town was still the long grade past the Fish Ranch and over the summit.

By 1887 Contra Costa County had appropriated $1,000 which had been spent on the Wagner Road, and at least another $1,000 had come from private subscription.[35] The dirt road was finished in both counties in 1889 but was not operated as a toll road. Wagner had given much of his experience as a surveyor as well as time to the project. The present Wild Cat Canyon Road leading through Tilden Park to the end of Spruce Street in Berkeley was the approximate route. It was a shorter way for Orinda residents to get to Berkeley, but it had serious problems of maintenance. In 1890 Wagner and James Miner were appointed by Orinda Park members as delegates to represent Orinda Park at a road meeting in Martinez and to discuss the problem.[36] By the following year rumors were around that the road would be abandoned, and interested citizens were appealing to keep it open.[37]

The road seems to have been kept open to some degree. In 1897, "Old December," an Orinda spokesman, wrote, "We are in need of a fence on either side of the Berkeley Road

BROADWAY LOW LEVEL TUNNEL

Ground Breaking Ceremonies

SUNDAY, JUNE 17th, 1934

Guests of Honor

HONORABLE FRANKLIN DELANO ROOSEVELT

HONORABLE FRANK F. MERRIAM

JOINT HIGHWAY DISTRICT No. 13, STATE OF CALIFORNIA

Directors

THOS. E. CALDECOTT - *President*
HARRY M. STOW - *Secretary*
HENRY L. HINMAN - *Treasurer*
ARCHIBALD B. TINNING - - - - - - - - - - - - - - - - - - - *Attorney*
WALLACE B. BOGGS - *Engineer*

Boards of Supervisors

ALAMEDA COUNTY	CONTRA COSTA COUNTY
Thos. E. Caldecott	W. J. Buchanan
William J. Hamilton	James N. Long
George A. Jansen	H. M. Stow
Ralph R. Richmond	R. J. Trembath
Clifford Wixon	H. L. Cummings

OAKLAND AND BERKELEY JUNIOR CHAMBERS OF COMMERCE
COMMITTEE ON ARRANGEMENTS

DUDLEY W. FROST - *General Chairman*
FRANK W. TEASDEL - - - - - - - - - - - - - - - - - - - *Vice-Chairman*
EDWARD H. SIEMS - *Secretary*
H. BUFORD FISHER - *Treasurer*

FL

that there may be an end to the obstructing gates. We should not be compelled to cross a muddy road with a gate on our shoulders and polished shoes on our feet. . . . Our taxes are as genuine and substantial as others. . . . People here have inhabited this section for many years and the only route to market was by way of Fish Ranch Road, inconvenient to this place, as our market is largely in Berkeley."[38] The road went up the hill past the Orinda Park School, past Souza's Hog Ranch and then on past the Curran Ranch. The summit of the ridge between the Curran Ranch and San Pablo Creek was called Cape Horn by the local people because of the wind that always blew there.[39] Now known as Inspiration Point where the passerby has a wide panoramic view of the northern part of Orinda, the spot is also well-known to the many kite-flyers who gather there in the spring.

In the 1930's E. I. deLaveaga tried to get the road improved to help serve his property that had been developed on the east side of the hills. In 1935 help came for the road which was by then called the Wild Cat Creek Road. DeLaveaga wrote, "After a terribly arduous week's work in which every political string was pulled, we were able to secure from Alameda County's allocation of PWA funds, a quarter million dollars to be spent on the Wild Cat Creek Road. . . . If the county will fix up the Toyonal on the west side up to the Highlands, and this road connect with the Wild Cat Creek Road, it will obviate the use of the Tunnel Road for those wishing to come from Berkeley. It will thus relieve congestion on the Tunnel Road. It will form another means of reaching Orinda by those timid souls who are afraid to go through a tunnel. . . . In my mind, the Wild Cat Creek project is the beginning of the opening up of the EBMUD land for a metropolitan park."[40]

A new, and for the first time, paved, seven-mile road was planned to replace the old rough road, but in 1937, the Orinda Association was still requesting the Board of Supervisors of Contra Costa County that the remaining 2–1/6 miles be surfaced.

Caldecott Tunnel

Even with the opening of the tunnel by 1904, problems of transportation were not completely solved. Soil conditions were such that the road was hard to keep open due to the many slides in winter, or the tunnel would have to be closed for repairs of various sorts.

In 1912 a section of the road to the tunnel was closed for at least six months during the winter while twenty men and teams worked on a section from Fish Ranch towards the tunnel.[41] The following June the road was open again as repairs were completed. While the tunnel was closed, the floor had been lowered two feet and macadamized.[42] This was a great improvement. However, in 1915, the road was again closed for a year, not opening until the following July.[43] When the tunnel was closed, the old problem of how to get to Oakland or Berkeley had to be faced. If it were summer, the Wagner Road might be a possibility, or the old Fish Ranch Road over the summit, or even the long way around by San Pablo.

So it was for good reason that the tremendous project of building a low-level tunnel through the hills was discussed by residents and supervisors for many years. Teams were no longer the problem as automobiles began to travel State Route 24 in larger and larger numbers. This highway was constructed in Contra Costa County through the actions of supervisors of both counties who formed Joint Highway District 13 in 1928. State Highway

24 was voted into existence by the legislature in 1931 and incorporated the road from the tunnel's east portal to the town of Walnut Creek.

Plans were prepared; rights of way for the highway and new tunnel acquired; and within two years, work on the project was started. On December 5, 1937, ceremonies were held to dedicate the new Broadway Low Level Tunnel and to celebrate the opening. The natural barrier to traffic which had remained since the beginning of California finally was breached. Thomas F. Caldecott was president of the Board of Directors of Joint Highway District No. 13 and, subsequently, was honored when the tunnel was rededicated in his name.

The tunnel is actually two bores. The twin tunnels, each 3,000 feet long, are concrete-lined, lighted with incandescent electric lights, and ventilated with a forced air ventilation system. They are 310 feet lower than the old single-bore tunnel. Curved at the ends, they join in a single portal building at each end, but the roadways between are 150 feet apart. The openings of the old tunnel, closed and boarded, are now concealed by dirt and natural growth.

In the next twenty years, continued growth of the bay area increased traffic through the two low-level tunnels to the point where they were becoming inadequate. A third bore was built and also dedicated with the name of Thomas Caldecott on October 6, 1964. The new bore cost approximately $11,000,000, whereas the old tunnel built in 1903 had cost $46,000. Mr. Walker's toast that it be "the first child of a large family of progress"[44] had certainly been fulfilled.

Orinda soon will become the gateway to Contra Costa County as the east portal of a $31,000,000 twin bore tunnel has its exit here as part of the Bay Area Rapid Transit System.

Slides

Even after the marvel of the low-level tunnels, the nature of soils along the highway occasionally caused problems. In December of 1950, an area between the tunnel and Orinda, comprised of the old Siesta slide, dumped tons of dirt onto the highway in heavy rains. The road was closed for two days. Fortunately, the slide occurred on a Saturday, and by Monday, after working night and day, the State Division of Highways cleared a narrow detour for traffic. Cars used El Toyonal Road leading into the shortcut to the summit and Wildcat Canyon Road while the highway was closed. Traffic was also routed through San Pablo and Redwood Canyon.

Other slides continued to come down on the road each winter, but through the years, the old banks and cuts have been well terraced and now seem to be under control.

Bus Service

On the completion of the low-level tunnel, bus service was possible for the first time to Orinda and other Contra Costa towns. The Sacramento Northern Railway received approval from the California Railway Commission to inaugurate the first bus service to the area from Oakland and San Francisco.[45]

In 1932 the Orinda Country Club had started a private bus service to Oakland for the convenience of residents, but its existence was brief. Otherwise, up to the opening of the tunnel, commuting traffic was dependent upon private means of transportation.

"A recent slide looks like a big thumb-print" —Orinda side of tunnel (December, 1950)   OFD

The Sacramento Northern Bus Service was available for $13.52 per month for the regular commute book, and W. A. Mitchell, president of the company, cooperated with citizens in trying to work out schedules.

In 1940 Rhodes States, Inc. inaugurated service to Berkeley with the Tunnel Road Line.[46] The bus came to the Orinda Store to pick up passengers from Orinda. Within a year the line was taken over by the Greyhound Corporation.[47] Except for brief interruptions, Greyhound service to Oakland and San Francisco has continued to the present time. It is planned now that Rapid Transit will replace all bus service.

In April 1952 a bus shelter for Orinda was completed, under the auspices of the Orinda Chamber of Commerce.

San Pablo Dam Road and Moraga Road

Since the days of the Castros, the people from the San Pablo and Richmond areas found their way into the area that is now Orinda by following the San Pablo Creek. The road remained a dirt road until paving work, started in 1920, was completed in June 1923. Now for the first time drivers could enjoy paved road all the way from Richmond to Moraga. Parts of the road had already been improved; the bridge on the road through the Orinda Village was built in 1920 and still stands with the date visible, although the bridge itself is battered and bruised. In the 1950's a new, wider and less curved San Pablo Dam Road was constructed.

The road from old Telegraph Road to Moraga did not always extend from the Crossroads. It was not until 1893 that a good wagon road was built by the Grant Bros. in conjunction with the California and Nevada Railroad and the Glorietta development. Several branch roads were also graded, and bridges were constructed between Glorietta and Lafayette by way of John Taylor's place.[48]

When the Charles Nelson family moved to Orinda to the historic "old yellow house," Moraga Road was still an unpaved wagon road. Nelson often had to harness a team of horses at night to pull a stuck motorist out of the mud during the winter months, while the oldest Nelson boy held a lantern for his father.[49]

In 1921–22, a construction company, headed by a woman, Mrs. Ellen E. O'Brien, built a new road on the old roadway into the Moraga Valley from Tunnel Road. The newly paved link was over four miles long, and although work was started after the paving of the San Pablo Road began, the completed road was celebrated in October, 1922, more than half a year ahead of the longer road. Moraga, in the spirit of the old times, feted the occasion with a barbecue, exhibits of local products, and sports of the old days of the roundups. The highway was christened by Mrs. Horace H. Breed, wife of one of the owners of The Moraga Company.

A construction camp was located about one-quarter of a mile past Glorietta Boulevard on the right side of the road going toward Moraga. Nelson would take milk from his herd of cows each day to supply the workers. The workers used solid tire trucks, and the concrete mixer required several men to operate it.[50] Four creeks had to be dammed to get enough water to mix the concrete.

After 1928, St. Mary's College contributed to some increase in traffic on the road; other

Fish Ranch in 1910   LLS   View of Sleepy Hollow from Boysen Lake (1942)   CC than that, the road was little used except on weekends when sightseers drove through the local countryside.

When the old highway developed many cracks, the road was tarred and graveled in the late 1930's, and in 1951 the road was widened. The old Nelson house was now five feet closer to the road than before.

Now one of the most heavily traveled roads in the county for its size, a new entrance to Moraga is planned from Highway 24 along Gateway Boulevard.

Local Roads

Many of the Orinda roads remain as they were planned long ago by the farmers and first subdividers. Most of the old bridges which crossed the roads have been replaced by culverts or newer bridges. Miner Road winds up the canyon approximately the same as when James Miner built it in 1879, following the old trail used by Smith and Lauterwasser, in 1939 a major bottleneck was relieved by the completion of the bridge-culvert at the end of Miner Road where it joins Camino Pablo, which is what the San Pablo Dam Road is now called in this section. A culvert also replaced the bridge at Camino Lenada this same year. In 1965 a $38,500 culvert was constructed across Lombardy Lane at Lauterwasser Creek to replace the old inadequate one which caused flooding in the winter.

Other roads throughout Orinda have a similar history of development. Many are named after local citizens. All the roads have been straightened when possible and widened, but many still remain narrow and with sharp turns due to the natural terrain of the countryside. Before most roads were taken over by the county, many individual neighborhood groups were responsible for their maintenance.

Due to the necessity for enlarging the utility services, particularly during the 1940's and 1950's, the local roads seemed to be in an upheaval much of the time. Every Orindan who lived here in that period will understand the following article that appeared in the Orinda News in December 1950:

IT COULD ONLY HAPPEN HERE

The other day the County Road men were in the Village pouring inches and inches of nice smooth tar and gravel, and making the highway into the kind of a thoroughfare on which you could take Grandma for a comfortable little jaunt in the family bus. There were "hot pots" and smoothers and scrapers and red trucks, and everyone was happy, even the road men. The long anticipated resurfacing of the Orinda Highway was in the happy process of becoming a reality.

Hardly anyone saw another truck drive up and stop about 100 feet back on the stretch of newly finished highway, still warm. The men in the second truck, which belongs to one of the utilities, unloaded tools and with gusto, fell to tearing out a nice chunk of the brand new road—digging for something, Providence knows what. • • •

In 1967 Miner Road was torn up while sewer lines were enlarged, and other roads still suffer similar fates.

The community has often struggled to beautify the main roads. In 1938 many trees were planted on the stretch of road from the Tunnel Highway to Orinda Village in an arrangement with the Improvement Association and the citizens. Plane trees and sycamores were selected. A few of these trees remain, but most were lost as the road was widened in 1940. In recent years the Orinda Beautification Committee has contributed to landscape improvement, with other community organizations assisting, and visible progress has been made.

A list of some of the roads in the deLaveaga subdivisions shows the Spanish flavor of the community and deLaveaga's close sensitivity to the land.

Camino Sobrante	From the Spanish grant Rancho Sobrante—surplus	Miner Road	Named after the Miner family who lived at the end of the road
La Espiral	The spiral	Camino Lenada	The shaded or wooded road
La Plaza	The plaza or square		
El Patio	The courtyard	La Senda	The path
Mira Loma	View of the hills	El Sueno	The dream
Linda Vista	Beautiful view	El Sereno	The road of serenity
La Cuesta	The summit	La Cintilla	The ribbon
El Caminito	The little road	Dias Dorados	Golden days
Las Cascadas	The Cascades	La Campana	The bell
Los Aromas	The aromas	El Campanero	The ringer of the bell
La Vuelta	The turn	La Puerto	The point
Dos Posos	The two wells (There were two wells along the road)	Via Hermosa	The beautiful road
		El Gavilan	The eagle
		Los Dedos	The fingers
La Noria	The draw well (here was an old well which supplied Bien Venida, the deLaveaga home)	El Pulgar	The thumb
		Las Vegas	The fields
		El Verano	The summer
		Via Floreado	The flowered way

and on the west side of the highway:

El Toyonal	The road of the toyon berries	Mariposa	The butterfly
		Vallecito	The little valley
Ardilla	The squirrel	Madronal	The road of the madrones
Bonita	Beautiful		
Rio Vista	View of the river	La Encinal	The road of the oaks
Los Conejos	The rabbits (cottontails)	Camino Diablo	The devil's highway
		Monte Vista	View of the mountains
El Dorado	Gold		

Moraga School children picture (1892) shows Miss Jennie Bickerstaff, teacher   GS

X

The Schools

The first school buildings in Orinda did not much resemble those of today. They were generally one-room wooden buildings heated by a wood stove. Then, more than now, the schools faced problems of shortages of teachers and books, inadequate facilities and lack of funds. Attendance was very sporadic due to many factors, including the season of the year, work at home and the distance to the school. However, the first two schools in Orinda remained in their original locations for many years, and a school has been established here for over a hundred years.

The Moraga School

The first school in Orinda was located near Glorietta Boulevard on Moraga Way. It was erected on property of the Moraga family and was called Moraga School. At that time the nearest school to this area was Willow Springs School, located where the town of Moraga is now. Willow Springs District had been authorized February 4, 1857.[1]

Sometimes schools were in existence in a haphazard sort of way before the districts were formed, wherever the population warranted it. Boundaries for school districts were very flexible, often being expanded to include new settlers.

By 1859 there were quite a few families living along the new Telegraph Road, the approximate path of the present freeway, and several of the Moragas had married and started families of their own and were settled on the ranch outside of the adobe. Without doubt there were enough children to make a new school necessary, one that would save them the long trek to Willow Springs. The Moraga School District, however, was not officially formed until November 5, 1861, when the Board of Supervisors granted the petition of L.W. Perry and others for a separate district. The order read that "said District be divided by a line commencing at the source of the San Pablo Creek including in said district the house of Joe Moraga, thence in a northerly direction including the premises of Wm. Dougherty and thence in the same direction until it reached the easterly line of said District of Willow Springs."[2]

It was common practice for a landowner to give permission for a school to be located on his property without deeding the property to the district. No specific conveyance of the sites to the school districts was ever made.[3] After the property was not in use for a school for a period of time, or the school trustees released it, the property automatically reverted to the owner. This happened in the case of the Moraga School and also in the case of the Orinda Park School situated on Wagner's land.

Mrs. Gladys Shally, a resident of Canyon, who has done a series of articles on local schools, tells us that in 1864 the Moraga School had twenty students, while neighboring

Lafayette had forty-three pupils and Willow Springs had twenty-seven. The local district then had $20.78 in cash on hand, received $41.43 in state aid and was further supported by $127.13 from the county taxes. The budget included $40.00 for a teacher's salary. O. S. Hough was the first recorded school board clerk.

In later years Willow Springs School District changed its name to Moraga School District (1927) after Moraga School District in Orinda had consolidated with Orinda Park School District in 1923, and the resulting joint district was named Orinda Union School District. This action straightened out a mix-up of names which was confusing, as Willow Springs was in Moraga and the Moraga School in Orinda.

Mrs. Shally found the first record of a county school tax was .03, levied in 1851 which was the first year that the county was in full operation. In 1855 the tax went from .05 to .10 which was still the tax rate in 1861 with a total tax rate of $2.80. The total assessed value of property in the county was less than $2,000,000. Occasionally a special tax was levied on an individual school district where a deficit was shown.[4]

In 1908 Moraga School had 49 pupils, Orinda Park 14, Willow Springs 56 and Mount Pleasant 32.[5] However, old school records of attendance and expenses do not give the whole picture. Circumstances sometimes occurred where there was no teacher for a time, or a school might not open for a year while another would remain open for ten months.

We are fortunate to have the memories of Addie Gerow Allen who had attended both the Moraga and the Orinda Park School, both being within reach of her home at her father's blacksmith shop at the crossroads. Mrs. Allen remembered having Edith Mills as her teacher in 1880. Her father, Edward Gerow, was a trustee at Moraga School from 1892 to 1898 and perhaps longer.

Mrs. Shally has also recorded the memories of Mrs. William Rosenberg (Jennie Bicker-staff) who taught at the Moraga School from 1892 to 1898.[6] Mrs. Rosenberg lived to be 94 years old and taught in Contra Costa County schools until her retirement in 1936. Her home was in Lafayette when she taught in Orinda, and, at first, she commuted side-saddle across the countryside on her mare, Topsy, for the three miles to school. There were five gates to open and one shoulder gate which she had to dismount to open. When the Grant Brothers built their wagon roads in 1893 from the railroad station at the crossroads into the new Glorietta area they were trying to develop, she drove on five miles of county dirt road with a horse and cart. She was twenty years old when she started teaching. For the seven years of her tenure in Moraga School, the same three men remained as trustees. They were Edward Gerow, the blacksmith, Daniel Huested, a renter and farmer on Moraga Ranch who lived near the school, and John H. Olive. Trustee Huested laid a fire in the winter for the teacher, then Miss Bickerstaff, to light when she arrived at the school.

To collect her salary, Miss Bickerstaff had to ride horseback to Olive's home at the Fish Ranch to pick up a warrant from Trustee John Olive, and then she had to ride or drive her horse and buggy to Martinez to collect the payment in gold.

One of her pupils was Olivette Moraga, granddaughter of John Olive of Fish Ranch. John Olive's daughter, Ella Olive, had married Gabriel Moraga. Olivette was born in 1881 and had lived in the adobe until the family's eviction in 1886. The family then lived in the grandparent's home on the Fish Ranch, but Olivette attended the Moraga School located on her family's land grant. Miss Bickerstaff remembered that her pupil brought fresh trout to school instead of an apple for the teacher. Olivette died at the age of 87 in 1968 in San Francisco.[7]

There were also two more Gerow children in school by then, Henry and Esther Gerow. Miss Bickerstaff would often give the children a lift in her cart as she went by the home and blacksmith shop at the corners, and sometimes she would sample the fresh baked bread and butter that Mrs. Gerow invited her to try.

Many of the children at the Moraga School were related to the Moraga family through marriage. A report from the Moraga Valley School in 1881 shows a pupil list of six Arreagadas, an Avilla, Angelina, Gilbert Moraga, Andrew, Mary and Willie Mulholland, Eudocia Van Duyn and Rinaldo Nino.[8] The Mulholland family had settled on the ranch in the 1870's.

Other families on the ranch whose names are known today included the Carroll family who came to the ranch in the early 1860's and the Williams family who purchased even earlier. The Carrolls and the Williams, who owned the land where Rheem is now located, were two of the families who were able to prove their titles to the land before the final decree of partition of the Moraga Ranch.

In 1892 there were seven Avillas and four Arreagadas still on the school list, and, during the nineties, among the pupils were members of the Bello, Fagundes, Jacinto, Silva, Joaquin, Feely, Manuel, Reynolds, Jenkins, Huested, Moraga, Joseph, Neves, Allen, Boyer, O'Neil and Bettencourt families.

Some of the teachers in the 1870's and 1880's at the Moraga School were Lizzie Swain, Edith Mills, Nellie Lawless; in the 1890's Ella Tryal and Jennie Bickerstaff were the teachers. In the 1900's Annie Johnson taught, and when the Moraga School was about to close its doors in the 1920's, Malvaina Madden was the teacher. Lorene Johnson (Mrs. Giles Crandall) took her place when she left and was the teacher who came to the new consolidated school in 1925. Mrs. Crandall remembers teaching three Nelson children and five Domingos children at the old Moraga School. The Domingos brought fresh mushrooms as gifts and rode to school from their ranch on a big white horse which was tethered during the day.[9]

Trustee Charles Nelson was paid $5.00 a month to supply and haul water daily to the school as there was still no water on the premises in 1924 after almost seventy years.[10] The Nelson home (the old yellow house) was almost across the highway from the school and had two wells located on the property.[11]

The school building itself was not much different when it closed from when it opened years before. After the building had not been used for school purposes for a year, the land reverted to the Moraga Company in accordance with the conditions of a deed in which the Moraga Company conveyed to the Moraga School District the property on which the school was located on January 8, 1920.[12] The new Orinda School District delivered a quit claim deed of the premises to the Moraga Company in February 1927.[13]

The minute book of the Board of Trustees of the consolidated Orinda and Moraga School District reads on March 20, 1925: "Mr. Nelson was appointed to move the flagpole from the old Moraga School to the new yard. Mr. Nelson and Mr. Brockhurst are the

Upper Orinda Park School (1900) FS   *Lower* Orinda Park School (1921) GK

committee to change the fences from the old Moraga School to the new school."[14] Thus, the flag came down for the final time from the first school in Orinda, which had been in use for close to seventy years.

In 1929 Gus Nordquist purchased the old building and moved it closer to the highway near his home to use for a taxidermy shop. It was later moved again and became the kitchen of a home on Moraga Highway.

The Orinda Park School

The next closest school to Orinda Park was the Mount Pleasant School to the north, located on the southeast corner of the Fargo Ranch near Kelley's Creek in Sather Canyon as it came down from Mount Pleasant. This District was formed August 11, 1863.[15] The location is now under the waters of the San Pablo Dam. The families of the northern ranches in the Orinda and Bear Creek area attended this school because it was more accessible to them. One of the students who attended Mt. Pleasant School, later becoming a prominent Orinda citizen, was George Brockhurst. The school closed when the water company bought up the property.

After settlers purchased Camron's land in the Orinda Park subdivision, they found that they needed a school closer than the Mount Pleasant School or the Moraga School. It was just about impossible to travel very far over the muddy roads during the stormy season.

The Orinda Park School District was formed in 1881, and a school was built on Theodore Wagner's land in 1882. It was at the present junction of Bear Creek, San Pablo Dam and Wildcat Canyon Roads. Until the San Pablo Dam Road was built on its present path, it joined with the Bear Creek Road on the northern line of the Rowland property further north than the present intersection. Later, the San Pablo Road was straightened and followed more closely the line of the old California and Nevada Railroad. Both roads came together and then branched again; one went to the Wagner Berkeley Road and the other followed the San Pablo Creek through Orinda. The school was on the hill above the San Pablo Road to the left of the Wagner Road as it started its winding way to Berkeley.[16] The location was only a short distance across the highway from where the newest Orinda school is located—the Wagner School.

After the forming of the Orinda Park School District, it took more than a little planning to build the school. The building of the school was up to the community. Seven of the men living in the area raised $700 and built the school in 1882 during time snatched from their farming or their business. Among them were Eugene Sullivan, Richard Rowland, William Minto, John Gray, Theodore Wagner and James Miner.[17] Most of these men served as trustees at one time or another.

Before the school opened, Frederica de Laguna, a university student, came out to tutor a few pupils, and when the school opened, Miss Nettie Parkhurst, 22, was hired as the teacher at $60 a month.[18] Fourteen children attended the first year the school was open, while nineteen enrolled at the Moraga School. Miss Parkhurst remained for six years. Later Martha Rowland from nearby Rowland Ranch taught for awhile. Addie Gerow (Allen) remembered attending the new school with her brother, Will, in 1883. The Gerows had been asked to come from Moraga School to help the total number needed for the school to open. She also remembered the two Wagner girls, Carrie and Lulu; Emily Rowland; Hugh and Jack O'Brien; and Herb, James and John Sullivan.[19]

The school's location on the hill was such that it was visible to many of the homes up and down the valley which made it convenient to hoist a red flag to say "no school today" when winter storms made the roads impassable. Winter vacations might last for a couple of months if rains continued and the local adobe turned to a sticky mud.

Eddie Rowland could see the school from his bedroom window, and on October 6, 1885, he looked out of his window at 11 p.m. and saw the school in the moonlight. But at 3 a.m. he awakened to see the reflection of flames leaping high in the sky. The school was completely destroyed by fire, and vandals were suspected as there had been no fire in the stove for months. Fortunately, there was $600 insurance with the Home Mutual Company of Oakland. This was promptly paid. A reward of $250 was offered for the arrest and conviction of the person who had set the fire. With the insurance money and $250 secured by a tax levy, a new school was built and equipped. Mr. Willarts of Berkeley was the builder.[20] The school now had the luxury of water piped into the cloakroom, but the old wood stove remained in the center of the room.[21]

By 1892, when Mrs. Harriet B. Foye taught, there were 26 students, including three Fastine children, three Gray, five of the Martinez family, four Fleitz, three Sullivan and two Rowland children. There were now ten grades in the little schoolhouse.[22]

Following Mrs. Foye as teachers were Lydia Atterbury, Lizzie McCauley, and Francis Gray in 1900.

A couple of years later, Miss Fanny Tyrell, a graduate of the University of California in 1900, who had taught in Clayton for awhile, arrived to teach. In Orinda she met Woodward J. Martinez of the Martinez family near Bear Creek, who had attended the Orinda Park School along with his brothers and sisters. They soon were married. Fanny and Woodward Martinez later moved to Berkeley but had a summer house in Canyon where they were responsible for starting the school in 1918. They subdivided land in Canyon City in 1919. Woodward was on the first school board. The first term Canyon needed three more students to start the school, so the Martinez family stayed in their summer home so the school could open. Woodward built a railroad in the school yard at Canyon which was extremely popular with the children.[23]

Another teacher at Orinda Park School was Kate Applegarth who was there from 1904 to 1907. Next was Florence McNeil (Sullivan) who taught for several years, followed by Gladys Hoagland. Florence McNeil married James Sullivan in 1913, so at least two teachers at the little country school found romance in Orinda. Mrs. Sullivan taught again in 1917 for awhile. She remembers among her students the Symmons, Baptistas, Silvas, Rowlands, Gerows, Lawrence Greer, Leslie Wigstead, Signey Chester, Ezevedas, Bettencourts, Brunos, and Dion Barrack.[24]

Grace Kendall followed Florence Sullivan and remembered that the day school opened only two students arrived; she was afraid the school would close, but by Christmas there were forty-nine students. She remembered that when the Symmons family moved to Walnut Creek in 1917 because the water company needed their ranch, they took ten children away from the community.[25]

Upper Teacher Florence Sullivan, Orinda Park School   FS
Lower Alma Reynolds, Olivette Moraga, Jennie Bickerstaff (teacher) and Esther Symmons,
pupils at Moraga School 1892–8   GS

Upper Tree planting day, Orinda School, March 7, 1925   GK   *Lower* Students (1926)   GK

In 1922 Ostrid Iverson (Ruidi) arrived to teach, and like many of the other teachers, she was often included in the social events of the community. Following her was Maude Woodin who was teaching in 1924 when the Moraga School District and the Orinda Park School District combined to form the Orinda Union School District. When the new school was built, she was the first principal and taught the upper grades.

On April 17, 1925, the Orinda Park Schoolhouse was auctioned off at 4 p.m. by Frank Enos who acted as auctioneer. The pupils had moved to the new school in January of that year. The building sold for $62.50 to Frank Teiche along with two patent toilets that went for $3.00 each.[26] The old school built in 1882 had come to the end of its days.

The land reverted to the water company. No specific conveyance of the school site in the 1880's to the school district had ever been made. The school simply was in possession of the property with the knowledge and consent of, first, Theodore Wagner, and later, the East Bay Water Company.[27]

Orinda Union School District

On August 1, 1923, the first meeting of the Board of Trustees of the new consolidated Orinda Park School District and the Moraga School District was held. It was unanimously voted to call the consolidated district the Orinda Union School District.[28] William Hanlon, County Superintendent of Schools, presided over the meeting.

The first important item on the agenda was to choose a site for the planned new school, and several were considered. One was on the Teiche property, one on the deLaveaga property where the Fleitz family operated the dairy, and one on the East Bay Water Company property. E. I. deLaveaga, whose lease to Fleitz was to expire in October 1923, offered to remove "the barn, dairy house, house and outhouses, and the manure from the corral," as well as to supply "an adequate supply of drinking water and connection to a sanitary and proper sewage disposal system."[29]

The final choice of the Board was the water company site of 3.7 acres in exchange for the release of the old school site and $600. The site is the one on which the school is today. James Narbett was the architect for the new building. The first trustees were E. P. Tenney, T. N. Vinther, Charles A. Nelson, George A. Brockhurst and Frank Enos. Harry W. Mears, Grace Kendall and E. I. deLaveaga filled the first openings on the Board.

A bond election was held on February 29, 1924 and 23 votes were cast, all in favor of the $22,000 bond issue. This was the second election held on the bond issue, as the first one, in which 42 votes were cast for and one against, was declared illegal as the polls had closed at 6 p.m. rather than the new 8 p.m. time, as specified by recent legislation.

Water problems were solved later in the year when the East Bay Water Company permitted the school to connect to a pipe line which they were installing about a thousand feet above the site.

In January 1925 the school was ready for occupancy. Maude Woodin came from Orinda Park as principal, and Lorene Johnson came from the Moraga School. Miss Woodin remained as principal for several years, and Agnes Horton replaced Lorene Johnson as primary teacher in 1926. May Clausen took Miss Woodin's place for a brief leave of absence in 1926.

On March 7, 1925, a "tree-planting day" was held, and each child planted a tree along with many of the adults. Trustee Brockhurst had previously prepared the ground for planting with his horse and grader, and deLaveaga contributed landscape plans. The new school was formally dedicated April 11th at impressive ceremonies, with trustee deLaveaga giving the main address. Citizens from all over Contra Costa County attended this major step in the progress of Orinda schools.

The Orinda Nursery in the village, owned at that time by Scanlon and Klemmer, made an agreement with the trustees on May 21, 1926, to construct and maintain the gardens. When Mr. Vaughn purchased the nursery in 1927, he cooperated with the Board on the gardens.

That active member of the Martinez family, Woodward, who had married the school teacher from Orinda Park School, who had been the first rural mail carrier, and who had founded Canyon as well as the Canyon School, now contracted to install electroliers for the school grounds for $198.

Henry Jansen was given permission in 1927 to use the school piano for children's instruction at 50 cents for a 30-minute lesson after school hours. His classes were probably the first music instruction in a local school.

Alfred W. Elkinton, a trustee in 1927, wrote to the P.T.A. to see if they would serve hot lunches during the winter season to the pupils. They agreed to do this, and a total of $1.00 per day was allotted to the P.T.A. for each school day on which they served a hot lunch during January, February and March. If there was any slack in the funds, the P.T.A. took it up as their contribution. Gradually, the school became the center for a great deal of community activity.

Gus Reuter took Charles Nelson's place on the Board in April 1928. Now, both Reuter and Enos, who had successfully run the Canary Cottage at the east end of the tunnel, and who had both opened establishments in Orinda, were on the school board.

The Orinda Union School District roughly extended to the northern end of the San Pablo Reservoir, to Charles Hill to the east, to Moraga and Canyon School Districts on the south, and to the east portal of the tunnel on the west. The boundaries were rather flexible as may be seen from a letter received by the Board from Superintendent Hanlon in 1928 stating that, in his judgment, there was nothing to be done to prevent children living in the extreme south end of the district from attending Moraga School (the old Willow Springs School) and that Mr. Brockhurst should take the matter up with the trustees of the Moraga School to see what could be done.

In 1929, during the financial depression, when so many of deLaveaga's buyers failed to complete their purchases, a problem was encountered in finding a sufficient number of children to attend school to keep the minimum average to qualify for state aid. A happy solution was found when the trustees hired Mrs. Lillian Dorrington, a widow with four eligible youngsters, as custodian.[30] She lived in a cottage behind the school, and later became an invaluable school secretary, a position she held for over twenty years.

Expansion of the Orinda Union School

The development of the community can be followed through the development of the schools. After the spurt of population growth in the middle 1920's, the depression slowed down the growth of Orinda for some years. From 1933 there seems to have been a slow, but steady, advance in the school population as is evident by the five-year statistical report.

FIVE-YEAR STATISTICAL REPORT OF ORINDA UNION SCHOOL DISTRICT

| Year | Assessed Valuation | Elementary School Tax | | | Average Daily School Attendance |
		Oper. & Maint.	Bldg. Bonds	Total	
1933	$ 778,830	.08	.22	.30	26 pupils
1934	781,025	.077	.14	.217	41 pupils
1935	1,206,780	.20	.11	.30	49 pupils
1936	1,360,035	.11	.105	.215	50 pupils
1937	1,632,830	.14	.085	.225	70 pupils

ORINDA NEWS 12–1–1937

When Mrs. Vance, principal in 1937, resigned, Doris Park took her place. Marian Jost was the second teacher. With seventy pupils more help was needed for the first time in the school history, and two student teachers came to assist, without any cost to the district.

With the completion of the new low-level tunnel and the rapid increase of building in the area, it was obvious that the school would soon be inadequate. In May 1938 a new bond election was held with 210 votes cast as follows: 164 for and 46 against, which gave the necessary majority.

In September more adjoining land was acquired from the East Bay Municipal Utility District for new school playgrounds. With the combined effort of the citizens, and help from the Lafayette Sun, Walnut Creek Kernel, Oakland Tribune and the Martinez Gazette, they succeeded in getting the price of the land reduced from $6,250 to $2,800. Lonie Bee, a well-known artist living in Orinda, did two very effective cartoons in behalf of the drive.

Early the next year possibilities of adding on to the school were explored, and the sad fact was found that, owing to poor materials used in the original building, it would practically have to be rebuilt. Another bond election had to be held on February 15, 1939, which was overwhelmingly passed. Now a large stone wall was built along the edge of the playground, and a new raised playground was constructed with the dirt removed from the site of the new addition.

On October 20, 1939, the new and enlarged school was dedicated. There were now six classrooms, an auditorium, kitchen, two play rooms downstairs, a principal's office, library, storage room for books and supplies, janitor's storeroom and modern lavatories with tile floors.[31]

By 1940 a fifth teacher was added, and the following year Richard Davis became principal. He resigned in 1948, and Joseph Sheaff took his place. There were by then seventeen teachers. Joe Sheaff was the superintendent of the Orinda Union School District until June 1969 when he retired. He participated in the tremendous growth that took place in the district since his arrival in 1948. Dr. William W. Fisher is the new superintendent.

131

In January 1968 there were 253 employees. The 1967-68 budget was $2,684,129. Enrollment, as of January 12, 1968, was 3,419.[32]

The growth of Orinda cannot be told more graphically than to look at the growth of the Orinda Union Elementary School District between the years of 1940 and 1953. During this period there was a 999.4 per cent increase, or a growth of 112 students to 1,225.[33] Since that time, population growth has been such that many additional schools have been built.

Additional Schools

In 1939 children from this area were still being bussed to Richmond by driver, Joe Miller, to attend high school. On October 24 bonds for the new Acalanes High School, amounting to $330,000, were passed by the voters of the district, which included Walnut Creek, Lafayette, Canyon, Moraga and Orinda, by a vote of 884-195.

The site for the school was the present location of the Acalanes High School.

In the Orinda Union School District, the following schools have been added:

Orinda	1924	Pine Grove	1956 (January)
Glorietta	1949	Inland Valley Elem.	1960
Sleepy Hollow	1953 (January)	Inland Valley Intermediate	1961
Del Rey	1953 (November)	Wagner	1968

In the Acalanes High School District are the following schools:

Acalanes	1940	Del Valle	1959
Las Lomas	1951	Campolindo	1962
Miramonte	1955		

Pre-Schools

A kindergarten was not added to the Orinda School until 1942, so before that time, in 1938, Mrs. G. A. Woods started a kindergarten and nursery school. Mrs. Robert Bennett assisted Mrs. Woods for a time, and in 1941 Mrs. Bennett and Mrs. Mary Gibbons took over the organization, and school was held in the Gibbons home.

The Orinda Park Play Center, which was sponsored by the W.P.A. under its recreation program, also formed a pre-school for awhile which met in the Orinda Park Pool Building.

By 1943 so much interest in nursery schools had developed, along with a desire on the part of the mothers to participate, the school became the Cooperative Nursery School. It was held in the guest house of Mrs. Stanley Allen three mornings a week for children from two to five. The next year attendance increased, and the children were divided into two groups. The younger ones now met on Tuesdays and Thursdays with Mrs. Laura Mallory (later postmaster) supervising. Mrs. Myrtle Patterson and Mrs. Maxine Laney directed the older group. Mrs. Patterson, who became the School Director, retired in 1967 after many years of dedicated service.

In 1946 the Orinda Mothers' Cooperative Nursery School met temporarily at the Orinda Park Pool while waiting for its permanent quarters at the Community Church site.[34]

The Nursery School group purchased a building for $500 from the Naval Flight School, held at St. Mary's College during the war, but they lacked means and a place to erect it.[35]

The Community Church had a site but no building, so they helped out, and the building was located on their land. The 31 x 65 foot building was moved on Friday, December 5, 1947, while highway traffic was stopped for half an hour as the building made the turn from Orinda Highway into the church property. The narrow Moraga Road created problems for the movers, and a full day was required to pull up over the 15 per cent grade to the church property.[36]

The Orinda Cooperative Nursery School still meets in this building.

The Orinda P.T.A.

The following article from the Orinda News in 1937 tells the history of the Orinda P.T.A.: "On September 19, 1924, parents, friends and teachers of the Orinda Union School met at the school house for the purpose of organizing a Parent Teachers Association. Mrs. C. P. Woodbury was elected president. There were sixteen charter members: three of these were men, Mr. Brockhurst, Mr. E. W. Jensen, and Mr. T. C. Kendall. Mr. Brockhurst was elected treasurer.

"By October, the treasury consisted of $6.40 which sum had been increased to $30.65 by December as the result of a benefit whist part at the home of Mrs. T. C. Kendall. By June of the following year the treasury boasted $102.81, eighty dollars having been raised by a dance at the school auditorium.

"By November of that first year, 1924, new members were Mr. E. I. deLaveaga, Mr. F. W. Enos, and Captain H. Oakley. Then, having fathered their offspring and watched it past its first toddling steps, they left it to the care of the ladies, for no longer do the names of the men appear on the membership lists.

"The first Father's Night was celebrated on the evening of Founder's Day, February, 1925. A number of fun-provoking stunts were performed. The fathers trimmed their wives' Easter bonnets. A pillowcase race between the ladies and men followed—and the men won. . . . Supper was served at long tables, and Mrs. Woodbury cut the birthday cake. Mrs. Rowland of Walnut Creek told fortunes. . . . The total amount derived from these 'extortion schemes' was $12.50.

"But the early spontaneity of the thrill of a new venture began to pall as the years went on. Interest lagged and attendance dwindled."

By the time the above article was written, interest had again revived, and the P.T.A. was thriving. A garden party was held to raise money, and thirty-six paid-up members were counted. Mrs. Sidney K. Rosenfeld was president.

In the fall of 1942, Mrs. Melvin Jacobus became president, with Mrs. Kendric Morrish, vice-president; Mrs. Donald Badgley, recording secretary; Mrs. Kenneth Courtright, membership chairman; and Mrs. Richard Laney, hospitality chairman. Some of these women are still participating in community affairs.

In 1945 Mrs. Morrish was president, and during that year, the group voted to become an independent Mother's Club. In 1948 the president was Mrs. Donald Krotz who has been and is still an active participant in community affairs. Today, independent Parent's Clubs are found at the various schools.

Although not in Orinda, St. Mary's College is located on 420 acres of picturesque Moraga Valley, on a portion of the Moraga grant. It is conducted by Brothers of the Christian Schools and has achieved national recognition as a liberal arts college. Its athletic teams have also been known throughout the country.

St. Mary's College built its first campus in San Francisco on old Mission Road in 1863. By 1889 it was overcrowded and moved to Oakland. Despite a damaging fire in 1894, and another in 1918, the college existed until 1928 when city life encroached upon the building.

The acreage in Moraga was purchased after a 100-acre gift to the college from the Moraga Company in 1928. Beautiful Spanish-style buildings were erected on a site bordering the banks of Las Trampas Creek. A country club had been built here during a 1913 attempt at subdividing in Moraga.

During World War II, a Pre-Flight School of the U.S. Navy was commissioned here. From 1942 until 1946, the college shared its facilities with the Navy. More than 15,000 cadets were graduated from the Pre-Flight School.

The enlarged campus in its beautiful setting is now a welcome landmark in the area that is a near neighbor to Orinda.

XI

The Churches of Orinda

Santa Maria Catholic Church

It was in keeping with the community's historic Spanish and Mexican background that the first church in Orinda should be Catholic. Marie LeBreton deLaveaga and her husband, Miguel, built their lovely home in Orinda in 1888. The closest Catholic Church was reached either by a long, difficult trip over the twisting, hilly road to Oakland, or by the dirt road to Walnut Creek, where a church had been for a decade. In stormy weather the roads were practically impassable. All of the area of Moraga, Orinda and Walnut Creek at that time was under the care of Father Lawrence Serda of Sacred Heart Church in Oakland.

Marie deLaveaga was a devout Catholic and wanted to build a chapel in Orinda on the deLaveaga estate for the use of the family and for the community.[1] She donated 60/100 of an acre for a site and built the lovely chapel of Santa Maria, deeding it to the church in 1892.[2] The building was modeled after Sainte Marie DuBois Church in France. It was located at the beginning of Miner Road, and now, two residences are in its place.

It was a sad experience for Miguel and his three children when Marie deLaveaga died from complications of childbirth on October 4, 1892, only a few days after the dedication of the church by Archbishop Riordan of San Francisco. Marie had made and fitted the altar coverings and done all of the planning for the little chapel before she became ill and unable to attend the dedication.

Children from nearby were in an organized Sunday School class which had been under the instruction of Father Serda, and they received Holy Communion at Santa Maria on the first Sunday in October 1892.[3]

This same year, the Walnut Creek church was placed under the care of the Dominican Fathers at Martinez. In Orinda at Santa Maria, mass was celebrated every other Sunday by Father Serda or Father Sampson of Sacred Heart Parish until Miguel deLaveaga's death in 1914. The family's donation had provided for the services, and with its cessation, the chapel was closed for many years except for brief times when some devout Catholic would undertake all of the work entailed in having Sunday mass.

On the third Sunday in February 1927, largely through the efforts of Mr. and Mrs. Joseph Miller, the church was reopened. Mass was celebrated when Miller arranged for various priests to come to Orinda, including Father Turco or Father Riberon from St. Mary's College after its establishment in Moraga in 1928. Other Orindans did a great deal to help keep the chapel open intermittently. One was Mary Gallagher who, during her job as manager of the Orinda Country Club in the early 1930's, took a great interest in the chapel. She rejuvenated the garden, spending all of her spare time there, and she interested others in improving the building. Services were held as often as possible.

135

In the summer of 1936, Mrs. Andrew Welch (Julia deLaveaga), the daughter of Marie and Miguel who had built the chapel more than forty years before, generously helped to repair the building even though she was not a resident of Orinda. Lucia deLaveaga Ward helped to organize the Santa Maria Church Association to carry on the affairs of the chapel. The first members were Mr. Joseph Miller, Mr. J. H. Craig, Mr. and Mrs. Charles Malone, Mr. and Mrs. George Pitt, Mr. W. J. Martinez, Mr. and Mrs. Harrel Ward and Mrs. Edward deLaveaga. Soon Mr. and Mrs. Roy Warren, Mr. and Mrs. William Siefker and Miss Mary Siefker were added to the group.

The Dominican Fathers from St. Albert's College in Oakland celebrated mass for a time. In 1938 Archbishop Mitty of San Francisco decided to include Santa Maria Church in the Danville Parish under Father Louis J. Miller.

A year later, Mr. Ralph Sisson, a well-known architect living in Orinda, designed a beautiful Wayfarer's Shrine in memory of Mr. and Mrs. Miguel deLaveaga at the request of some of the church members.[4] It was affixed to a giant oak tree that sheltered the church. Under it was placed a bronze plaque which read, "In memory of Marie and Miguel deLaveaga." The shrine and the lovely chapel were the subjects for numerous artists and photographers for many years. Classes of painters sitting by the side of the road with their easels were a familiar sight to the residents of the area. An excellent photograph of the chapel may be seen in Geoffrey Bangs' "Portals West," a folio of late nineteenth century architecture.[5]

Rev. Albert T. Duffy was the priest in 1947 as Orinda became an official parish and was the first resident pastor. He was followed in 1951 by Rev. Thomas F. Scahill who remained for a year until Father David Harrington was appointed in February 1952.[6] Father Harrington was pastor until 1968 when Father Michael Tobin, who had been assistant pastor since May 1965, took his place. Father Harrington is still pastor in 1970.

In 1947 a heavy windstorm caused most of the huge oak tree next to the church to snap and fall to the ground, but to everyone's joy, the part of the tree on which the Shrine of the Madonna was attached was left standing. The flowers at the foot of the shrine were still in place after the storm.

The population had so increased by 1954 that the little chapel with its nineteen pews was no longer adequate. A new Santa Maria Church, which can seat over six hundred, was built in its present location on Santa Maria Drive. The first mass was celebrated on Christmas Eve. The parish includes a rectory, convent, and a school which opened in 1960.

Community interest was aroused to try to save the historic old chapel in 1955 when the property on which it stood was sold, but at the time no way was found to save it. The citizens of the bay area suffered a loss when the unusually attractive and historic chapel was destroyed to make way for two homes. Orinda boys found a treasure of square nails in the debris, nails which had been used in building the sixty-three-year-old structure.

Orinda Community Church

The idea for the Orinda Community Church began in 1923 when Orinda newcomers, the Alfred W. Elkintons, who had built their home in the first deLaveaga subdivision, gathered together a few local boys and girls into a Sunday school which was held in their garden. The

Santa Maria Church, built in 1892 CL

Elkintons played a most dedicated part in the building up of the Christian Endeavor and Sunday School groups until the church was established enough to go on its own. For years the groups met, first in a store in the village, in a house on Canon Road, or wherever possible. The only other Protestant Sunday School in Orinda had met occasionally in the old Orinda school house at the foot of Wild Cat Canyon Road, when, in the years past, a clergyman could be persuaded to make a visit.

In 1935, after meeting intermittently for over ten years, Mrs. Ralph C. Sisson and Mrs. Elkinton discussed organizing a new church. In the full of 1936, with the assistance of Mrs. James Dieterich, a house to house canvas was made and enough enthusiasm found to plan for the future. A Women's Guild held its first meeting in November at the home of Mrs. Sisson, wife of the architect who designed the shrine for the Santa Maria Chapel.

The new church group managed to meet for a while in a retreat cottage owned by St. Mark's Church of Berkeley, when it was available. Here the roof leaked, and, in the winter, the floors, which the ladies had carefully swept the day before, were apt to be covered in the morning of the service with a thin sheet of ice.

Funds to pay the rent on various rooms occupied were provided by the Elkintons with assistance from Mrs. Mock, Mrs. Kenneth Gelwix and the Women's Guild, of which Mrs. Sisson was the first president. In 1937, through the efforts of Marie Bennett, rooms in the Casa Verana were leased. Henry Adams, a student at the Seminary in San Anselmo, came over to officiate at the Sunday service.

The following year, a forward step took place in the progress of the Community Church when Dr. Miles B. Fisher was secured as part-time minister to the pastorate. Dr. and Mrs. Fisher were honored at a reception given by the Women's Guild. Galen Fisher, a brother, had recently built a large home near the golf course in Orinda.

Through Dr. Fisher's encouragement, a formal constitution of the Orinda Community Church was adopted on May 3, 1939, and within a month seventy-three charter members were received into the interdenominational church. In 1944 an affiliation was made with the Congregational Christian Churches.

June 1940 saw the purchase of 1.06 acres for a building site on the highway adjoining the Orinda Union School, and that fall the church was incorporated. After the coming of Reverend Fred Morrow in 1945, the now greatly enlarged congregation began to look to the future and to plan for building. For a brief period after Dr. Fisher left, Rev. Palmer Williams had been the minister, but he was soon forced to leave because of war-time duties.

The only building that had been erected so far on the site was a boys' clubhouse, built by the boys themselves out of salvaged lumber. Services were still held in other locations.

In January 1947 the church lot was exchanged, by mutual agreement, with the Orinda Association, for one slightly north and above the one they had.

The Orinda Nursery School, which had purchased the St. Mary's Naval School band building, now turned it over to the church, who had the building site to place it on and the funds to remodel it. The building was moved from St. Mary's down the Moraga Highway and up the hill to the church property.

The nursery school was allowed week-day use of the building, which was also made available for many community activities when not in use for church requirements.

This shrine was placed on a tree
alongside of Santa Maria Church LAV

Orinda Community Church remodeled the St. Mary's Naval School band building in 1948 DB

On Sunday, April 18, 1948, Fellowship Hall was dedicated. In the belfry was an old church bell, donated by Alfred Elkinton. A new children's unit was dedicated in January 1949, and a chapel and classroom unit on October 21, 1951. Under Reverend Morrow the church grew in membership and much was accomplished.

Reverend Chauncey Blossom, the present minister, came in January 1956, following the brief service of Reverend Willis Wygant.

A survey soon showed the need for a much larger sanctuary with greater parking facilities. $212,000 was raised, and the remaining Orinda Association land, adjacent to the present church, was exchanged, through their cooperation and that of the East Bay Municipal Utility District, for land purchased from the water company northwest of the crossroads. Within two years, groundbreaking took place for the present beautiful and spacious building, with formal dedication festivities on June 7, 1959.[7]

St. Stephen's Episcopal Church

Due to interest in establishing an Episcopal Mission in Orinda, a committee was formed in 1950 composed of Mr. and Mrs. Clinton Easterbrook, Dr. and Mrs. Alvin P. Wold, Mr. and Mrs. William A. Sparling, Mr. and Mrs. Walter Christie, and the Mesdames James E. Sullivan, Paul Slattery, Paul S. Booth, T. E. Haley, H. S. Doane, Robert Moorehead, William H. Brailsford, Jr., W. E. Joslin and S. A. Ballard to petition the Diocesan Council.

Bishop Karl Morgan Block named Reverend John M. Green, Jr. as temporary vicar. Reverend Green conducted the first service of Morning Prayer on October 15, 1950, in the Orinda Boy Scout hut.

Ninety interested Episcopalians gathered together at the home of the William Sparlings for a pot-luck supper in honor of Bishop Block.

When he became ill, Reverend Green was replaced by Dr. Frederick A. Shilling.

At a December meeting, the name Saint Stephen's was selected for the new mission.

For a time the group met in various available temporary locations—the old village bakery, a store building on Brookwood Road, and the Community Church. In September 1951, 9.022 acres of land were purchased between Las Vegas Road and Honey Hill Road as a site for the proposed church building. In August the Reverend William M. Fay was appointed the first permanent vicar but only remained a short time when Reverend Charles F. Whiston took his place as temporary vicar. A year after the purchase of the land, Reverend Charles M. Hill became the permanent vicar.

A financial drive produced $68,000, and groundbreaking ceremonies for the new building were conducted in July 1953, with 200 in attendance. A vicarage was built, and in December, the cornerstone for the new church was laid at ceremonies conducted by the Rt. Rev. Henry Shires. Dedication of the church took place on March 14, 1954 with Bishop Block officiating.[8]

Following Reverend Hill, Albert Lucas became the vicar in 1955. He remained for four years during which period the church grew considerably in membership. After his departure in August 1959, Reverend C. Corwin Calavan became the minister, arriving on September 15, 1959.

Groundbreaking to extend the church and to build a new chapel took place on September 23, 1962. Also in September of that year, St. Stephen's opened an Episcopal Day School, which was discontinued in June 1966. In its place the Canterbury School at Diablo was established.

While Father Calavan was at St. Stephen's, the church building was enlarged to take care of the expanding membership.

On Saturday, November 27, 1965, a tragedy befell the parish when Reverend Calavan was accidentally drowned while fishing on the rugged coast north of Santa Cruz. Memorial services were held on December 13th at St. Stephen's with the Rt. Rev. G. Richard Millard as celebrant.

During the following months the assistant minister, the Reverend George A. S. Hollywood, remained as associate while Reverend Spencer M. Rice served as temporary minister. In June 1966, Reverend B. Jean Clark, the present minister, was elected to be the Rector.

First Church of Christ Scientist

Early in January 1935 a small group of Christian Scientists held their first service in the Orinda Village in an empty store in the Corder Building which had been converted into their church home. For three years Sunday School was held, and the church services were read there. In the fall of 1938, the Corder Building was sold and the church relocated in the old Casa Verana building. Then a reading room was opened to the public one day a week.

A permanent church site was decided upon and purchased in 1940 next to the Orinda School, but in 1948, the school needed room to expand, and the church site was exchanged for an adjacent lot. A year later, groundbreaking took place and site-leveling was started. The first portion of the present building was completed early in 1950.

In 1955, as growth continued, it was decided to build a separate Sunday School and to enlarge the church building. The following fall the new addition was completed and services were expanded.

As all Christian Science Churches are required to be free of debt prior to dedication, it was not until 1965 that formal dedication took place. Three services were held for the dedication of the First Church of Christ Scientist.

A reading room was opened in 1967 in a new building in the village at No. 1 Camino Sobrante.

Shepherd of the Valley Lutheran Church

Reverend Edward R. Andersen, Jr. led the organization of a congregation to form the Shepherd of the Valley Lutheran Church in 1953. In November, worship services were held in the parish house. Three years later, the Reverend Albert E. Hidy, Jr. was installed as pastor. He remained until 1963.

The first church building at 433 Moraga Way was dedicated on October 23, 1960. Three years later, Reverend Richard M. Bennett was installed as pastor. Under his leadership, a drive was held in 1964 for a Christian Education building and other additions. The new buildings were dedicated in November 1965. In 1966 the Reverend Kenneth Bancroft, Jr. was installed as associate pastor.

In April 1969 there were over 500 active confirmed members of the church.

St. Mark's Methodist Church

One of the newest churches in Orinda is St. Mark's Methodist at 451 Moraga Road. Groundbreaking took place on their 7-acre site near Oak Road in October 1961. Rev. John L. Dodson was the minister. The congregation had been organized only eighteen months before the building was started with funds donated by the new members and with the ground donated by the California Methodist Conference.

The first unit of the building consisted of a diamond-shaped chapel and education building. In 1962 the St. Mark's Nursery School was opened, which has operated under the direction of Mrs. Irene Wickland ever since.

In 1965 the Reverend Wilton Vincent was at St. Mark's, and in June 1966, John W. Sublett took over as the pastor, a position he still holds.

During the period Reverend Sublett has been at St. Mark's, two notable events have taken place. In September 1966 the congregation held a Service of Dedication for the Memorial Gardens planted and set aside in memory of three persons who had been important in the congregation.

In March 1967 a new building was completed and put into use as an education building. The nursery school also is in the building.

The congregation has now grown to approximately 300 members.

Lafayette-Orinda Presbyterian Church

Although the Lafayette-Orinda Presbyterian Church is located at 49 Knox Drive, Lafayette, many Orinda residents attend, and it serves both communities. It was chartered June 6, 1954, with 133 members. The steering committee consisted of Mrs. Mark Vallory, Mr. Kenneth Colemans, Mr. James A. Leppard, Mr. Earle F. Glenk, Mrs. Ralph Hickcox, Mrs. Aakon Johnson and Mr. Theodore S. Ockels.

Reverend Carl Thomas was the first minister, and the present minister, Reverend James S. Little, was appointed October 25, 1964. Membership is now 1,596.

The first Orinda Fire House was built in 1924 KC

Remodeled in 1935 with a room added for Orinda Library KC

XII

Community Services and Utilities

Orinda Fire Department

Today Orinda has a very efficient fire department with modern equipment and several fire stations, but this was not always the case. When the disastrous fire in the 1880's destroyed the Wagner home and another equally bad fire in 1915 destroyed the deLaveaga home, the only firefighters were the few neighbors, farmhands and cowboys who rushed to assist.

E. I. deLaveaga remembered the experience of the fire at his family home, and a firehouse was uppermost in his mind when he began to subdivide his land. At the fourth meeting of the new Improvement Association on July 10, 1923, the matter of fire protection was taken up. The minutes state: "By request of Mr. Alfred Elkinton, President E. I. deLaveaga spoke on fire protection, and he graciously offered to subscribe one dollar for every other dollar subscribed toward fire apparatus."[1]

At the next meeting, on August 28, the Orinda Volunteer Fire Department was formed, as members present subscribed $420 toward a goal of $2,500. A benefit dance held shortly after netted some $300. In November the Association voted $500 for the erection of a fire-house and $400 to purchase a siren and other apparatus. On April 1, 1924, deLaveaga kept his promise by paying $746 into the Fire Department Fund which matched the sum raised.[2]

When the firehouse was erected, it was the second building in the village and was located almost opposite The White Swan across the road and on the other side of the bridge. Built late in 1923, it was originally just large enough for one truck and looked a little like a garage. In 1935 the building was remodeled and enlarged to about double its original size. The old firehouse is, at present, part of the building on Orinda Way, which has grown up around it.

The Volunteer Fire Department was an important part of the community. Originally, their equipment consisted of a truck loaded with two barrels of water, rakes, axes, buckets, shovels and ropes. Wet sacks were used, and backfires often set. A siren called the volunteers when they were needed. This siren was moved in 1942 to a newer building on Avenida de Orinda, and during the Second World War, it was used for community civil defense alerts.

There were from 50 to 100 men in the volunteer company, and all were citizens of the community. Warren Harrold was a leader, serving as Chairman of the Board of Fire Commissioners for many years. The first fire chief was Edward Jensen, who was present when the Association first planned a fire department. Other chiefs have been Philip Donaldson, Joe Varni, Everett Wyatt and Allen P. Winsor. Ewart Phair, owner of the Orinda Store, was honorary chief and acting chief in 1943-45. Fire Marshall William Koch was known to all of the community, when he was active, for his intensive community fire prevention program. Chief Winsor has been with the Orinda County Fire Protection District since 1945 and became chief on April 1, 1960. He is retiring in 1970.

145

During the 1920's and 1930's the fire department sponsored many community affairs such as benefit parties, dances on the old dance platform near Sleepy Hollow, and Christmas parties for the children. Each child received a personal written invitation from the Orinda Volunteer Fire Department announcing the date and time when Santa Claus would be at the firehouse with a present and a bag of goodies for him. For many years the popular Joe Varni was the Santa Claus. Proceeds from all of the parties went for new equipment or gear.

In 1939 Fire Chief Joe Varni formed a Junior Fire Department which was open to all boys of the Orinda Fire District under 15 years of age.[3] Drills were held, and actual firefighting practices of extinguishing burning sheds were held. The boys watched for and removed fire hazards in the community. This activity proved to be extremely popular and beneficial. Some of the boys went on to become volunteer firemen for the department for many years.

The Orinda County Fire Protection District was established on February 6, 1933. A five-man Board of Fire Commissioners was appointed to administer the affairs of the district. The Volunteer Fire Department turned over equipment worth $9,250,[4] including the little firehouse which was enlarged two years later.

In 1942 the second firehouse building was erected on Avenida de Orinda at a cost of $22,802, of which $3,990 was for land. The building would have cost much more except for the services donated by Ralph Sisson as architect, William P. Mott, Jr. as engineer, and Milton E. Selby as legal counsel.[5]

As new subdivisions and tracts in Orinda were opened, land outside of the Orinda Fire District was annexed. At present there are three stations: the headquarters station at 33 Orinda Way; station two, located at the corner of Moraga Way and Orchard Road; station three, at the corner of Honeyhill and Via Las Cruces. A fourth station is projected for the Sleepy Hollow area. Station one is now located on a half-acre site on Orinda Way, not far from the previous location but with better access to public roads than the dead-end street, without danger of the flooding that the station on Avenida de Orinda faced several times and with room for larger apparatus. The station was erected through a $400,000 bond issue approved by the voters on March 5, 1968. The new firehouse of 14,000 square feet was dedicated October 18, 1969, in memory of Charles W. Langridge who served on the fire commission from January 1952 until his death in 1969. The fire department personnel has increased to 32 at the present time.

Orinda County Fire Protection District maintains a rescue unit which has been credited with saving many lives during the relatively few years it has been in use. It is geared for answering calls dealing with accidents, drownings, impaired breathing, heart attacks and similar emergencies.

Orinda Post Office

The first post office in Orinda was established on March 18, 1888, in the old blacksmith shop, near the junction of the three roads to Berkeley, San Pablo and through Bear Valley.[6] The following year it moved to the Orinda Park Hotel which advertised "Post Office on premises."[7] Carrie Wagner used to meet the old stagecoach, which ran from Berkeley to Walnut Creek twice a week over the old Summit Road, and take the mail to their ranch on which the hotel was located.

On May 10, 1895, the post office was moved to the John Hoyt ranch near the location of

Fire Station on Avenida de Orinda (1942) DB   Old bridge to Manzanita Road LLS

the present Orinda Filter Plant. Richard Chester was the postmaster for a time.[8] All of the residents had to walk or come by horse and buggy to get their mail, and getting mail and newspapers was definitely an exciting occasion.

Then on September 10, 1903, a big step forward took place when a rural free delivery route was established out of the Berkeley Post Office, and the first mail boxes began to appear in Orinda.[9] Woodward Martinez, the first carrier, had a route from Berkeley, out to San Pablo, back through the valley to the crossroads and through the new tunnel,[10] when it was open. There is probably little doubt that the rural free route was established because of the newly built tunnel through the hills which was formally dedicated in November. Communication between Berkeley and Orinda was made somewhat easier. The first mail route was limited to 24 miles.

The rural free delivery system continued until November 16, 1945, when the first separate and independent post office was established in Orinda in the Vashell Building. This major achievement followed the ever increasing business and a great deal of effort by the citizens. From 1903 until the 1920's, the rural carrier sold stamps, registered letters, mailed parcels and obtained money orders. He was a one-man post office. In the 1920's E. I. de-Laveaga advertised a post office in his Orinda Store. The Orinda Postal Station was under the jurisdiction of the Bureau at Washington which supervised rural delivery service. The carriers came from Berkeley, which was the official post office.[11]

Luther Dunlap, Superintendent of Mails in Berkeley, reminisced in 1937: "When I first entered the Postal Service, Mr. Stowell was the carrier on the Orinda route, and I can recall many times that he returned to the office after dark and reported that he had left his buggy in the mud somewhere and completed the delivery on horseback. Later, Homer Read had the route under slightly improved conditions and he was succeeded by George Parker, who was the first to use an automobile. And then during the war days, this was one of the few routes served by a woman carrier. Miss Eunice Ricketts, famed for her sweet smile and kindly service, was the carrier until her death in 1926. After several temporary appointments the present carrier, Mr. Stephen E. Babson, was transferred from his former route at Sacramento. . . ."[12] Miss Ricketts was so popular with the residents that she was included in many local social affairs.

The delivery service expanded with the population, and if four additional families could be served within a mile, an extension was the rule, if roads and route were feasible to travel. A petition had to be filed and the change approved by a bureau of the Post Office Department in Washington. With the sudden increase in building in 1936 and 1937, a plan for numbering the houses in Orinda became necessary. By 1939 the number of families served by the carrier had risen from less than 100 to over 350, with many residents calling for their mail or having post office boxes in the Orinda Store which then maintained the Orinda Station.[13]

By 1938 the carrier was regularly coming through the new low-level tunnel instead of up the San Pablo Dam Road to Orinda. In two years it was necessary to employ a helper for the rural carrier, and Stanley Richardson of Lafayette was employed. He met the carrier, Stephen Babson, at the Orinda Station and took all of the mail for the residents on the east side of the highway.[14] Babson was the Orinda mail carrier for ten years until he left in 1940.

Opening ceremonies for Orinda's first post office, November 16, 1945, included Paul Vashell, Stanley Allen, Grace Kendall, Milt Nelson and Frank Whiting   GK

Through the 1940's the residents of Orinda began to look for ways to improve the postal service, as Berkeley RFD No. 1 was now serving over 800 families and service was felt to be inadequate for the rapidly growing community. A petition was circulated in 1941, and 300 signatures were obtained on the document which was sent to Washington requesting the establishment of an Orinda Post Office at the crossroads.[15] When the Orinda Store decided in 1943 that the Postal Station must soon move out, due to their need for space, the situation became more acute. In August 1944, a telegram was received from Albert Carter, Congressman: "Am pleased to advise that I have been successful in persuading the Post Office Department to establish a post office at the Orinda Crossroads as soon as suitable quarters can be provided."[16]

Orindans, Inc. had carried on a campaign for months under the leadership of Stanley Allen, President, for the establishment of the post office. A site had already been chosen in one of the store rooms in the Vashell Building across from the theatre. Mrs. Grace Kendall, who had been handling one of the Orinda routes, received her appointment as postmaster. However, it was not until Friday, November 16, 1945, that the Orinda Post Office became an independent third-class unit.[17]

A dedication was held on November 29th with many notables present, and the oldtime resident, Mrs. James Symmons, addressed the group.

By 1949 the Orinda Post Office had outgrown its quarters. It had jumped to a second-class office within six months after its opening. Because of her health, Mrs. Kendall had resigned in 1946 as postmaster and accepted a clerkship, with Mrs. Laura Mallary becoming the postmaster. A bid for the needed new location was awarded to Donald Rheem in 1950, who built a new building just behind the Orinda Theatre. In July 1951 another major change took place as the post office became first-class. Mrs. Kendall retired in 1960 after watching the office grow from receipts of $8,000 to $128,000, and from two rural routes and one clerk to nine routes and four regular clerks.

Others who assisted in the post office in the early years were Josephine Dawson, Helen Vurek and Myrtle Patterson. The first regular clerk was Jim Doyle, who came in 1946 and is the present assistant postmaster, taking this post in 1957. Mrs. Mallory was postmaster until 1964 when she retired. Robert Ross, who had become a clerk in 1951, became postmaster, a job he held until 1970. W. D. "Bing" Crosby joined the post office in 1947 and Edward J. Kuenzli, in 1949. Edmund Richard, Orville Rakestraw and Joseph Guisto were regular carriers. Guisto and Harold Eggers are now in managerial positions.

The Orinda Post Office again outgrew its space in 1961, and the present building on Orinda Way was built. The office staff now consists of 47 employees and 17 mail carriers.

Orinda Library

The Orinda Library was built from funds privately raised by the residents of the community, who take a great deal of pride in this beautiful building. Over a period of three years, residents of Orinda raised $115,000 to build the library.

It seems that as early as 1915 there were enough people in Orinda interested in a library so that a small book collection was kept by the county in a deposit station. The part time librarian was Mrs. Artie Barbie who kept the books in the local school.[18]

In 1925 the library occupied a three by four foot bookcase in the original Orinda Store. There was very little supervision of books and the county system was about to remove the Orinda Branch when Mrs. J. W. Dieterich, under the sponsorship of the P.T.A., made plans for moving the library into a nearby vacant store. Members of the P.T.A. were to take turns on duty from two to five o'clock on Monday and Friday afternoons, but this rather loose arrangement was greatly improved when Mrs. E. A. Dawson took over the responsibility of first librarian. Mrs. Dawson received a salary of $10.00 a month, and the first few months her salary went toward accumulating a fund with which to buy wood and coal for the stove. During the 1929 depression, her salary was reduced to $7.50 per month. When the store was rented, the library moved to another empty store space. The landlords received no rental for the stores at any time when the library occupied them.

In 1935, at the suggestion of Mrs. J. W. Dieterich, the Orinda Improvement Association asked the fire commissioners if they would consider building an addition to the firehouse as they remodeled to house the library. This was approved by the commissioners, and due to the prompt work of architects W. P. Stephenson and Ralph Sisson, local citizens who donated their time and talents, an addition was started within a month. On April 5, 1935, the minute book of the Orinda Improvement Association shows that the State Employment Relief Administration approved a project for this addition and the alterations to the firehouse. The library remained in this addition to the firehouse until the building was sold by the county in 1944, the fire department having moved to their new location. Books were put away, and the library closed for several years.

In January 1949, with the cooperation of the Orinda Community Church, the Orinda Lions Club donated part of the cost and all of the labor to build and install shelving for a library in a rough space underneath the new Children's Unit of the Community Church. A Mothers' Club committee, headed by Virginia Phair, had obtained the cooperation of the county library authorities and interested the Lions Club in the project. Mrs. Dawson was again requested to become librarian.

It was not long before the community felt the need for larger quarters than the 400 feet in the church building, and in March of 1954 citizen interest in a library was expressed at a meeting of the Orinda Association Civic Affairs Committee.

Within the year the Orinda Junior Women's Club and the Lions Club began to awaken community interest both in the present location and in planning for a future building. A questionnaire was sent out by the Orinda Association who found community interest in obtaining an adequate library. The Orinda Women's Club contributed shelves for 500 more books and the Lions Club, a space for another 1,000. The status was now changed from a deposit station to a branch library, and weekly hours increased from 11 to 27. The Women's Club held fashion shows and rummage sales to contribute to the library, and both groups kept the community interested in the possibility of a new building. On October 28, 1954, Mrs. Elizabeth Lieberman became the new librarian.

A major step in progress toward a new library was taken when the Orinda Library Board, Inc., was formed as a non-profit organization. The move was headed by the Orinda Junior Women's Club and the Lions Club.

In 1955, when the interchange of the highway at the Orinda Crossroads was completed,

Orinda women and County Librarian Bertha Hellum listen to Perc Brown
tell plans for a new library

the local improvement clubs and civic organizations sponsored a revival of an old community celebration—the Orinda Fiesta. It was held on May 15 and 16 and proceeds of $5,200 which were received were later turned over to the library building fund by the Fiesta committee. Weekly hours increased again following the demand for 40 hours per week, and a part-time assistant was employed for 20 hours per week.

The following year, Perc Brown, a local citizen with a background of interest in libraries, became chairman of the fund drive. Brown was also a well-known collector and a director of the Friends of the Bancroft Library. One of the first donations was from the Women's Club for $1,000, and other groups followed shortly with donations. The location on Irwin Way was approved and obtained through the cooperation of the Orinda Association, and the property of 1.4 acres was deeded outright to the Orinda Library Board in 1958 by the Association.

During the campaign for funds, members of the Library Board were: Lloyd L. Farrar, Mrs. John J. Madison, Mrs. E. F. Wilford, Perc S. Brown, and Ernest I. Spiegl, who was the legal counsel. Under general chairman Perc Brown, the following were the active committee chairmen: William Fleager, Administration; Walter N. Boysen, Major Contributions; Melvin S. Jacobus, Treasurer; Mrs. Donald P. Krotz, Field Chairman; John W. Watson, Public Relations-Publicity; George H. Hauerken, Library Building; Odie Monahan, Fund-raising Consultant; and committee members included Marvin C. Baker, J. C. Roos, Walter E. Friberg and Robert E. Gemetti, Jr.

On November 14, 1958, the new building was dedicated with Dr. James D. Hart, present director of The Bancroft Library, as the keynote speaker. The finished library was 4,800 square feet and had a book capacity of 20,000. The figures showing circulation of books over the years tell the story of growth of the library and community.[19]

1914–15	344	1953–54	22,673	1960–61	177,561
1924–25	213	1954–55	37,770	1961–62	167,175
1934–35	1,199	1955–56	63,579	1962–63	157,516
1944–45	3,732	1956–57	72,287	1963–64	178,078
1950–51	14,397	1957–58	94,733	1964–65	188,634
1951–52	15,556	1958–59	130,630	1966–67	200,726
1952–53	18,365	1959–60	156,457	1967–68	208,431

The figures for 1961–62 and 1962–63 do not represent a drop in circulation but reflect a change in the extension of the loan period from two to three weeks in 1961 with the saving in renewals.

Librarians through the years have been Mrs. Josephine Dawson, Mrs. Elizabeth Lieberman, Mrs. Sara Malinowski, Mrs. Joan Kasten, Mrs. Betsy Gordon, Mrs. Ann Clark, Mrs. Elizabeth Faragoh, Mrs. Ann Sprowls, and Mrs. Laurie Delarueulle. During an absence of Mrs. Malinowski, Mrs. Elizabeth Faragoh and Miss Mary Rupp were temporarily acting librarians.

Funds for a new addition to the library, which includes a children's wing, have been accumulated through County Service Area Lib-8. Construction has been completed and the area of the present library approximately doubled. Formal dedication is planned for Fall, 1970.

Since its formation, Orinda Library Board, Inc. has maintained a diligent interest in the library. The active working group of the organization is known as Friends of the Orinda Library, formed in 1959. Members, numbering over 600, are residents of the community who pay a nominal dues and who are voting members of Orinda Library Board, Inc. They elect a board of directors as well as have their own working board and committee heads. The purpose of the Friends of the Orinda Library is to foster closer relations between the library and the community. The group has a constant program to improve facilities of the library. Dues and money raised from outside events go to further this aim.

Activities include four coffee hours and programs each year, held at the library, open without charge to the public, with speakers from the bay area representing various cultural fields. A major event of the year is a book fair held outdoors in the village. In this event several other groups participate with all proceeds from exhibits or projects going to benefit the library. In 1968 and 1969, Orinda Art Center, The Orinda Garden Club, Orinda Women's Club, Knights of Orinda, Camp Fire Girls, Girl Scouts, Boy Scouts, Ailanthus, M.O.L. —Teen Drop in Center, and Junior Friends of the Orinda Library participated.

Through efforts of the Friends groups, Orinda Library Board, Inc., headed by President William Fleager, was recently able to contribute $10,000 from its treasury to be used for furnishing for the new wing.

Always lending a helping hand to citizen interest in the Orinda Library and other county libraries is the dedicated Contra Costa County Librarian, Mrs. Bertha Hellum, who was appointed in 1954. Her cooperation with local groups and her untiring efforts in their behalf have played a large role in the development of the entire library system.

Water System

East Bay water companies were organized by the 1860's. Temescal Dam was constructed in 1869 with an original capacity of 188,000,000 gallons.[20] Contra Costa Water Company eyed development of water from San Pablo Creek, Wild Cat or Little San Pablo Creek, Cordonices, Cerrito, San Leandro and San Lorenzo and their sources and tributaries. Three water companies, Contra Costa Water Company, Syndicate Water Company, and Richmond Water Company were taken over by Peoples Water Company, incorporated in 1906.[21]

The Peoples Water Company was interested in developing local watershed resources for public usage. Property in the area of the present San Pablo Dam was bought up, and the San Pablo Creek, Bear Creek, and smaller tributaries were developed with reservoirs, pipes, flumes, aqueducts and mains to serve parts of Alameda and Contra Costa County.[22]

In 1906 the Richard Rowland property of 442 acres was taken over by Peoples Water Company.[23] Development of watershed land was actually taking place in Orinda, but none of the water was available for local use.

In 1888, Moses Hopkins, who was financially interested in water companies, had petitioned the Board of Supervisors of Contra Costa County for the privilege of laying water pipes. The November 24, 1888, issue of the Contra Costa Gazette reports that he was authorized to lay pipes and maintain them along the public road from the east side of the ridge, between San Pablo and Wildcat Creeks, to his land on the west side of the ridge. As mentioned earlier, he purchased the Wagner ranch in Orinda, and, eventually, all of this land also went to the water company.

In 1917 Peoples Water Company became part of East Bay Water Company whose objective was to supply water to Alameda and part of Contra Costa County. San Pablo Reservoir, holding 14 billion gallons, was completed in 1920 by Bates, Borland and Ayer, contractors for the job. Water service to the East Bay was improving, but Orinda was not yet included. Only a year later, deLaveaga had to develop the first of three small local water companies to serve his subdivisions.

EBMUD was voted into existence in 1923 by residents of Alameda and Contra Costa County. Then a thorough study of water problems was made and the Mokelumne River project was planned. Pardee Dam was built the following year. Within a few years, East Bay Water Company, with its 40,000 acres of watershed land was purchased through a $26,000,000 bond issue approved by voters in 1927.

A large filter plant was build in Orinda as a result of the Mokelumne River project; the main pipeline from the mountains goes through Orinda, then on under the Alameda-Contra Costa hills. Mokelumne water reached the local district system in June 1929. Since that time, two more Mokelumne aqueducts have been constructed and Briones Dam built in Orinda.

A serious accident occurred in Orinda on Thanksgiving Day in 1926. A cofferdam had been built by contractors during the construction of the water tunnels. The dam was to hold back and divert the waters of San Pablo Creek near the entrance to the tunnel. A terrific rainstorm caused the waters to rise, and while the dam was still being strengthened, the night shift, as usual, went down the 75-foot shaft into the tunnel. A roaring torrent, unleased by the cofferdam's bursting, caught ten men below the surface of the ground without any chance to escape. Within fifteen minutes the entrance to the tunnel began to cave in. The San Pablo Creek, which can become a raging torrent in a heavy, continuous rain, had claimed its victims.[24]

Orinda Water District was formed February 5, 1932 and was not dissolved until October 1952 when water was purchased directly from EBMUD.

The $28,000,000 Briones Dam and reservoir was begun in 1961. Bear Creek Road which followed the course of the creek had to be realigned on higher ground. Many old ranches in the area were inundated. Dedicated in May, 1965, the huge earth-fill structure will impound nearly 20 billion gallons of water when filled.

Gas and Electricity

The early Orinda resident did not just flip a light switch and see a room flooded with light. General Wagner, and perhaps a few of the others, had a generating system, but it was not until 1922 that E. I. deLaveaga, developing his first subdivision with its twenty-one residences, requested power from the Great Western Power Company of California. They tapped a 12,000-volt line which had originally been installed on a temporary basis to provide power for the construction of the San Pablo Dam. Great Western built a transformer

NOT TO BE USED UNTIL MARCH 1, 1938

ORINDA
TEMPORARY
TELEPHONE DIRECTORY

MARCH 1938

SPIRIT OF COMMUNICATION

THE PACIFIC TELEPHONE and TELEGRAPH
COMPANY

SEE PAGES I TO VI FOR EXTENDED SERVICE, EMERGENCY
CALLS AND OTHER IMPORTANT INFORMATION

MS

bus structure to reduce the 12,000 volts so that it could be used for residential service at 110 volts. DeLaveaga was the first to be connected in August, 1922.

Power for Orinda originated at Station F in Berkeley, at McGee and Hearst Streets. From there it was apparently transmitted to Ridge Station on Glendale Avenue, Berkeley, and then taken "over the hill" to Orinda.[25] The Pacific Gas and Electric Company later took over the Great Western Power Company, but some of the old substations remain in service as a part of P.G.&E.

In 1926 Great Western Power Company of California constructed a 60,000-volt line to the Orinda Substation from the old Bay Counties Power Company 60,000-volt line between South Tower and Elmhurst Station in what is now Oakland. The Orinda Substation was equipped with a 60,000-volt to 4,000-volt transformer to reduce the power to local distribution voltage.

The gas service to Orinda came when a four-inch main line was constructed by Coast Counties Gas Company from Walnut Creek through Lafayette to Orinda in 1937. From Charles Hill the line followed a private right of way to the head of Las Aromas Street, proceeding through Orinda along Las Cascadas following the west side of Lake Cascade to Camino Sobrante and thence along Camino Sobrante to the San Pablo Highway, with distribution systems then north, south and west of there.[26]

The first residence in Orinda to be connected to the new gas service line was that of Geoffrey W. Mayo on Las Cascadas on November 9, 1937. Coast Counties Gas Company was also a predecessor of Pacific Gas and Electric Company in the area. The company became a part of P.G.&E. in 1954.

From these beginnings gas and electric service has grown with the community.

Telephones

When it was founded on October 18, 1881, the telephone exchange in the neighboring city of Martinez was the ninth in California to have a telephone central office providing local as well as long distance service. The first exchange on the Pacific Coast and the third in the world had been established at San Francisco in 1878, followed a year later by one in Oakland.[27]

The first telephone in Contra Costa County was installed in the Southern Pacific depot where the secretary of the Contra Costa Telephone Company, James H. Borland, was acting as agent for the railroad company. Equipment was leased from the Pacific Bell Telephone Company.[28]

As early as 1881, connections were made from Martinez to Pacheco, Concord, Clayton, Somersville, Antioch, Walnut Creek, Danville and San Ramon.[29] The following year a line was connected to Lafayette. The Philip Lamp family, who had farmed on the Moraga Ranch for fifteen years before this, had the distinction, on January 11, 1882, of sending the first regular message over the newly connected telephone line to Walnut Creek to summon Dr. Hook when one of the sons of the family injured his arm.[30]

Telephones to the Orinda area evidently came from Berkeley rather than Martinez. The following announcement appeared in Berkeley on the 17th of June, 1882: "Telephones are about to be placed in various houses and public buildings of Berkeley. . . . Switches and branch lines will be extended to the school for the blind and to the University. A line will go to General Wagner's and to the Colton Ranches. . . ." Soon Theodore Wagner, N. M. Hoyt and E. I. deLaveaga all had phones listed at their residences. The numbers were Main 91⁵, 91³, and 91⁴, respectively.[31]

In 1937 the telephone company put in a new cable from Berkeley to Orinda. Orinda did not have its own telephone exchange until 1938. Permission was granted to the Pacific Telephone and Telegraph Company to open a separate exchange here on February 2, 1938. The first temporary telephone book for Orinda was printed in March 1938. There were 225 subscribers. Before this time, Orinda had been included in the Oakland book. By May 1942 there were 893 subscribers.

In 1940 a program started which was to place the telephone wires underground in the village. By 1957 the old building, which had adjoined the Orinda Store, and is now a part of it, was outgrown. A new 6,500-foot central office building was constructed on Santa Maria near San Pablo Dam Road. The number of telephones then had reached 5,600.

Sanitary District

Before 1947, at almost any social gathering of Orindans, the conversation would turn at some time to septic tanks. Each family would eventually have a tale to tell of his tank or his neighbor's; sometimes serious and often humorous. The problems created in part by the heavy adobe soil increased as more and more homes were built in the county.

In 1945 a report was presented to the County Board of Supervisors, recommending formation of a sanitary district in Contra Costa County along watershed lines including about 52,700 acres. This proposal was defeated. A much smaller area including only Moraga, Lafayette, Walnut Creek and a corridor to the Treatment Plant and embracing 23,000 acres was incorporated July 15, 1946 as the original district. Most of the Orinda area was annexed in 1947. Other areas have been annexed since that time so that the present Central Contra Costa Sanitary District boundary includes over 60,000 acres (93 square miles).

General obligation bonds in the amount of $2,400,000 were voted for the construction of trunk sewers, pumping stations, and treatment plant in June 1947. An Orinda Pumping Station was completed two years later, and a second Orinda Pumping Station completed in 1960. An additional $8,900,000 bond issue was approved by the electorate in 1956.

XIII

Community Organizations and Plans

A local improvement association was the most effective voice of the citizens in the 1920's, and an organization of this type has continued to represent them to this day. When the community was smaller, the organization was extremely effective in acting in the interests of the citizens. Today, the Orinda Association is made up of representatives who are elected from the various districts by the members of the Association who pay nominal dues. The Association represents a large group of citizens on local affairs, listing over one thousand members.

Orinda Improvement Association

The Orinda Improvement Association was inaugurated on May 22, 1923, according to the old minute book kept by Secretary, Mrs. A. P. Tenney. Edward I. deLaveaga was the first president.

One of the first items on the agenda was a petition to the telephone company for more adequate service. Within a few months "two additional hen party lines were secured."[1] There were other vital needs for the growing community: education, fire protection, transportation, and improved mail facilities.

It was through the efforts of the Association that the Moraga and Orinda Park School Districts were consolidated into the new Orinda Union School District and the school bonds passed. By August 1923 the Orinda Volunteer Fire Department had been formed and money raised. A building was erected for a fire house by early 1924. A postal station was generally maintained in the Orinda Store, and the Association was vigilant over the years to seek better service from the Rural Free Delivery out of Berkeley and, eventually, an Orinda Post Office.

Bus transportation was anxiously sought after through the Railroad Commission and bus companies. There were continuing efforts to secure a new tunnel through the hills and, in the meantime, a straighter approach to the old tunnel. It was through the efforts of this group that Orinda spoke, periodically, along with other county towns, for the new tunnel which was finally completed in 1937.

Throughout the years, the group met informally and kept in touch with community affairs. In May 1937, with evident growth to the community brought by the easier access to Orinda, the Orinda Improvement Association adopted a revised constitution and by-laws[2] and elected new officers. Warren Harrold was given the post of president, and, under his enthusiastic leadership, the Association began many more years of active community service. The other officers were vice-president, Lowell Barry; secretary, Donald Badgley; treasurer, C. E. Donaldson; and trustees, Frank D. Bryant, George H. Pitt, and W. D. Scott. Standing committee chairmen were: program, J. W. Dieterich; membership, George H.

Pitt; publicity, Harrison L. Ketcham; safety and public welfare, R. R. Dennis; transportation, roads and highways, W. P. Stephenson; entertainment, Joe Varni; reception, Harry R. Oakley. Special committee chairmen were: incorporation, Ralph Sisson; west of Orinda, Sidney K. Rosenthal; south of Tunnel Road, Herbert Hauser; east of San Pablo Highway, G. B. Schuyler; west of San Pablo Highway, A. W. Elkinton. Oldtimers will recognize these men who contributed so much for their fellow citizens.

The active head of the entertainment committee, Joe Varni, planned parties and dances to raise money for the various plans of the Association. One of the first things the revised Orinda Improvement Association planned was an official publication.

The Orinda News

The first volume of The Orindan had been published in 1927³ by Warren Harrold ten years before the new Orinda News was started. Before this time, the only other local publication was Hayseed Siftings,⁴ published in 1893 by a local citizen according to Mrs. Delight de-Laveaga. Neither paper lasted long. The Orinda News, however, was extremely successful and eagerly looked forward to by residents.

The newspaper was run on a non-profit basis as was the Association which charged dues of $1.00 per year. The first issue was published July 7, 1937, and was sent to all of the members. There was a monthly news report of the Association's activities, and, later, minutes of the meetings were included. The aim was to print topics of general interest, notices of local projects, reports of the Improvement Association, local organizations' activities and other items of importance. Warren Harrold personally financed the cost of the first copy, helped by local friends who purchased advertising space. Advertisers supporting the paper made it possible to distribute it without charge.

The Orinda News was published consistently until the spring of 1943 when the war years caused the community to turn its energies elsewhere. Publication was resumed in September 1946, and continued through 1953. It was resumed again in 1956 for a brief period, and seven years later, another attempt was made to continue the paper. Only a few issues have been printed since that time. The size of the community by then made the local intimate spirit of the paper a thing of the past.

The Orinda News made a large contribution during the rapidly growing years. Everyone knew what was going on; town meetings were announced, community efforts to achieve goals were unified, problems of zoning were reported, and master plans for the community aired. Road problems, fiestas, and all varieties of plans mentioned in the paper caused the community to have a closeness of purpose and a unity that was, for years, individual to the community of Orinda.

Neighborhood Organizations

As the various neighborhoods and smaller subdivisions developed, local improvement organizations were formed to take care of their specific and individual needs. The Orinda Improvement Association, before 1940, was basically interested in the original subdivisions. The local organizations have included: Minerinda, Moraga Highway Improvement Association, Orindans, Inc., Canyon Ranch Improvement Association, Encinas del Moraga

San Pablo   The O-I-C-NEWS   Moraga
Valley   Orinda, Contra Costa County, Calif.   Valley

"In the Valleys where the Sunshine meets the Stars"

March 15, 1937
Published by the Orinda Improvement Club

This club sponsors the Orinda Troop No. 1, Boy Scouts of America

IF YOU WANT

THE

BROADWAY TUNNEL

AND THE

TUNNEL ROAD

COMPLETED

BE AT THE MASS MEETING AT THE ORINDA SCHOOL AT EIGHT O'CLOCK

NEXT FRIDAY EVENING, MARCH 19th, 1937

The following speakers have already accepted our invitation to be present: Mr. Thomas E. Caldecott, President of the Berkeley Tunnel District and Mr. E. G. Poss, State Construction Engineer of our District. Others have also been invited.

Bring your suggestions and complaints. Questions from the floor will be in order after the regular speaches. Do you know why we continue to have such bumpy roads? Why the Detours? What is going to be done about the slides? Why the hill on a turn making a dangerous blind spot? How are the children to be protected at the Cross Roads? How are you going to make a left turn at the Cross Roads? When will the Tunnel be open for traffic? Its safety ventilation etc.

These questions and many others will be asked and answered. There are no people more interested in these questions than ourselves and every resident and property owner should make it a point to be on hand and lend his support. Your voice and vote count here.

EVERY RESIDENT AND PROPERTY OWNER INVITED

Meeting in charge of Special Committee appointed by the Chairman at last meeting: Herbert Hauser, Dr. N. Austin Cary and Ralph Wilson.

HAYSEED SIFTINGS.

VOL. I.   ORINDA PARK, CAL., APRIL, 1893.   NO. 2.

OUR SECOND ISSUE has been delayed beyond the time originally fixed for it. Since we have no subscribers we owe no apologies for this delay. The cause was principally the bad weather which made it impossible for many to attend our last meeting, and hence it was deemed best to delay the publication of another issue until this meeting. Interest is increasing in this novel venture, and it is having a good effect upon our young people. The regular newspapers, so far as they have noticed our venture at all, have treated us leniently and kindly, for which we thank them. It rather seems as if one of them was disappointed because they did not find us different from other people. That paper evidently expected HAYSEED SIFTINGS to be full of hayseeds, i. e., full of outlandish and boorish ways and ideas, and we feel highly complimented that they did not find us so. However, if the editor's conclusion that HAYSEED SIFTINGS was started to boom the Hog business is correct, it would fill us with vanity, for the Hog business is booming, but HAYSEED SIFTINGS is too modest to claim the credit for it.

LOOKING over our experiences since the last issue of HAYSEED SIFTINGS (which was also the first), we have good reason to be thankful that they are passed. They were vexatious and trying.

Our California and Nevada Railroad, in which we alone have faith, had almost forsaken us entirely.

It would seem almost as if the old trusty engineer who has left it and gone into the butcher business has hoodooed it, or perhaps it is the new engineer who is the hoodoo; at any rate, we find that we miss it when it does not run.

We have found out that a railroad train is very convenient even if it is not always on time, and that a railroad train even if not on time is better than no train at all.

But our late experience has been somewhat discouraging, and our faith in the California and Nevada has been sadly shaken.

Our Supervisors have not taken much interest in us either, as even our wagon roads were almost impassable.

To meet such an emergency in the future it may be necessary to organize a Pedestrian Club, and award prizes to the best walker.

In this way we will accomplish three things: *first*, show our independence; *second*, boom the shoemaking business; *third*, save our money on railroad tickets.

THIS DAY, April 1st, closes the Lenten season, which to Christian people is, or ought to be, a time of self-denial and sacrifice.

But fasting or abstaining from pleasures is not all that is expected from us; they ought merely to serve us as reminders, and turn our thoughts upon our lives, upon what we have done and to the things that perhaps we have left undone.

In such a retrospect we will, no doubt, view with regret many of our actions.

This season of fasting and self-denial, if properly observed, will be apt to bring these matters home to us, and thus will aid us in avoiding similar mistakes and regrets in the future.

If our backward view reveals to us any good actions, things in which we may justly feel pride and satisfaction, whatever sacrifices we may have made will find a sufficient reward in the deed itself, and the comfort and satisfaction it thus gives to ourselves.

Abstaining for a brief time from the ordinary pleasures of the table and from amusements is no hardship, and is rather calculated to make us appreciate them at their just value.

But, having passed that season of repentance, we all gladly welcome Easter day, a day of promise, of new hope and new life.

We wish the young people of Orinda Park, especially, much enjoyment at their next entertainment, as we think they deserve it for having observed the Lenten season as they did.   ED.

So much unlooked-for poetical talent has been developed at Orinda Park that it has given rise to the suspicion that the author of "Ta-ra-ra-boom-de-ray" hails from there. There seems to be a poetical inspiration attached to the shores of San Pablo Creek, as it is known that even married ladies have perpetrated poetry upon their husbands after even a temporary residence or brief visit to this locality.

Homes Association, Glorietta Improvement Association, Hacienda Homes Improvement Association, Inland Valley Improvement Association, Lake Orinda Highlands, Lincoln Estates, Lost Valley Improvement Association, Lost Valley Estates, Los Amigos Home Owners Association, Meadowlands, Monte Vista Improvement Club, Moraga del Rey, Moraga Highlands, Moraga Meadows Association, Moraga Woodlands Improvement Association, Oak Springs Homes Association, Ranchitos de Moraga Association, Rheem Highlands Association, Sleepy Hollow Improvement Association, Snug Harbor Improvement Association, Orinda Estates Owner's Association, and Orinda Oaks Association.

Orinda Association

The rapid growth south of the crossroads in Orinda brought about the incorporation of a new group called Orindans, Inc. in 1944. Both groups now offered membership to residents in the entire Orinda area. By 1945 it was clear that the two organizations were often duplicating each other. The result was the incorporation of the new Orinda Association formed from Orindans, Inc. and the Orinda Improvement Association.

The new organization now served all of Orinda, and all of the neighborhood groups were entitled to representation in the Orinda Association. Also represented were the Orinda Chamber of Commerce, Orinda Community Church, Orinda County Fire Protection District, Orinda Garden Club, Orinda Junior Women's Club, Orinda Lions Club, Orinda Mothers Club, Orinda Nursery School Association, Orinda Park Pool, Santa Maria Altar Society and the 12.15 Club. The various groups formed the Civic Affairs Committee.

The present Orinda Association functions with nine directors selected by vote by the distinct geographical areas of Orinda. The Association cooperates with approximately twenty-eight other local organizations. It tries to serve as a community sounding board and spokesman. It concerns itself with issues and problems that are of general community interest and concern, and meetings are run more or less on the old "town hall" basis. Goals pursued actively at the present time include better police protection, a community center, careful planning and zoning, improved political liaison, central area beautification and planning for traffic and roads.

When the enlarged Orinda Association was formed in 1945, William Penn Mott, Jr. became president. Throughout the years, he has dedicated many hours of service and much of his talent to plans for the development of the community. Now Director of the Department of Parks and Recreation for the State of California, he maintains his interest in Orinda and has kept his home here.

Clarence Betz became Secretary-Treasurer of the newly formed organization. Betz has been active in innumerable Orinda organizations and is well-known for his talents in helping various local groups.

In January 1968 Clark Wallace became president of the Orinda Association. Membership expanded under his leadership, and a newsletter was printed and sent to members giving the highlights of the Orinda Association meetings and plans. Harry Clemons was president in 1969 and became the first president of the newly-formed Orinda Historical Society, a group formed by citizen interest after a committee was appointed by the Orinda Association to

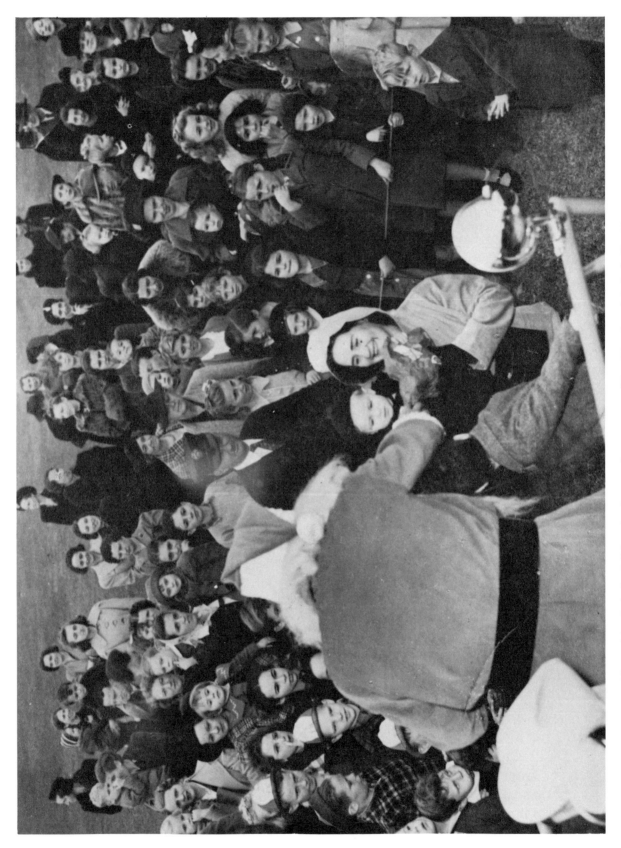

Santa Claus visits Orinda children in the 1940's, courtesy of Joe Varni and Orinda Fire Department   KC

investigate the potential of such a group. Charles Ivy was his successor to head the Orinda Association.

Master Plans for Orinda

As early as 1937 the farsighted Warren Harrold advocated the purchase of land opposite the Orinda School for future community development—of schools, auditorium or town hall. Since that time, several plans for Orinda have been presented and zoning ordinances concluded. Efforts have been made to keep Orinda residential.

In 1946 Orinda's first "master plan study" was completed by Howard Moise of the Department of Architecture at the University of California.[5] Moise felt that central community facilities should be grouped on the east side of San Pablo Dam Road from the Orinda School to the crossroads. His plan showed a community center at the Pine Grove and a high school adjacent to it with joint use of facilities. Today the Pine Grove Intermediate School is near the area, but the Pine Grove is gone.

At the crossroads Moise planned a plaza-type shopping center with ample off-street parking and architectural harmoniousness. The design was not followed, and the crossroads grew into a heterogenous assortment of buildings and parking. His plan for roadways did come closer to actuality.

On June 6, 1949, the Board of Supervisors of Contra Costa County adopted an ordinance, No. 485, which placed Orinda under the "Precise Land Use Master Plan of the County of Contra Costa." Orinda citizens and civic groups contributed to the zoning plans.

In January 1954 Francis Violich was retained by the Orinda Association as Planning Consultant. After receiving the results of a community questionnaire, Mr. Violich developed further plans for a commercial zone, designated the Pine Grove as a site for future community facilities, and proposed that San Pablo Dam Road be realigned behind the village.[6]

A "General Plan for Orinda" was then conceived by the Master Planning Section of the County Planning Commission's technical staff. In the text of thirty pages the following was included: "The community center should be the focal point of the civic life of the residents of Orinda, dominating and functional in its design and location. . . . The Pine Grove site meets the above requirements."[7] A new road through Siesta Valley to Moraga was proposed, as well as a road linking Sleepy Hollow with Happy Valley.

Incorporation

Orinda is generally referred to as the area that is embraced by the Orinda Union School District and contains approximately 23 square miles. Incorporation was first thought of as early as 1938,[8] when people and businesses began to appear in larger and larger numbers. Population of the community was 767 at that time.

Two years later the population was 3,200, increasing to 3,500 by 1946. After the war years, the population jumped to 9,500 by 1955. A postmaster's estimate of the population in 1970 is 19,740.

In 1953 the Association made a study of the possibilities of incorporation. Nothing developed from this study, but in 1956, a strong movement toward incorporation was begun as Mr. Fred Rust headed a research committee of the Orinda Incorporation Committee. Disagreement arose from the beginning with many citizens questioning the proposed figures for the new city. Petitions were circulated to obtain signatures in the summer of 1956 and part of the following year. A town meeting was held in May of 1957 to discuss the pros and cons of incorporation. However, the petition failed short of the twenty-five percent of the assessed land necessary to place the issue on the ballot.

In late 1963 a special committee was appointed by Association President, Harry Fledderman, to make an objective fact-finding study of the incorporation question. The committee report ran to some fifty pages and was available to Orindans for examination. The Association did not take a partisan point of view.

It was not until July 1966, when the population was over 18,000, that a drive was again started to give the people of Orinda the opportunity to incorporate if they so desired. Supporters of incorporation again sought a petition from owners of twenty-five percent of the assessed valuation of the land. This time the petition was a success, and an election was scheduled for September 26, 1967. The area was to include the school district with minor modifications. Opposition tried to get a petition from owners of fifty-one percent of the assessed valuation but failed in their attempt. Bruce Geernaert headed the Orinda Incorporation Committee with Clarence Betz the chairman of the "unincorporation movement."

At the same time, it was necessary to vote for city councilmen. An excellent group of men were persuaded to run on the five-man council, including Joseph Long, Joseph Lohman, O. W. Campbell, Clark Wallace and James Halloran. There were fifteen candidates to choose from, but the five mentioned pooled the most votes in order. However, after the seeming success of the drive for incorporation, the headlines of the Orinda Sun on September 29, 1967, were: "Incorporation Beaten at Polls by Landslide Margin."

Thus, the first time incorporation for Orinda was placed on the ballot it was defeated 4,413 to 1,913 with seventy percent of Orinda voting. With the failure of incorporation, a study was proposed for the Chamber of Commerce and the Orinda Association on the subject of police protection for Orinda.

Community Center

The absence of a community center for many years was not for lack of trying. The subject occupied many dozens of meetings and discussions. When publication of the Orinda News was resumed in September, 1946, one of the prime interests of the Orinda Association was to foster plans for a community center. Three acres of land behind the Orinda School and the original church properties on the highway were planned for purchase as soon as funds could be raised. Architect Wayne Littlejohn[9] and Landscape Designer William Mott[10] drew tentative plans for a building and a master plan for the center. These included a playhouse, natural amphitheatre, tennis courts, picnic area, and a community center building.

The Association began a drive for funds under the leadership of President Mowry Irwin and sponsored an essay contest, "Why I Think Orinda Needs a Community Center." The Orinda School auditorium was, up to this time, the only place large enough for any local affairs or meetings.

By November 1946, only $10,000 of the original goal of $20,000 had been raised, and according to the understanding made by the Association, contributions already made could be reclaimed if the goal was not reached by October 31. Hope was expressed that the project would somehow still succeed and donations were left in the fund by unanimous decision.

Several civic groups suggested that the Orinda Elementary School District take over the operation of the proposed project and that all of the land except the church properties and the road be deeded to the school district. The school trustees asked community wishes by sending a letter to residents of Orinda,[11] listing the restrictions it would consider mandatory before it could consider this project. At this time 10 acres were considered for development, of which one-third would be owned and developed by the Community Church. In 1948 it was decided by the Association that title to the community center property would be held in the name of the Orinda Association in case of the future unification of the Orinda Union School District with other districts. By this time, about $19,000 had been raised, more was pledged, and a final deed to the property was imminent. On October 1957 formal dedication of the Community Center site was held. The road into the property was named Irwin Way in memory of Mowry Irwin who had recently died and who had been a moving force behind the Community Center plans. Gates were erected at the road entrance in December 1948.

For the next few years, plans for the center were constantly discussed at meetings of the Association, but it was felt a further attempt to raise funds for a building was not timely. The property had been purchased from EBMUD for $15,000. The Association shared with the Community Church the cost of grading and paving the road to the property, so that the fund had only a balance of $1,200.

In 1950 a questionnaire sent to residents returned a 457 to 284 no vote on interest in further development of the center on a voluntary contribution basis. The property now began to be a liability as taxes and sewer assessment costs brought expenses to $700 a year.

With the cooperation of the Association, 1.4 acres was made available for a new library building for which the community had expressed a desire. About the same time, in 1956, the Orinda Community Church had plans for expansion and needed more land. The Association land adjacent to the existing church was exchanged in a transaction between the EBMUD, the Community Church, and the Association for 9.83 acres of land northwest of the crossroads.

In June 1965 the land near the Orinda Crossroads was sold to Bay Area Rapid Transit for $67,000.

Money held in trust by the Orinda Association was transferred in 1969, through legal action, to an extended library service area (LIB-8) in order to purchase the old Orinda firehouse in the village for a community center. Plans are underway for remodeling the building.

The Pine Grove

Today there remains one lone pine of an old group of trees that formed what was known as The Pine Grove. The Pine Grove, and the larger area of over 300 acres on which it stood, has been the object of many community controversies. The area had been suggested for a community center location in the first "Master Plan."

The venerable old trees were planted in the early 1900's, but whether by the Syndicate Water Company who purchased the property in 1906, or more likely, the Peoples Water Company who in turn purchased it on January 2, 1907, is not certain. It is thought that the

Orinda's first Boy Scout Troop: Jimmy Dieterich, Remy Zuur, Bob Elkinton, Charles Rosenthal, Wing Wong Quong, Wilbert Sorensen, Alfred Ahlquist, Nowell Martin, Donald Donaldson, Fred Elkinton, and Teddy Zuur (1933)   SKR trees were part of a nursery of trees grown for the benefit of watershed lands. Tree plantings were started in 1906 and evidently continued for about six years.[12] The East Bay Water Company bought the property in 1917, and this land then went into the EBMUD holdings in 1928.

The problems of the Pine Grove started in 1953 when EBMUD wanted to sell the land as it was increasing in value and was not necessary as watershed land. Plans proposed included a shopping center and parking space. In 1955 the Pacific Intermountain Express Company purchased the land with the idea of building offices for their employees. The public was aroused when the County Planning Commission recommended that the area be rezoned for business. A poll was taken locally which showed a 3,298 to 1,460 vote against rezoning.[13] Many articles were written about PIE coming into the area, and the company, finding themselves unwelcome by many of the citizens, decided against building in Orinda. A faction of citizens, however, felt that PIE would have followed their plans for Cliff May's design for office buildings similar to the Sunset Magazine offices, which he had designed, and that they would have developed the remaining area in a satisfactory way. PIE sold the property to a group of private buyers.

Part of the Pine Grove tree section was lost when the highway expanded in 1953. Since that time, the remaining tree section has been removed by the owners and regraded by Bay Area Rapid Transit. The Pine Grove Student Council recently planted 200 Monterey Pines on the school property hoping that eventually the beauty of the old Pine Grove, which was a landmark for years, will be restored. Some of the students did the digging while others watered and cleared the land.

The property was purchased in 1958 by eight men, including the present four developer-owners who hope to develop Orindawoods, a 187-acre project. The architect for their plan is Gordon Hall. The plan which calls for open space, single family and multiple residences, has appealed to many citizens but has had opposition by the Orinda Homeowners, Inc. Two other plans, Bernard Muth in 1961 and Orinda Cerro in 1965, failed to materialize. Rezoning was approved in 1969 by a unanimous vote of the County Planning Commission.

During its life, the Pine Grove was the subject of many controversies. Arguments about this area have continued even though the trees have now disappeared.

The Fiestas

Older residents of the community well remember the Orinda Fiesta. In April 1938 Warren Harrold, then president of the Orinda Improvement Association, recommended in his annual report the adoption of an annual Fiesta Week by the citizens.

The following year, April 22 to April 28, was proclaimed Fiesta Week, the purpose being to show pride in the Spanish background of the area with its "genuine hospitality and festive gaiety." The fire siren sounded three times to open the week on April 22, Saturday, at 3 p.m. Fiesta attire was worn by the residents and festivities ended with a dance and entertainment at the Orinda Country Club.

A second Fiesta was held in May 1940, with three days of festivities which included a kangaroo court, children's parade, dance, and a grand parade led by the honorary mayor, E. I. deLaveaga. A horse show was held across from the Orinda School followed by a Spanish barbecue. Lowell Berry was chairman and master of ceremonies, and Joe Varni acted as chief cook. All horsemen in the county were invited to take part in the show. The parade of horses started at Santa Maria Church on Miner Road, continued to the crossroads and ended in the showing field opposite the school. Over 130 horses were entered in the event. This community fun was not only happily participated in by all Orindans, but $376 was the net return for the Orinda Improvement Association.

In May 1941 a third Fiesta was held in which the local improvement clubs and organizations participated. The parade included a color guard unit of the Twelfth Naval District from San Francisco, the Acalanes Union High School band, various marching organizations, 150 horses and riders, floats, the Orinda Fire Department, the Piedmont High School Kiltie Band, and the Orinda Troop of Boy Scouts. This year the march was from the filter plant to the field opposite the grammar school where another horse show was held.

The Fiestas ended with the war years, but in 1943, celebrations were held at the opening of the newly improved highway. A Fiesta was revived in May 1955, when the interchange and overpass at the Crossroads was completed. $5,200 of the proceeds were later turned over to the building fund of the Orinda Library by the Fiesta Committee.

Unfortunately, the growth of the community and lack of space has eliminated the old type Fiestas. A day long Fiesta was held on Labor Day, 1969, to benefit the new Orinda Community Center. This was the first one to be held in many years.

Boy Scouts

When the Sidney Rosenthal family, who had moved to Orinda in the 1920's, had a son who wanted to be a boy scout, there was no other way than to start a troop. Sparked by Mr. Rosenthal, the interest in scouting grew. It was not a simple task to find enough boys to start a troop. One family in Orinda had a Chinese houseboy, and they consented to his becoming a scout so there would be the legal number. Wing Wong Quong was a charter scout in Orinda. The other charter members were Patrol Leader Jimmy Dieterich, Remy Zuur, Bob Elkinton, Charles Rosenthal, Wilbert Sorensen, Alfred Ahlquist, Nowell Martin, Donald Donaldson, Fred Elkinton, and Senior Patrol Leader Teddy Zuur. Mr. Rosenthal acted as scoutmaster until the arrival of Mr. F. Foster, and the Parent Teachers' Association sponsored the troop.

The Orinda Troop received its charter at an elaborate dinner held at the Orinda School on Friday evening, February 24, 1933. The program was conducted by the officers of the Berkeley-Contra Costa Council, Boy Scouts of America, and Eagle Scouts from several of the county troops.

In 1935 sponsorship was taken over by the Orinda Improvement Association. Lack of sufficient adult leadership caused some problems, and it took a letter from the District Executive, Mr. W. R. Whidden, to the Association to arouse enough interest so that the scouting move could continue.

The same year, two Orinda Scouts, Charles Rosenthal and Forest Shakley, attended the World Jamboree. The Improvement Association also took more interest, and the following year, Dr. Austin Carey reported that the Orinda Troop was properly organized and a real credit to Orinda. Since that time steady growth has resulted in the formation of other troops and a large body of scouts.

Charles Rosenthal became the first Eagle Scout in Orinda; then when his brother, Kenneth, was ready to become a Cub Scout, no Cub meetings had yet been held in Orinda. Again the Rosenthal family started interest in scouting at the Cub Scout level. By 1937 two dens were functioning. Mr. Vinson Brown, a well-known naturalist, was the first cubmaster. Orinda was represented again at the National Jamboree of scouts, this year by Sheldon Kales and Donald Trucker.

Other men who gave of their time to promote the early scouting movement were Harold Martin, L. V. Dana, T. Edson, J. Schmelz, J. McNeill, Austin Cary, Donald Badgley, Franklin Kales, George Pitt, A. Scott, G. Shepherd, J. W. Snook, J. Cathcart, Vinson Brown, Harold Symes, Richard Breuner, Melvin Jacobus, Jack Neal, Harry Craviotto, Henry Gentry, Kenneth Thompson, Kenneth Gelwix, Lowell Berry and Grovel La Velle.

Girl Scouts and Camp Fire Girls

In 1936 the girls, not to be outdone by the boys, were interested in some form of group activity. Both the Girl Scout program and the Camp Fire Girls activities were investigated. Mrs. Sydney Rosenthal, president of the P.T.A., had representatives from both groups speak at the monthly meeting. A secret ballot was taken, and it was decided that the P.T.A. sponsor a Girl Scout Troop.

The charter members of Troop 27 included Mary Bennett, Carol Kales, Lily Dorrington, Beatrice Clebourne, Georgia Shepherd, Connie Pearson and Betty Lou Gunn, under the leadership of Mrs. G. F. Hickok. By July 1937 Vida Schworer, Harriet Morgan and Nancy Harrold had joined the group. Mrs. Lloyd Farrar took over the duties of leader of the troop.

At a formal Court of Awards, held in the school on May 11, 1938, Jacklyn Mean, Connie Pearson, Nancy Harrold, Betty Lou Bennett, Carol Kales and Lily Dorrington received their second class badges from Mrs. Leceister H. Williams, Berkeley Girl Scout Commissioner.

From then on, the girls were active, presenting pageants and having parties, as well as studying and learning crafts and participating in charitable and community affairs.

Although the Camp Fire Girls movement was delayed by the vote taken in 1936, a group was formed in 1957 by Marian Rand, with Ann Copenhagen as assistant. Blue Birds followed in 1960, and both have been active since that time.

Twelve-Fifteen Club

One of Orinda's earliest groups is a small organization of women, its purpose social and philanthropic, which started when Orinda was a small community—the Twelve-Fifteen Club. On December 12, 1933, a group of women met at the home of Mrs. Ralph Sisson and organized the group. Mrs. E. Casterline was elected chairman and Mrs. H. Mack, secretary-treasurer. The first members included Mesdames Casterline, Sisson, Dieterich, Alexander, Rich, Deadrich, Mack, Sullivan, Harrold, Kendall, Lake, Elkinton, Pasteris and Donaldson.

On December 3, 1963, the club celebrated its thirtieth birthday with its annual Christmas party. Meetings are still held at the present time.

Founded in 1937, the group is interested in the beautification of the community, exchange of ideas pertinent to gardening, and cooperation in protection of wild flowers, native trees and plants. Founding members were: Mesdames Richard Breuner, Ernest J. Hadden, Harrison Ketchum, Dorothy Lamb, Harold Martin Jr., P. D. Richardson, W. P. Stevenson, Harold B. Symes and Leon Woolsey. Monthly meetings are held at the Orinda Country Club and occasionally in members' homes.

In the past thirty years the Garden Club has contributed much toward the beautification of Orinda. Early projects included: planting trees in the village in front of the first Orinda Grammar School; scattering wild flower seeds on the hillsides; planting trees and shrubs around Lake Cascade such as the cork oaks which are now good-size trees; conducting house tours to many of the gardens in Orinda, including one in 1942 which raised funds for the local volunteer fire department; and participating in the Oakland Garden Show.

In the "A Wish to Keep Orinda Clean" campaign during conservation week in 1958, wishing wells of redwood were placed throughout the village and at the crossroads for use as litter containers. Poster contests were sponsored in the schools for litterbug campaigns, with prizes given for the winning slogans and posters.

When the Orinda Library was completed, the Orinda Garden Club put their efforts into the large landscaping project involved in the grounds around the library. Following a plan by Robert M. Babcock, Landscape Architect, garden club members donated the plants and shrubs and did the planting of the Orinda Library grounds. The Garden Club participates each year in the Book Fair held, for the benefit of the Library, in the Orinda Village.

Other community plantings include the circle at the Crossroads. The large tree was decorated every Christmas by members with the help of the Orinda firemen. The Beautification Committee of Orinda has now taken over this project.

In 1965 the members began a cleaning up campaign for Lake Cascade and continued planting more native shrubs and trees around the lake. Many weeping willows and silk trees were planted, as well as oleanders, toyons, bottle bush, wild rose, broom, manzanita, white birch trees and bulbs and wild flowers.

One active group of the Orinda Garden Club is the FAGS (Flower Arrangement Group) who make monthly small bedside arrangements for the patients at the county hospital in Martinez. From 250 to 300 arrangements are taken to the patients.

The Garden Club contributes to plantings in many parts of the community, such as for trees along the highways and village and for the school baseball diamond at Pine Grove School (Randall Field). They support various conservation projects throughout the state. A memorial tree planting program for Orinda utilizes funds contributed "In Memorium."

For their work throughout the years, the Orinda Garden Club has received many awards. In 1958, for the "Wish to Keep Orinda Clean" campaign, they received the California Garden Club award and received this award again in 1958–59 for the beautification of the circle at the Crossroads. Also, that year they were given the Civic Beautification Award for planting 1000 seedlings along the freeway. Other awards included: The Richfield Award for landscaping and planting around the library, 1959; an award for litterbug campaign,

Orinda boys in fire training program sponsored by Orinda Fire Department   MS

1960; and the Richfield and Sears Awards for the lake project, 1964–65. The 1966 Lake Cascade award money went to help landscape the Mary Thom Memorial reading pavillion at the Sleepy Hollow School. In 1968 the club again received the Sears Award for the Memorial Tree Planting Program.

The Dramateurs

Known throughout the area of Contra Costa County as well as to many residents of the East Bay is our local amateur theatrical group, The Dramateurs. Since 1958 the Dramateurs have leased the Town Hall in Lafayette on a year-round basis.[14]

The old Town Hall was built in 1914. At that time the Lafayette Improvement Club decided a community center was necessary, and land for the project was donated by Mr. and Mrs. Frank Ghiglione. The building was opened on May 1, 1914, and a community affair was held with supper served downstairs and a dance upstairs. For many years dances were held at the Town Hall on Saturday nights, and they proved to be very popular. The Oakland, Antioch and Eastern Railroad (Sacramento Northern) provided extra trains on dance nights and waited until the last person was ready to leave in the early morning hours before departing. In time the popularity of the dance parties waned, and the building was used for other purposes.

Boy Scouts, Campfire Girls, American Legion, Lions Club and other civic groups have met in the old Town Hall, and similar to Orinda's Casa Verana, it has at various times housed a church, a public school classroom and a library until each found its permanent quarters. For a time it was the home of "The Straw Hat Revue."

Although the plays are given in Lafayette, roots of The Dramateurs were started in Orinda, in 1940, when a group interested in theatricals organized the Barnstormers. Several plays were produced.[15] In 1944 some of the Orinda housewives produced a Christmas play for the children, and soon husbands were also involved in presenting plays for adult and family audiences. Several of the original members are still active in the Dramateurs, and players have always participated not only from Lafayette and Orinda but also from other local communities. Early meetings and rehearsals were held in private homes, while sets were constructed in workshops, barns, garages and driveways.

Since the 1958 occupancy of Town Hall, The Dramateurs have grown to the point where four or five major productions a year are staged, each running two evenings a weekend for six to eight weeks, consecutively. Carl Rasmussen became the director in 1954, and since then, over fifty plays have been produced. Thousands of bay area residents have attended.

In October 1964 changes made in local fire and building regulations forced the closing of the old Town Hall. The Dramateurs by this time had installed a new stage, permanent seating, and light and sound equipment. Studies made of the situation showed that approximately $30,000 would be needed to fix the building to comply with the new building codes standards. A goal of $50,000 was set to enable the group to also add improvements for the comfort of the audiences and to improve the quality of the productions. This was the first time that public funds were solicited by the group since its founding. The drive was successful, and the building was improved.

For a time the Orinda Chapter of the Society for the Preservation and Encouragement of Barber Shop Quartet Singing in America flourished and gave free programs for the community. Organized in 1946, the "Barber Shop" Chorus presented their first musical for the community in December 1948.

Members included: Clyde Bumgarner, Ken Courtright, Oakley Bradley, Bill Bradley, Mike Murphy, John Ogden (Director), Don Skilling, Bill Simpson, Joe Dorst, Frank Callahan, Ray McDaniels, Claude Hazlett, Keene Pettengill, Don Krotz, Howard Pettijohn, John Armstrong, Mort Ingls, Paul Pease, Iver Jacobson, Bill Courtright, Larry Osborn, Irwin Johnson and Monte Murphy.

Orinda Art Center

Mr. Joseph Sheaff, former Superintendent of the Orinda School District, is credited with passing the idea of an art center in Orinda on to Mrs. Doris Fraser, a local artist. She gathered together an enthusiastic group of local ladies who immediately went to work in the fall of 1949 to create the Orinda Art Center. The purpose of this group was to assist in the furthering of the artistic ability of talented Orinda children.

Originally the classes were composed of children selected for their outstanding artistic talent. As Orinda grew, so did the art center, and today there are classes for all interested children as well as for adults. Over the years other types of activities such as dance, crafts, photography, lectures, tours to museums and places of artistic interests have been added.

Highlight event of the year is the Orinda Art Center's annual "Art in Springtime." This event features the childrens' art work from the current classes, an exhibit of local artists' work, and a guest speaker of renown, all woven together around the theme chosen for the year.

Members of the Art Center have participated in the Friends of the Library annual outdoor Book Fair, adding to the color of the occasion. They also maintain exhibits of paintings in the Orinda Library.

The Orinda Art Center is a non-profit organization whose activities are made possible by the nominal donations of interested members of the community. The sponsors' donations enable them to be eligible for the activities, classes, and tours offered by the organization.

Orinda Women's Club

Organized in May 1953, with 23 charter members, the Orinda Women's Club has grown to a present membership of approximately 50. Formerly called the Orinda Junior Women's Club, the goal is to promote the welfare of the community through social, philanthropic and educational work.

During the first year, the members participated in a survey of the residents of Orinda to determine what future developments were desired. The most obvious requirement was an adequate public library, and the Orinda Women's Club was instrumental in forming the Orinda Library Board together with other members of the community. Story hours were held, a fashion show and luncheon sponsored in March 1956, publicity given the current library, and new shelves and telephone services were furnished; all this activity was going on while the plans for the library were being formulated. Members took a large part in aiding in the drive for funds for the newly planned library; and from the club treasury presented Chairman Perc Brown with $1,000. The group has supported the library in various ways such as maintaining a record collection, donating funds with which a valuable Contra Costa history book was purchased, and giving many hours to the Orinda Library Board.

In recent years the club has made donations to the local schools for various types of needed equipment that has not been provided in the budget.

A study group of the club made a survey of the need for a community center in Orinda. With the availability of the old Fire House, a type of community center is now in the offing. The Women's Club is participating in the fund raising to refurbish the building purchased with the old Community Center Funds and has made a $1,000 donation to the fund.

The study made showed the desire and need for a Children's Park area. The Women's Club, in cooperation with Briones Park, has planned a $14,000 donation to establish a Children's Park area in the Briones Park District. Nine thousand dollars was allotted for the first stage Pre-School area which has been dedicated. The remaining $5,000 will go to a section planned for grade school children.

Newcomer's Club

The Newcomer's Club of Orinda was organized in October 1957 by a small group of Orinda women. Among the founders were: Mrs. J. J. Gannon, Mrs. James Nichol, Mrs. J. W. Bishop and Mrs. Harold Scott, some of whom are still active in the group.

The club has grown from a small number of residents to a membership of over 400, ranking it among the largest organized groups in the area. Membership is open to women who have lived in Orinda less than one year. However, once a member, she may remain as long as she wishes.

The Orinda group is strictly social and sponsors many activities within the club. Activities include: book review, garden, Cordon Bleu, choral, crafts and stitchery, drama, ball room dancing, painting, tennis, golf, bowling, canasta and seven bridge groups.

Monthly luncheon meetings of the general membership are held at various restaurants throughout Contra Costa County and the Bay Area. Highlighting the meetings are a wide variety of interesting programs.

Other Business, Service and Social Clubs

There are several other organizations in Orinda making various types of contributions to the community. The oldest of these is the Orinda Lions Club which held its charter meeting at the old Wild Duck Dining Room at the Crossroads on July 10, 1939. The club was active in the improvement of the library, and in donating funds toward this, as well as helping to awaken general interest in a new building in the 1950's. Members sponsor a Boy Scout troop, are interested in the foreign student exchange program, and particularly assist in blind student aid. They are active in various other community projects and maintain a community birthday calendar.

In 1946 the Orinda Chamber of Commerce was formed. The Chamber keeps its watchful eye on the problems of business, roads and signs, as well as parking, always working toward the best solutions for all. Among its services is the printing and distributing to all members of the community a yearly Orinda Business and Professional Directory. The Chamber has recently taken over the sponsorship of the Man of the Year Contest from the Jaycees. The Orinda Sun started the citizen award in 1949 and seeks nominees each year.

The Orinda Jaycees, although disbanded in 1969, sponsored for twenty years, with the Orinda Sun, a Man of the Year Contest. Orinda Men of the Year have been: Dr. Ralph C. Hall, Joseph Sheaff, D. Ramsay Underwood, Edgar Stewart, Ernest Rahmeyer, Jean Henderson, Frank Isola, Dr. George Prlain, Perc Brown, Robert Karplus, Ann Pollaczek, Gerry Cullen, William Koch, Clarence Betz, Allen Winsor, Dr. John Boulware, Walter Treanor, Barbara Parker, Sam Stovall, Richard Bartle and Clark Wallace. The group also sponsored a community swim meet each year and planned safety programs. An annual picnic for wards of the court in Martinez was held each year at McCosker's Ranch.

On February 17, 1949, the Orinda Rotary Club was organized with 19 charter members, and a charter granted April 20, 1949. A widely attended community event sponsored by the group is the Orinda Rotary Field Day held each year at the Orinda School grounds. The club raised $6,000 for the new library building in the 1950's; brought the first American Field Service Student into the area; sponsors Boy Scout troops; started Career Night at Miramonte High School; and has plans to furnish the community with an ambulance in the near future. There are 72 members at present.

The Masons have Orinda Lodge No. 521 with headquarters in the building they constructed in 1960 on Altarinda Way. The building is a center for various group activities. Organized locally with 40 members in 1950, the Masons met for some time in the Boy Scout Hut at the Park Pool site. They have sponsored a Demolay Chapter since 1962 for young men of the community. The boys helped in refurbishing the Orinda bus stop.

The Orinda Kiwanis Club had their charter presentation on July 11, 1964. The group provides and presents the awards at the yearly Sports Banquet at Campolindo High School; provides awards for the Orinda Science Fair; sponsors a yearly luncheon for the new teachers entering the Orinda School District and the Moraga School District; and makes donations mainly aimed at youth activities. In 1969 they took over sponsorship of the All-Orinda Swim Meet from the former Jaycees.

Among other organizations active locally are the Orinda Chapter No. 634 O.E.S., the Eastern Star; the Orinda Tennis Club; Lafayette-Orinda Professional Women's Club; Lafayette-Orinda Soroptimist Club; and the active Orinda Branch of the American Association of University Women.

The Orinda Sun

The weekly Orinda Sun, only local, professional newspaper covering the community, has come out every Friday since 1947. Its forerunner was the Orinda Homebuilder, started in 1938. The paper is part of the Contra Costa Sun group which has won many county, state and national editorial awards for excellence. The Lafayette Sun was begun in 1936; Moraga Sun, 1970, and the give-away Midweek Sun, 1968. Herman Silverman was editor-publisher from 1945–1963 when the Suns were purchased by Dean S. Lesher, major Contra Costa County publisher and Orinda resident.

Marie Monahan, an Orinda resident, was a feature writer for eight years prior to also becoming women's editor in 1964. Jane Putnam, Orinda news editor from 1961, has been involved in community issues.

An oil well on the Miner Ranch RB

XIV

Orinda

Climate and Wildlife

Orinda is in a most favored location in relation to climate which is mild throughout the year. On a typical summer day, the temperature might be in the 70's or 80's and average in the 50's in the winter. When the inland valley simmers in the summer heat, the natural air-conditioning of the bay region in the form of fog creeps through Wildcat Canyon and Shepherd Canyon and cools the Orinda area, after a few excessively warm days. In the middle of the day there may be a twenty-degree difference in temperature on one side of the Caldecott Tunnel from the other. The normal summer pattern is several days of warm weather and then the welcome cooling period. Even with the warmer days, the nights are cool, generally, with the presence of the fog on the ocean. As there is no local industry, the air is still smogless in contrast to some parts of the bay area.

Sometimes in the winter the tule fogs which form in the tule marshes of the delta spread as far as the Berkeley Hills and even through the gaps and into the bay area, but often these fogs are stopped by the hills. On many days, the winter fogs retreat from Orinda as the sun rises, leaving Orinda in the sunshine while the inland valley remains blanketed beneath the low fog. The tule fogs come to Orinda only occasionally, if at all, in some years, while other years find them lasting a week or so at various times.

This climate, which is so attractive to people, is liked by the many trees and shrubs, animals, and the birds. Throughout Orinda, when the first explorers came to settle, the native trees were much the same as they are now. Laurel, live oaks, deciduous oaks, buckeyes, manzanitas, alders, willows and redwoods, pines, madrones and ash are among the principal trees.

The animals, however, did not survive the coming of the white man as well as the trees and shrubs. The early settlers found the grizzly as well as other kinds of bear. As late as 1849, around 80 elk were counted in one herd nearby.[1] The antelope also roamed in herds. Deer were thick before the coming of the cattle and horses of the Spaniards. The elk, antelope and grizzlies have disappeared. In 1849 a grizzly was killed in the Carquinez Straits by General Sherman's mate. Dr. Marsh saw many of them on his ranch, and Jacob Harlan tells of the killing of a bear weighing 1500 pounds near San Pablo Creek.[2]

A bear regularly raided Captain Oakley's bee hives in the olive grove planted by General Wagner on the hill above his home. In the 1940's Captain Oakley and Jim Sullivan tracked one for two days. Although they got several shots at it, they lost it in the brush, only to find it some days later dead of its wounds on the banks of Bear Creek.[3]

A 250-pound black bear was killed on the road near the intersection of Bear Creek Road and the San Pablo Dam Road in 1961.[4] Naturalists from the bay region were amazed to hear

179

of a bear in these hills, but Orinda residents were not surprised. Frank Dutra, who has ranged cattle on the EBMUD property near Bear Creek Road, has seen many bear tracks in this area. His brother, Leroy, rode within ten feet of a brown bear in the 1950's while checking the cattle.

Other animals found in large numbers were squirrels, rabbits, gophers, raccoons and skunks; also roaming the land were mountain lions, coyotes and foxes of which a few have survived. Charles H. Allen remembers that, in July 1915, about 8 coyotes attempted an attack on the chicken house on the Wagner property where he was vacationing.

One small mammal that enjoys the climate and vegetation in Orinda is the mouse. Dr. Oliver P. Pearson, speaking at a meeting of the Friends of the Orinda Library, told about a scientific sampling conducted throughout the United States which showed that Orinda and the Tilden Park area had the highest mouse population in the country.

The streams were filled with fish, and it was only after the building of the San Pablo Dam that Orinda residents stopped fishing for the large steelhead that ran up the creek each year.

It is possible that coyotes and wildcats might have survived in larger numbers except for the fact that they were a menace to the stock. In 1894 Philip Lamp of Moraga Ranch collected $5.00 bounty for one coyote scalp from the county.[5] Bounties such as this were regularly paid for scalps. In 1925, the county, the federal government and the state maintained a corps of hunters who reported in a six-month period that 167 coyotes and 72 wildcats had been killed.

Paul Vashell in Orinda caught a small 27-pound mountain lion in 1939, and many bobcats were still seen at that time. There are still occasional reports of these animals. Only a few years ago a fox often came to lick a sticky barbecue grill at the end of Los Altos Road near water company property.

With their natural enemies gone, the deer are now quite plentiful; but in 1926, E. I. deLaveaga found them so scarce that he imported ten from the Crocker family down the peninsula. Three died in transit, but the other seven were turned loose to multiply. Shooting deer is prohibited in the area except by special permit. By some gardeners they are considered a nuisance, while other residents love to see them still roaming through the countryside.

Oil

Resources have never been successfully developed in the area of Orinda, but over the years there have been occasional flurries of excitement and interest in oil. In the 1860's considerable interest in crude oil seepage was evident throughout all of California.[6] The oil industry was in its infancy, and little was known of efficient methods of operation for obtaining the oil and gas.

The Contra Costa Gazette of May 17, 1862, reported a seepage of coal oil that was discovered a few miles south of San Pablo. A number of wells were drilled that year, one to a depth of 87 feet on the west bank of San Pablo Creek about four miles south of San Pablo toward Orinda.[7] Records show that this well had the apparent distinction of being the second well that was drilled in California.[8] About $25,000 was spent on drilling, fixtures, oil tanks, retorts and distilleries.[9] The operation was evidently not profitable for it was discontinued.

Many wells were drilled from 1888 through 1903 in the Miner Road area of Orinda and near Happy Valley in Lafayette.[10] There are records of the Berkeley Crude Oil Company,[11] a Charles L. Havern, lessee, and a Mr. Holbrook, evidently a promoter, drilling for oil in these vicinities.

Several older residents of Orinda remembered the Holbrook venture. A few of the old well and derrick sites can still be located by the adventurous. One old site is near the creek bed near Sycamore Road, one near Ranch Road and one above the Bruce Howard property on Miner Road where the seepage of oil and bubbling of gas can still be seen coming out of the old shaft in the ground.

Mr. R. B. Fearey, who owned the Bearinda Hereford Ranch on Bear Creek, now under the waters of the Briones Dam, recollected: "In 1897, I was working as a mechanic for the California and Nevada Railroad, installing air brakes on the flat cars, and the company loaned me for a while to Mr. Holbrook, so that I could erect a water tank for him on Miner Ranch. Then I stayed on for two months to run his donkey engine, which powered the boring drill. Altogether seven wells were sunk to various depths. As I recall the maximum depth reached was about 3,800 feet."[12]

Fearey continued, "July 4 was a holiday and everyone was away from the works. Next day when we returned, we found that someone had blown up the whole outfit—engine, tools and all. We members of the crew had been receiving practically no cash wages, but were paid mostly in stock by Holbrook. All that we and other stockholders got out of the debacle was about fifteen cents on the dollar; the other $250,000 invested had gone down the well."[13]

Mrs. Robert Macey (Anita Miner) said one well at 1,500 feet yielded five gallons of oil that were slowly fished up with a bottle, but that was the end of production from that well as the drill broke loose and could never be recovered.[14]

Evidently the company tried again in 1903 as the Contra Costa Gazette reported: "Oil, that has been sought by an enterprising company for years, has at last been discovered on the Miner Ranch. As the murky fluid shot up into the air it caught fire from lanterns hanging on the derrick, and workmen barely escaped with their lives. Much valuable machinery was destroyed by fire."[15]

Another attempt to get oil was made in 1929 by the Orinda Petroleum Company headed by O. G. Green. The effort was inspired by high grade oil seepage found when the Claremont Pipeline Tunnel was bored through the hills. Thirty thousand feet of lumber were built into a 122-foot derrick and the oil company proceeded to bore through 3,033 feet of the earth. Two years' time and $100,000 were consumed in the venture which was a failure.[16]

The location of this well was at a spot known as Coyote Flat near Upper El Toyonal Road. The Orinda Petroleum Company abandoned the lease on the property, and in 1939 the American Trust Company and Haciendas Homes, Inc. filed suit to quiet title to the twelve parcels of land. The derrick which was considered a hazard to the community was dynamited and removed.

Although Orinda is only a small area of Contra Costa County, there are many towns in California that might substitute the names of their citizens and ranchos for those mentioned in this book and a very similar tale would be told. The vanishing of the Indians, the brief period of Spanish and Mexican grantees, the rush of settlers to California after the American conquest and the discovery of gold, their struggles to keep the land, the gradual breaking-up of the large ranches, the development of towns, the towns becoming cities and suburbs—this panorama is not the story of one area but of most of California.

What is to be the future story of Orinda? What will happen to its remaining open land? Is Orinda some day to be part of a megalopolis, an urban concentration that we cannot yet visualize? Will future historians be able to write that today's residents were farsighted? The answers are unknown, but the story of Orinda is continually expanding, and there will be many additions to it before long.

APPENDIX

Some Common Plants Growing Wild in the Orinda Area
Lauramay Dempster

Liliaceæ (Lily family)
  Brodiæa pulchella – Blue Dicks
  Brodiæa laxa – Ithuriel's Spear, Grass Nut
  Brodiæa elegans – Harvest Brodiæa
  Allium species – Wild Onions
  Calochortus venustus, etc. – Mariposa Lilies
  Calochortus tolmiei, etc. – Globe Lilies, Pussy Ears
  Clorogalum pomeridianum – Soap Plant
  Disporum hookeri – Fairy Bells
  Fritillaria lanceolata – Mission Bells, Checker Lily
  Smilacina species – False Solomon's Seal
  Trillium chloropetalum – Common Trillium
  Zigadenus fremontii – Star Lily, Death Camass
Iridaceæ (Iris family)
  Iris douglasiana – Douglas' Iris
  Sisyrhinchium bellum – Blue-eyed Grass
Corylaceæ (Hazelnut family)
  Corylus rostrata – California Hazelnut
Fagaceæ (Oak family)
  Quercus agrifolia – Coast Live Oak
  Quercus lobata – Valley Oak
  Quercus kelloggii – Kellogg Oak
Polygonaceæ (Buckwheat family)
  Eriogonum species – Wild Buckwheats
  Rumex species – Sorrels
Portulacaceæ (Purslane family)
  Calandrinia ciliata var. menziesii – Red Maids
  Montia perfoliata – Miner's Lettuce
Caryophyllaceæ (Pink family)
  Silene gallica – Windmill Pink
  Stellara media – Common Chickweed
  Arenaria, Cerastium, Spergula, etc. (all inconspicuous)
Ranunculaceæ (Buttercup family)
  Aquilegia species – Columbine
  Delphinium nudicaule – Red Larkspur
  Delphinium, several species – Blue Larkspur
  Ranunculus californicus – California Buttercup
Lauraceæ (Laurel family)
  Umbellularia californica – California Bay Laurel
Papaveraceæ (Poppy family)
  Eschscholtzia californica – California Poppy
  Platystemon californicus – Cream cups
Cruciferæ (Mustard family)
  Barbarea orthoceras – Winter Cress
  Brassica campestris, etc. – Mustard
  Capsella bursa-pastoris – Shepherd's Purse
  Cardamine oligosperma – Bitter Cress
  Dentaria californica – Milk Maids
  Lepidium nitidum – Pepper Grass

  Raphanus sativus – Wild Radish
  Thysanocarpus curvipes – Fringe-Pod
Crassulaceæ (Stonecrop family)
  Sedum spathulifolium – Broad-leaved Stonecrop
Saxifragaceæ (Saxifrage family)
  Heuchera micrantha – Alum Root
  Saxifraga californica – California Saxifrage
  Lithophragma affinis – Woodland Star
  Ribes malveceum, etc. – Wild Currant
  Ribes, other species – Currants and Gooseberries
Rosaceæ (Rose family)
  Fragaria californica – Wood Strawberry
  Heteromeles (Photinia) arbutifolia – Toyon, Christmas
    Berry
  Holodiscus discolor – Cream Bush
  Osmaronia cerasiformis – Oso Berry
  Potentilla species – Cinquefoils, Silverweed
  Rosa gymnocarpa – Wood Rose
  Rubus parviflora – Thimble Berry
  Rubus vitifolius – Wild Blackberry
Leguminosæ (Pea family)
  Astragalus species – Loco Weeds
  Lathyrus species – Wild Sweet Peas
  Lotus purshiana – Spanish Clover
  Lotus, other species – Lotus
  Lupinus albifrons – Blue Bush Lupine
  Lupinus micranthus
  Lupinus succulentus
  Lupinus, many other species
  Melilotus species – Sweet Clover
  Psoralea physoides – California Tea
  Trifolium, many species – Clovers
  Vicia, several species – Vetches
Geraniaceæ (Geranium family)
  Erodium species – Filaree, Scissors, Stork's Bill
  Geranium species – Wild Geranium, Cranesbill
Anacardiaceæ (Sumac family)
  Rhus diversiloba – Poison Oak
Malvaceæ (Mallow family)
  Malva parviflora – Cheese Weed
  Sidalcea malvæflora – Checker Bloom, Wild Hollyhock
Aceraceæ (Maple family)
  Acer macrophyllum – Big-leaf Maple
Sapindaceæ (Buckeye family)
  Aesculus californica – California Buckeye
Rhamnaceæ (Buckthorn family)
  Rhamnus californicus – Coffee Berry
Violaceæ (Violet family)
  Viola pedunculata – Johnny Jump-up, Wild Pansy

Viola, other species – Violets
Onagraceæ (Evening Primrose family)
    Clarkia (Godetia), various species – Farewell-to-
        Spring, Godetia
    Clarkia concinna – Red Ribbons
    Epilobium species – Willow Herbs
    Oenothera ovata – Golden Eggs
Umbelliferæ (Parsnip family)
    Conium maculatum – Poison Hemlock
    Heracleum lanatum – Cow Parsnip
    Lomatium utriculatum – Bladder Parsnip
    Osmorrhiza chilensis – Sweet Cicely
    Perideridia species – Queen Anne's Lace
    Sanicula bipinnatifida – Purple Sanicle
    Sanicula crassicaulis – Pacific Sanicle
    Scandix pecten-veneris – Shepherd's Needle
    Many others
Garryaceae (Silk Tassel family)
    Garrya elliptica – Silk Tassel Bush
Cornaceae (Dogwood family
    Cornus californicus – Creek Dogwood
Ericaceae (Heath family)
    Arbutus menziesii – Madrone
Polemoniaceae (Phlox family)
    Collomia heterophylla – Varied-leaved Collomia
    Gilia capitata, etc. – Gilias
    Navarretia species
    Phlox gracilis – Slender Phlox
Hydrophyllaceae (Water-Leaf family)
    Nemophila menziesii – Baby Blue Eyes
    Phacelia californica – California Phacelia
    Phacelia distans – Fern Phacelia
    Pholistoma auritum – Fiesta Flower
    And others
Boraginaceæ (Borage family)
    Amsinckia intermedia – Common Fiddleneck
    Cryptantha, several species – White Forget-me-not
    Cynoglossum grande – Hound's Tongue
    Plagiobothrys, several species – Popcorn Flower
Labiatae (Mint family)
    Monardella species – Coyote Mint
    Salvia columbariæ – Chia
    Satureja douglasii – Yerba Buena
    Scutellaria tuberosa – Skull Cap
    Stachys rigida – Hedge Nettle
Solanaceæ (Nightshade family)
    Solanum umbelliferum – Blue Witch
    Solanum xantii – Purple Nightshade
    Solanum nigrum – Black Nightshade
Scrophulariaceæ (Figwort family)
    Collinsia heterophylla – Chinese Houses
    Collinsia sparsiflora – Blue-eyed Mary
    Castilleja species – Indian Paint Brush
    Diplacus aurantiacus – Sticky Monkey Flower
    Mimulus guttatus – Common Monkey Flower

    Pedicularis densiflorus – Indian Warrior
    Orthocarpus purpurascens – Purple Owl's Clover
    Orthocarpus erianthus – Johnny Tuck
    Orthocarpus, other species
    Scrophularia californica – California Bee Plant
Plantaginaceæ (Plantain family)
    Plantago erecta – Dwarf Plantain
    Plantago major – Common Plantain
    Plantago lanceolata – English Plantain
Rubiaceæ (Madder family)
    Galium aparine – Goose Grass
    Galium nuttallii – Bedstraw
Valerianaceæ (Valerian family)
    Plectritis species
Cucurbitaceæ (Squash family)
    Marah fabaceus – Manroot, Wild Cucumber
Caprifoliaceæ (Honeysuckle family)
    Lonicera species – Wild Honeysuckle
    Symphoricarpos albus – Snowberry
Compositae (Sunflower family)
    Achillea millefolium – Yarrow, Milfoil
    Agoseris species – Dandelions
    Anaphalis margaritacea – Pearly Everlasting
    Anthemis cotula – Mayweed
    Baccharis pilularis – Chaparral Broom, Coyote Brush
    Bæria species – Gold Fields
    Centaurea melitensis – Star Thistle, Napa Thistle
    Cirsium species – Thistles
    Erigeron species – Fleabane
    Eriophyllum lanatum – Woolly Sunflower
    Grindelia species – Gum Weed
    Helenium species – Sneezeweed
    Hemizonia species – Tarweeds
    Layia platyglossa – Tidytips
    Madia species – Tarweeds
    Matricaria suaveolens – Pineapple Weed
    Microseris species
    Senecio vulgaris – Common Groundsel
    Silybum marianum – Milk Thistle
    Solidago species – Goldenrod
    Tragopogon porrifolius – Oyster Plant, Salsify
    Wyethia species – Mule Ears
    Xanthium species – Cockle Burs
    And many others

References:

Jepson, Willis L. *A Manual of the Flowering Plants of California.* Berkeley: Associated Students Store, 1923-1925. Reprinted, 1963, by University of California Press.

Munz, Philip A. *A California Flora.* Berkeley: University of California Press, 1960.

Sharsmith, Helen K. *Spring Wildflowers of the San Francisco Bay Region.* Berkeley: University of California, 1965.

List of Birds Which Have Been Observed in the Orinda Area

Harry C. Adamson

Western Grebe	Aechmophorus occidentalis
Eared Grebe	Podiceps caspicus
Pied-billed Grebe	Podilymbus podiceps
Double-crested Cormorant	Phalacrocorax auritus
Whistling Swan	Olor columbianus
Canada Goose	Branta canadensis
White-fronted Goose	Anser albifrons
Mallard	Anas platyrhynchos
Pintail	Anas acuta
Gadwall	Anas strepera
American Widgeon	Mareca americana
Shoveler	Spatula clypeata
Cinnamon Teal	Anas cyanoptera
Green-winged Teal	Anas carolinensis
Wood Duck	Aix sponsa
Canvasback	Aythya valisineria
Ring-necked Duck	Aythya collaris
Lesser Scaup	Aythya affinis
Common Goldeneye	Bucephala clangula
Bufflehead	Bucephala albeola
Ruddy Duck	Oxyura jamaicensis
Common Merganser	Mergus merganser
Hooded Merganser	Lophodytes cucullatus
Turkey Vulture	Cathartes aura
Cooper's Hawk	Accipiter cooperii
Sharp-shinned Hawk	Accipiter striatus
Marsh Hawk	Circus cyaneus
Red-tailed Hawk	Buteo jamaicensis
Golden Eagle	Aquila chrysætos
Osprey	Pandion haliatus
Sparrow Hawk	Falco sparverius
California Quail	Lophortyx californicus
Common Egret	Casmerodius albus
Great Blue Heron	Ardea herodias
Green Heron	Butorides virenscens
American Coot	Fulica americana
American Avocet	Recurvirostra americana
Killdeer	Charadrius vociferus
Spotted Sandpiper	Actitis macularia
Greater Yellowlegs	Totanus melanoleucus
Common Snipe	Capella gallinago
Glaucous-winged Gull	Larus glaucescens
Herring Gull	Larus argentatus
California Gull	Larus californicus
Ring-billed Gull	Larus delawarensis
Mew Gull	Larus canus
Bonaparte's Gull	Larus philadelphia
Caspian Tern	Hydroprogne caspia
Band-tailed Pigeon	Columba fasciata

Mourning Dove	Zenaidura macroura
Roadrunner	Geoccyx californianus
(Now probably extinct in Orinda area; observed by H. Adamson on west side of San Pablo Reservoir in 1946.)	
Screech Owl	Otus asio
Great Horned Owl	Bubo virginanus
Barn Owl	Tyto alba
Anna's Hummingbird	Calypte anna
Rufous Hummingbird	Selasphorus rufus (migrant only)
Allen's Hummingbird	Selasphorus sasin
Calliope Hummingbird	Stellula calliope (migrant only)
Belted Kingfisher	Megaceryle alcyon
Red-shafted Flicker	Colaptes cafer
Nuttall's Woodpecker	Dendrocopos nuttallii
Acorn Woodpecker	Melanerpes formicivorus
Yellow-bellied Sapsucker	Sphyrapicus varius (winter only)
Hairy Woodpecker	Dendrocopos villosus
Downy Woodpecker	Dendrocopos pubescens
Western Kingbird	Tyrannus verticalis
(one record—one mile west of Rheem Shopping Center, 1956)	
Ash-throated Flycatcher	Myiarchus cinerascens
Black Phoebe	Sayornis nigricans
Say's Phoebe	Sayornis saya
Western Flycatcher	Empidonax difficilis
Western Wood Pewee	Contopus sordidulus
Olive-sided Flycatcher	Nuttallornis borealis
Barn Swallow	Hirundo rustica
Cliff Swallow	Petrochelidon pyrrhonota
Violet-green Swallow	Tachycineta thalassina
Tree Swallow	Iridoprocne bicolor
Rough-winged Swallow	Stelgidopteryx ruficollis
Steller's Jay	Cyanocitta stelleri
Scrub Jay	Aphelocoma coerulescens
Common Crow	Corvus brachyrhynchos
Chestnut-backed Chickadee	Parus rufescens
Plain Titmouse	Parus inornatus
Common Bushtit	Psaltriparus minimus
Wrentit	Chamæa fasciata
Dipper	Cinclus mexicanus
(one record at waterfall at a small dam crossing Bear Creek Road.)	
White-breasted Nuthatch	Sitta carolinensis
Brown Creeper	Certhia familiaris
House Wren	Troglodytes aedon
Winter Wren	Troglodytes troglodytes
Bewick's Wren	Thryomanes bewickii
Rock Wren	Salpinctes obsoletus

(on ridge between Bald Knob (Vollmer Peak and Orinda—not far from Grizzly Stables or upper end of El Toyonal, October 1947)

Mockingbird	Mimus polyglottos
California Thrasher	Toxostoma redivivum
Robin	Turdus migratorius
Varied Thrush	Ixoreus nævius
Townsend Solitaire	Myadestes townsendi
Hermit Thrush	Hylocichla guttata
Swainson's Thrush	Hylocichla ustulata
Western Bluebird	Sialia mexicana
Golden-crowned Kinglet	Regulus satrapa
Ruby-crowned Kinglet	Regulus calendula
Water Pipit	Anthus spinoletta
Cedar Waxwing	Bombycilla cedrorum
Loggerhead Shrike	Lanius ludovicianus
Starling	Sturus vulgaris
Solitary Vireo	Vireo solitarius
Hutton's Vireo	Vireo huttoni
Warbling Vireo	Vireo gilvus
Orange-crowned Warbler	Vermivora celata
Yellow Warbler	Dendroica petechia
Myrtle Warbler	Dendroica coronata
Audubon's Warbler	Dendroica auduboni
Townsend's Warbler	Dendroica townsendi
Black-throated Gray Warbler	Dendroica nigrescens
Yellowthroat	Geothlypis trichas
Wilson's Warbler	Wilsonia pusilla
House Sparrow	Passer domesticus
Western Meadowlark	Sturnella neglecta
Red-winged Blackbird	Agelaius phoeniceus
Brewer's Blackbird	Euphagus cyanocephalus
Brown-headed Cowbird	Molothrus ater
Bullock's Oriole	Icterus bullockii
Western Tanager	Piranga ludoviciana
Black-headed Grosbeak	Pheucticus melanocephalus
Lazuli Bunting	Passerina amoena
Purple Finch	Carpodacus purpureus
House Finch	Carpodacus mexicanus
Pine Siskin	Spinus pinus
American Goldfinch	Spinus tristis
Lesser Goldfinch	Spinus psaltria
Rufous-sided Towhee	Pipilo erythrophthalmus
Brown Towhee	Pipilo fuscus
Grasshopper Sparrow	Ammodramus savannarum

(at least one record—Mulholland Hill, May, 1950)

Lark Sparrow	Chonestes grammacus
Slate-colored Junco	Junco hyemalis
Oregon Junco	Junco oreganus
Chipping Sparrow	Spizella passerina
White-crowned Sparrow	Zonotrichia leucophrys
Golden-crowned Sparrow	Zonotrichia atricapilla
White-throated Sparrow	Zonotrichia albicollis
Fox Sparrow	Passerella iliaca
Lincoln's Sparrow	Melospiza lincolnii
Song Sparrow	Melospiza melodia

Notes and Sources

CHAPTER I—*Explorers and Indians*

1. Herbert Eugene Bolton, *Outpost of Empire* (New York: Knopf, 1931), p. 22.
2. Herbert Eugene Bolton, *Fray Juan Crespi, Missionary Explorer on the Pacific Coast 1769–1774* (Berkeley: U. C. Press, 1927), pp. xxvi, 211.
3. Zoeth K. Eldridge, *The Beginnings of San Francisco* (San Francisco, 1912), I, 42.
4. Herbert E. Bolton, *Anza's California Expeditions* (Berkeley: U.C. Press, 1930), IV, 424, 427.
5. *Ibid.*, III, 137–142; IV, 361, 375.
6. *Ibid.*, IV, 346.
7. *Ibid.*, III, 389.
8. *Ibid.*, III, 393–394, 400–401.
9. James A. Bennyhoff, "An Anthropologist Looks at the Maltby Mound," *Contra Costa Chronicles* (Martinez: Contra Costa Historical Society, Fall, 1967), pp. 23–25.
10. A. L. Kroeber, *Handbook of California Indians* (Berkeley: California Book Co., 1953), p. 465.
11. George F. Coles. Talk before the Contra Costa Historical Society, Concord, California, December 1, 1966.
12. *Orinda News*, December 9, 1946.
13. Mr. Edward deLaveaga. Interview, December, 1966.
14. Franklin Fenega, "Before Moraga Settled," *Orinda News*, December, 1948.
15. Bolton, *Anza*, IV, 368.
16. *Ibid.*, III, 419.
17. Kroeber, *op. cit.*, p. 471.
18. Coles. Talk, December 1, 1966.
19. Kroeber, *op. cit.*, p. 467.
20. Bolton, *Anza*, III, 417.
21. *Ibid.*, p. 267.
22. Kroeber, *op. cit.*, p. 468.
23. *Ibid.*, p. 467.
24. Wilma Cheatham, *Story of Contra Costa County* (San Francisco, 1942), p. 43.
25. Thomas A. Brown Papers, Candelario Valencia to Don Buillermo Leidesdorff, September 2, 1847. Misc. Vol. III, Contra Costa Library, Pleasant Hill. Leidesdorff was appointed by Thomas O. Larkin as U.S. Vice Consul in 1845, and in 1847, he was in San Francisco a member of the city council, treasurer, and a member of the school committee, as well as an active businessman. Information about Leidesdorff from Hubert Howe Bancroft, *History of California* (San Francisco: 1886), IV, 711.
26. Contra Costa County, Deeds, IV, 317.
27. *El Rancho*, Moraga Historical Society, Mimeographed Bulletin, May, 1966.
28. Kroeber, *op. cit.*, pp. 464, 881.
29. *Ibid.*, p. 883.

CHAPTER II — *The Land Grants*

1. Eldridge, *op. cit.*, p. 216.
2. *Ibid.*, p. 217.
3. Copy of Report of the Land Commission, 590, Petition of Joaquin Moraga and Juan Bernal, Moraga Historical Society Collection, St. Mary's College Library.
4. *Ibid.* Expediente signed by Jose Castro.
5. *Ibid.* Document for the Superior Political Chief of This Territory, Father Jose Maria de Jesus Gomez.

6. Ruth Mary McGinty. "Spanish and Mexican Ranchos in the San Francisco Bay Region." Unpublished M. A. Thesis, University of California, 1921, p. 39.

7. W. A. Slocum, *History of Contra Costa County* (San Francisco, 1882), p. 293.

8. Copy of Report of Land Commission, 590, Statement of Juan B. Alvarado, July 31, 1841, Monterey, Moraga Historical Society Collection, St. Mary's College Library.

9. Sketch of the Adobe by Ella Moraga, Bancroft Library, University of California, Berkeley. Ella Moraga says here that it was not finished until 1848, that it was three years in construction, and that her husband, Gabriel Ygnacio Moraga, was the first child born in the adobe, July, 1848.

10. Joseph Lamson, *Round Cape Horn* (Bangor, Maine, 1878), pp. 139–144.

11. Contra Costa County, Deeds, I, 387, 556.

12. Robert Cleland, *Cattle on a Thousand Hills* (San Marino, 1941), p. 43.

13. William Heath Davis, *Sixty Years in California* (San Francisco, 1889), p. 87.

14. Eldridge, *op. cit.*, pp. 218–219.

15. Paul W. Gates, "California's Embattled Settlers," *California Historical Society Quarterly*, XLI, No. 2 (June, 1962), 99–125. For an excellent account of the rights of settlers, see this article.

16. Eldridge, *op. cit.*, p. 219.

17. Cleland, *op. cit.*, pp. 56–57.

18. *Ibid.*, p. 149.

19. Sherwood Burgess, "The Forgotten Redwoods," *California Historical Society Quarterly*, XXX, No. 1 (March, 1951), 7–9.

20. Contra Costa County, Deeds, III, 10.

21. Contra Costa County, Deeds, VI, 295 (Bernal to Jones); V, 355 (Moraga to Jones).

22. Contra Costa County, Patents, III, 489.

23. Contra Costa County, Deeds, VII, 325; VIII, 42; IX, 126.

24. Contra Costa County Assessment Book, 1854–55, Louis L. Stein, Jr. Collection (hereinafter Stein Collection).

25. Contra Costa County, Deeds, V, 498.

26. Contra Costa County Assessment Book, 1858, Stein Collection. (Lists the owners of the Moraga half of the Rancho).

27. *San Francisco Call*, November 17, 1898.

28. Contra Costa County, Deeds, II, 6–8, 325–328.

29. *San Francisco Call*, November 17, 1898.

30. *San Francisco Chronicle*, February 21, 1918, p. 4; William Warren Ferrier, *Origin and Development of the University of California* (Berkeley, 1930), p. 578.

31. May Purcell, *History of Contra Costa County* (Berkeley: The Gillick Press, 1940), pp. 167–169. The story of the Moraga feuds is given here.

32. Contra Costa County, Deeds, XXVII, 109; XXVIX, 599.

33. *Ibid.*, LI, 165; Patents, III, 489.

34. *Contra Costa Gazette* (Martinez), July 30, 1887.

35. Contra Costa County, Deeds, XXXXIX, 144. The following heirs signed the deed: Gabriel Y., Joaquin B., Jose J., sons of Jose Moraga; Eudocia, Dolores, Natividad, Francisca M. Silva (wife of Frank Silva), Gumecinda M. Avila (wife of John S. Avila), daughters of Jose, deceased; Frank Silva (husband of Francisca); John Avila (husband of Gumecinda); John Van Dyne, Jr.; Denis Van Dyne and Eudocia Van Dyne, children of said John Van Dyne and his deceased wife; L. L. Baker; R. M. Hamilton; Librado P. Moraga (wife of Joaquin B.); and Ella F. Moraga (wife of Gabriel Y. Moraga).

36. Contra Costa County, Patents, III, 420; Final Report of the Referees in Partition of Rancho El Sobrante, Edson Adams et al. vs. Emily Hopkins et al., Stein Collection.

37. Papers on El Sobrante and Ward and Smith League (hereinafter El Sobrante papers), Juan Jose Castro et al. vs. the United States Land Commission No. 96, Petition of Juan Jose and Victor Castro, pp. 1–4, Contra Costa County Library, Pleasant Hill.

38. *Ibid.*, p. 4.

39. *Ibid.*, Deposition of Alvarado, pp. 4–5.

40. Contra Costa County, Deeds, II, p. 39.

41. *Ibid.*, p. 112.

42. El Sobrante Papers. See copies of various deeds for transactions during 1850's and 1860's.

43. Thomas A. Brown Papers, El Sobrante Rancho (hereinafter Brown Papers), Petition of Grover, Huertzel and Lauterwasser, Testimony of Juan Jose Castro, Vol. V, microfilm. Contra Costa Library, Pleasant Hill.

44. Contra Costa County, Deeds, II, p. 202. Castro agreement with John Wilson.

45. Slocum, *op. cit.*, p. 337.

46. For information on Edson Adams' interest in El Sobrante see Contra Costa County, Mortgages, A, 20; Deeds III, 328; V, 292, 307, 423.

47. Purcell, *op. cit.*, pp. 187–188. Account of squatter trouble on El Sobrante. Also see *Contra Costa Gazette*, September 7, 1878, October 12, 1878, November 30, 1878.

48. Map of the Rancho El Sobrante, Contra Costa County Survey, Thomas A. McMahon, July, 1893.

CHAPTER III — *The Ward and Smith League*

1. *A Kemble Reader, Stories of California 1846–1848*, California Historical Society (San Francisco, 1963), p. 37.

2. Slocum, *op. cit.*, p. 385.

3. Brown Papers. Testimony of Juan Jose Castro, September 2, 1861, V; Contra Costa County, Deeds, II, 39.

4. Brown Papers. Testimony of Jose de Jesus Martinez, September 2, 1861, V.

5. *Ibid.* Testimony of John F. S. Smith, September 2, 1861, V.

6. *Ibid.*

7. Slocum, *op. cit.*, p. 663.

8. Contra Costa County, Deeds, IV, 340, 416.

9. *Ibid.*, IV, 326, 548; V, 76.

10. *Ibid.*, VI, 202.

11. Brown Papers. Testimony of John F. S. Smith, September 2, 1861, V.

12. Edith E. Miner, Miner Family Scrapbook, possession of Mrs. James Roos, Orinda.

13. Louis Stein, Sr. Unpublished recollections, Stein Collection.

14. Contra Costa County, Assessment Books, 1860, 1861, Stein Collection.

15. Contra Costa County, Deeds, VII, 123, 200.

16. Brown Papers. Testimony John F. S. Smith, September 2, 1861, V.

17. El Sobrante Papers, p. 26.

18. *Ibid.*, p. 75.

19. Brown Papers. Testimony of Victor Castro, September 2, 1861, V.

20. El Sobrante Papers, pp. 75, 87.

21. Final Report of the Referees in the Partition of the Rancho El Sobrante, Edson Adams et al., Plaintiffs, vs. Emily B. Hopkins et al., Defendants (1909), Stein Collection. The "Specific Tracts" were designated:

Specific Tract A, Ward and Smith League, 3,762.21 acres
Specific Tract B, Kelly League, 4,098.25 acres
Specific Tract C, Thornton Tract, 1,000.00 acres
Specific Tract D, Baden Tract, 507.18 acres
Specific Tract E, Brisac Tract, 972.38 acres
Specific Tract F, Welch Tract, 70.40 acres
Specific Tract G, Castro Tract, 492.00 acres

Specific Tract H, Judo Boas Tract, 160.00 acres

22. Contra Costa County, Deeds, VII, 128.

23. Slocum, *op. cit.*, p. 345.

24. Contra Costa County, Deeds, VII, 267.

25. Slocum, *op. cit.*, pp. 345–346.

26. Contra Costa County, Deeds, VII, 266.

27. *Ibid.*, XVIII, 94.

28. *Ibid.*, XVIX, 7–8.

29. *Ibid.*, XXXI, 591; XXXV, 419; Maps, A–I.

30. *Oakland Tribune*, September 21, 1952, "This Is Your Town," Jack Burroughs.

31. Contra Costa County, Deeds, XVII, 515.

32. Mrs. Frank Leslie, *A Pleasure Trip from Gotham to the Golden Gate* (New York, 1877), pp. 215–216.

33. Contra Costa County, Deeds, XXXXVI, 274.

34. Contra Costa County, Deeds, C, 369 (Welch to Souza); CXV, 538–64 (Souza to Syndicate Water Co.).

35. Contra Costa County, Assessment Book, 1874, Stein Collection.

36. *Ibid.*, 1877, 1890.

37. Contra Costa County, Deeds, CCCLXXXVIII, 173–175.

38. Contra Costa County, Maps, XXII, 637–639, August 16, 1937.

CHAPTER IV — *The Beginnings of Orinda*

1. Contra Costa County, Mortgages, IV, 54.

2. Contra Costa County, Deeds, XII, 433–434.

3. Martinez Abstract & Title Co., Continuation of Abstract of Title to land described as portion of Ward & Smith League, Rancho El Sobrante, being Lot 3 of specific Tract A, Stein Collection.

4. *Berkeley Gazette*, February 27, 1943, "So We're Told."

5. Contra Costa County, Mortgages, IV, 375.

6. *Ibid.*, 229.

7. Remarks of William Walker Camron, Undated Scrapbook Clipping (around 1878), John Marsh Family Papers, Miscellaneous Box, Bancroft Library.

8. *Ibid.*

9. Contra Costa County, Deeds, XXXI, 306.

10. The Camron Family—A Brief History of the Family from whom Amy is descended. This sketch is in the John Marsh Family Papers, Box 3, Bancroft Library.

11. *Bay of San Francisco—A History* (Chicago: Lewis Publishing Company, 1892), II, 219–222.

12. May Fisher Purcell, *History of Contra Costa County* (Berkeley, 1940), p. 170.

13. *Contra Costa Gazette*, November 22, 1873.

14. Remarks of William Walker Camron. John Marsh Family Papers, Misc. Box, Bancroft Library. This survey map has not been found but is mentioned in all of the deeds on Camron's early sales.

15. George D. Lyman, *John Marsh, Pioneer* (New York: Chautauqua Press, 1931), pp. 194, 316.

16. "Katherine Philips," *Encyclopaedia Britannica* (1938), XVII, 734; Philip Webster Souers, *The Matchless Orinda; Harvard Studies in English* (Harvard Press, 1931); V. Samuel Johnson, *Lives of the Poets; The World Classics* (Oxford, 1955), I, 162.

17. Souers, *op. cit.*, pp. 41, 43. At the age of twenty, K. P. wrote to a friend in part:

> To My Dearest Lucasia
> But as there are degrees of bliss
> So there's no friendship meant by this
> But such as will transmit to fame
> Lucasia's and Orinda's name.

18. The word, Orinda, originally came from the Greek 'Opivons,' translated into Latin. It meant a seed from which bread is made peculiar to Ethiopia. A later Spanish dictionary gives three meanings: a seed crop (derived from Ethiopia; a bread made from this; a Spanish family name born for example by Martin Orinda, an architect who died in Valencia in 1655 after being employed by the Dukes of Calabria. *The Cook Book of Apicium Caelues*, II; *Harper's Latin Dictionary*; *Liddell's Greek Dictionary*; *Enciclopedia Universal Ilustrada* (Barcelona, 1907), XXXX, 464.

19. *Harvard Classics*, XXXX, 384–387.

20. Souers, *op. cit.*, p. 166. Here Souers quotes from Roscommon's *Poetical Works*, p. 144.

21. *Oakland Tribune*, September 21, 1952, "This is Your Town."

22. John Marsh Family Papers, A scrapbook clipping, Misc. Box, Bancroft Library.

23. Contra Costa County, Deeds, XXXVII, 236.

24. *Ibid.*, 234.

25. *Ibid.*, XXXIX, 98, 120; XL, 134, 360.

26. *Ibid.*, XL, 115.

27. *Ibid.*, XLI, 279.

28. John Marsh Family Papers, Scrapbook clippings, Misc. Box, Bancroft Library.

29. *Ibid.*, Box 3, Poem, "Camp Camron," Bancroft Library.

30. *Contra Costa Gazette*, June 11, 1881, "The Camron Sale."

31. *Ibid.*, Various clippings and letters; *San Francisco Examiner*, April 14, 1897.

32. Contra Costa County, Deeds, XLIII, 361.

33. Contra Costa County, Maps, F-143, Orinda Park Tract and Oak View Ranch.

34. Contra Costa County, Deeds, LIII, 33, 36.

35. *Contra Costa Gazette*, June 18, 1881, October 8, 1881.

36. *The Independent* (Richmond, California), December 18, 1965, Helen Follett Richards, "Yesterdays in Richmond, Contra Costa County and California."

37. Mr. Louis L. Stein, Jr. Interview, 1967.

38. Erle C. Hanson, "California and Nevada Railroad," *Western Railroader*, Issue 225, XXI, No. 9 (1958).

39. *Contra Costa Gazette*, April 4, 1888.

40. *Ibid.*, March 22, 1891.

41. Mr. Louis L. Stein, Jr. Interview, 1967.

42. Contra Costa County, Maps, March 27, 1888. F. 132.

43. *San Francisco Chronicle*, February 1, 1918, "Sketch of the Life of Horace Carpentier," Oakland Public Library.

44. Contra Costa County, Mortgages, XXVII, 57.

45. Moraga Land Company Brochures (1889, 1892), Moraga Historical Society Collection, St. Mary's College Library.

46. *Contra Costa Gazette*, April 29, 1893.

47. *Ibid.*, February 18, 1882.

48. *Ibid.*, March 22, 1891.

49. *San Francisco Chronicle*, April 7, 1894.

50. Mr. Edward L. deLaveaga. Interview, 1967.

51. *A. C. Transit-times* (Oakland), October, 1964.

52. *Contra Costa Gazette*, March 14, 1899, July 22, 1899.

53. *Ibid.*, February 5, 1899.

54. *Railroad Gazette*, *A Journal of Transportation*, *Engineering and Railroad News* (New York, 1902).

55. Contra Costa County, Mortgages, XXVII, 57; Deeds, LVI, 308.

56. Grant Burton. Talk before the Moraga Historical Society, January 6, 1966.

57. *Contra Costa Gazette* Centennial, May 29, 1959; Moraga Land Company Brochures (see 45).

58. *Contra Costa Gazette*, May 6, 1893.

59. *Ibid.*, April 7, 1894.

60. Contra Costa County, Deeds, LXIX, 202; Maps, D–81, June 28, 1893.

61. *Contra Costa Gazette*, September 8, 1894.

62. Ezra Nelson. Interview with the author, and letter to the author, 1967.

63. Contra Costa County, Deeds, LXXVIII, 104; LXXIX, 19, 79, 90.

64. Grant Burton. Talk, January 6, 1966.

65. Contra Costa County, Deeds, XC, 183.

66. *Ibid.*, LXXIX, 19; CXII, 63. A taped interview with the Bello family by Brother Dennis is in the Moraga Historical Society collection, St. Mary's College Library.

67. *Ibid.*, XCII, 431.

68. Harrison Sigworth. Interview, 1967. (Mr. Sigworth is the present owner of Casa Vieja.)

69. Contra Costa County, Deeds, CCLIV, 218.

CHAPTER V — *The People and the Life in Early Orinda*

1. *Orinda News*, January 13, 1947.

2. Miner Family Scrapbook in possession of Mrs. James C. Roos.

3. *San Francisco City Directories*, 1880–82, 1883–85.

4. Contra Costa County, Deeds, XXXIX, 88, 120; XL, 134; XLIII, 360.

5. Contra Costa County, Assessment Books, 1883, 1884. Stein Collection.

6. *Berkeley Gazette*, March 7, 1950, "So We're Told"; Contra Costa County, Deeds, XXXXVIII, 261.

7. *Orinda News*, March 1, 1938.

8. Louis Stein, Sr. Unpublished Memoirs, Stein Collection.

9. *Ibid.*; *Berkeley Gazette*, March 8, 1950, "So We're Told"; William Warren Ferrier, *Berkeley, California* (Berkeley, 1933), p. 165.

10. Interviews and walks on the property with Florence Sullivan, Louis Stein, and Charles R. Allen, 1966, 1967.

11. *Contra Costa Gazette*, September 18, 1886.

12. *Ibid.*, May 4, 1887.

13. *Ibid.*, October 8, 1887.

14. *Ibid.*, July 10, 1887, July 25, 1887.

15. *Ibid.*, August 13, 1887; Wagner Document, Stein Collection.

16. *Orinda News*, July 7, 1937.

17. *Contra Costa Gazette*, March 16, 1889.

18. *Ibid.*, July 6, 1889.

19. *Oakland Tribune*, July 13, 1961, "90's were Gay for Orinda."

20. Contra Costa County, Assessment Book, 1891, Stein Collection; *Contra Costa Gazette*, October 17, 1891.

21. *Berkeley Gazette*, March 8, 1950, "So We're Told."

22. *History of Contra Costa County* (Los Angeles: Historic Record Company, 1926), p. 910.

23. Wagner Document, Stein Collection.

24. *History of Contra Costa County* (Los Angeles: Historic Record Company, 1926), 1026.

25. Contra Costa County, Deeds, XXXVII, 236; XLV, 174.

26. Slocum, *op. cit.*, p. 377.

27. *Orinda News*, July 7, 1937.

28. Unpublished written memories of Orinda, Mrs. Florence Sullivan.

29. Contra Costa County, Deeds, XXXVII, 234.

30. *Ibid.*, LIII, 444.

31. Contra Costa County, Assessment Book, 1892. Stein Collection.

32. Contra Costa County, Deeds, CLXVI, 466.

33. *Ibid.*, ccc, 316.

34. *Ibid.*, cdlxxii, 136.

35. Oakland Tribune, May 28, 1963, "George Brockhurst Dies at 92."

36. *Ibid.*

37. *Orinda News*, January 13, 1947.

38. Contra Costa County, Official Records, viii, 123, Decree of distribution, Ann E. Miner.

39. Miner Family Scrapbook, possession of Mrs. James Roos.

40. Contra Costa County, Deeds, xl, 115.

41. Map of Orinda Park Tract and Oak View Ranch, Contra Costa County, Maps, f-143, April, 1882.

42. Slocum, *op. cit.*, pp. 306–334.

43. *Oakland Tribune*, December 23, 1945, "Bryant's Corners."

44. *Orinda Sun*, October 16, 1964, Jane·Putnam, "Local Landmarks."

45. *Oakland Tribune*, December 23, 1945.

46. *Oakland Tribune*, December 30, 1945, "Fish Ranch and Old Timers."

47. *Contra Costa Gazette*, May 30, 1896.

48. Contra Costa County, Agreements, lxii, 515.

49. *Oakland Tribune*, December 30, 1945.

50. Contra Costa County, Agreements, lxxi, 501.

51. *Orinda News*, July 7, 1937.

52. *Contra Costa Gazette*, May 13, 1899.

53. *Ibid.*, May 20, 1899; *Ibid.*, August 12, 1899.

54. Mrs. Henry Rudolph Ehlers, "History of Brenzel and Ehlers Family," Stein Collection.

55. *Berkeley Gazette*, May 20, 1948, "So We're Told."

56. Written Memoirs of Mr. Louis Stein, Sr., Stein Collection.

57. Information about Martinez family from telephone interview with Carmel Martinez, January 8, 1967; *Orinda News*, July 7, 1937; letter to author from Carmel Martinez, January 21, 1968.

58. Contra Costa County, Official Records, xxciv, 280; *Oakland Tribune*, April 30, 1953, "Dream Fulfilled."

59. *Contra Costa Gazette*, April 22, 1887.

60. *Ibid.*, November 4, 1888.

61. *Orinda News*, January 1, 1938.

62. *Ibid.*, October 1, 1937.

63. *Ibid.*, November 4, 1946.

64. *Hayseed Siftings*, Orinda Park, April, 1893, Stein Collection.

65. *Orinda News*, October 1, 1937.

CHAPTER VI — *From Old to New Orinda*

1. *Berkeley Gazette*, March 2, 1943, "So We're Told."

2. *San Francisco, Its Builders Past and Present* (San Francisco and Chicago: S. J. Clarke, 1913), i, 267.

3. *Ibid.*

4. *Ibid.*, liii, 413, 415.

5. March 24, 1888 a contract to build a road was filed with the Contra Costa County Recorder.

6. Interview with Edward L. deLaveaga.

7. *Orinda News*, March 10, 1947.

8. *Ibid.*, July 7, 1937.

9. Subdivision Map, Lake Orinda, 1920, California Subdivision Company, Oakland, California, Edward L. deLaveaga collection.

10. Contra Costa Deeds, see Grantors, 1922–23, E. I. deLaveaga.

11. Map of *Orinda Park Terrace and Vicinity*, Contra Costa County, J. H. L'Hommedieu & Company, Oakland, California, Edward L. deLaveaga collection; Contra Costa County, Maps, XVIII, 389–94, May 2, 1922; p. 414½, April 17, 1923.

12. *Orinda News*, March 10, 1947.

13. Letter from Alfred W. Elkinton, Carmel, January 16, 1968, author's possession.

14. *The News*, Walnut Creek, August 6, 1931, author's possession.

15. *Orinda News*, October 1, 1940.

16. *Ibid.*, May 1, 1938.

17. Sketch of deLaveaga property, Contra Costa County, situated northeast San Pablo Highway, Oakland, April, 1923, Edward L. deLaveaga collection.

18. Contra Costa County, Deeds, CCCLXXXII, 33.

19. *The Orinda Sun*, January 7, 1966, Sonia Levitin, "The Barn that Isn't a Barn."

20. Information about Marshall family from interview with Albert Marshall, Mrs. Eva Marshall Facelli, Tony Marshall, Santa Cruz, February 25, 1967.

21. Contra Costa County, Deeds, CCCXCVII, 429.

22. Interviews with Mrs. Frank Enos, Oakland, California, 1966, 1967.

23. Contra Costa County, Deeds, CDXVIII, 133.

24. *Ibid.*, CDXVII, 280.

25. *Ibid.*, CDXXVII, 200.

26. Bulletin printed in 1925, Orinda, collection Mr. and Mrs. Ernest Hadden.

27. Book of Minutes of Meetings—Orinda School Board, 1923–28, p. 45.

28. Booklet printed about June 1924, pp. 7–8, Edward L. deLaveaga collection.

29. *Ibid.*, p. 4.

30. *Ibid.*, p. 6.

31. *The Fairway* (San Francisco, Fairway Publishing Company, May, 1938), Vol. V, No. V, pp. 9, 11.

32. Haciendas del Orinda maps were filed in Contra Costa County:
No. 1: April 14, 1924, XVIII, 440–42; No. 2: October 15, 1924, XIX, 460–64; No. 3: February 16, 1925, XIX, 473–74; No. 4: June 1, 1925, XIX, 479–80; No. 5: August 4, 1925, XIX, 489–91; No. 6: January 5, 1926, XIX, 497–99; No. 7: June 25, 1926, XIX, 507–8; No. 8: October 18, 1927, XXI, 565; No. 9: November 29, 1936, XXII, 678–9.

33. Interview with Mrs. June Hadden, Orinda, California, 1967.

34. Interview with Dwight Chapman, Orinda, California, 1967.

CHAPTER VII— *Other Early Settlements North of the Crossroads*

1. Contra Costa County, Deeds, XC, 584.

2. *Ibid.*, CIII, 433.

3. *Ibid.*, CXCVIII, 435.

4. Contra Costa County, Maps, II, pp. 263–6, August 14, 1914, Orinda Villa Park Land Company.

5. Map of Orinda Villa Park, author's possession.

6. Interview with Florence Sullivan, 1966, Lafayette.

7. Interviews with Louis L. Stein, Jr., and Edward L deLaveaga, 1966, 1967, Orinda.

8. Letter from Mrs. Grace Kendall, January 21, 1967, author's possession.

9. Interview with Mr. and Mrs. M. C. Sorensen, January, 1966, Lafayette, California.

10. Sorensen interview.

11. Interview with Mrs. E. A. Dawson, June 3, 1967, and various conversations by telephone.

12. Interview with Albert and Tony Marshall, and Eva Marshall Facelli, February 25, 1967, Santa Cruz, California.

13. Contra Costa County, Maps, XIX, 466–69, 1924, Orinda Oaks; 492–93, August 7, 1925, Orinda Court; *Orinda News*, July 1, 1939.

14. Contra Costa County, Deeds, CDLXXVI, 391; CDXC, 108.

15. Contra Costa County, Maps, XXXII, 35–37, Snug Harbor.

16. Interview with Mrs. Sidney Rosenthal, June 3, 1967, Orinda; Contra Costa County, Deeds, CDLXXXII, 404.

17. Contra Costa County, Maps, XXVIII, 9–10, Lind-O-Rinda Estates.

18. Letter to Dear Fellow Orindans, April 15, 1953, author's possession.

19. Contra Costa County, Maps, XXI, 576, Fairway Acres.

20. *Ibid.*, XXIV, 780–82, October 10, 1940 (Orinda Estates); XXV, 827, January 20, 1941 (Orinda Vista).

21. *Orinda News*, September 3, 1942, pp. 1, 2, 5.

22. Contra Costa County, Deeds, CDLXXII, 136, June 3, 1924.

23. Contra Costa County, Official Records, CCCXC, 438, June 21, 1926.

24. Letter from Hanley Allen, Sonora, California, June 3, 1967, author's possession.

25. Contra Costa County, Official Records, CCXXVIII, 47, January 18, 1930.

26. Handbound booklet issued by the Sleepy Hollow Syndicate, date unknown, author's possession.

27. Letter from Hanley Allen, June 3, 1967.

28. Letter from Richard Rheem, San Francisco, May 8, 1968, author's possession; Contra Costa County, Official Records, CCCXCIX, 436; CDLIX, 45.

29. Contra Costa County, Maps, XXVIII, 13, 19; XXIX, 44.

30. Interview with Mr. Richard Breuner, Orinda, 1969.

31. Contra Costa County, Maps, XXV, 31–36, June 23, 1931.

CHAPTER VIII— *Development at the Crossroads and South of the Crossroads*

1. Information about the Moraga Company from a talk by Senator Arthur Breed, Jr., Moraga Historical Society, April 20, 1967; and from letter by The Moraga Company about sales and deeds titled "History of the Rancho Laguna de Los Palos Colorados," author's possession.

2. Talk by Arthur Breed, Jr. See 1.

3. Talk by Grant Burton before Moraga Historical Society, January 6, 1966.

4. Talk by Arthur Breed, Jr. See 1.

5. *Orinda Sun*, December 24, 1964, Sonia Levitin, "Moraga Milestones. Carr Ranch's Historical Roundup."

6. *Contra Costa Gazette*, May 19, 1894, says, "Mr. A. L. Fairchild, lately the hotel keeper at Bryant Station, has moved to Lafayette."

7. Letter from A. W. Elkinton, January 16, 1968, author's possession.

8. *Orinda News*, September 1952.

9. Louis L. Stein, Jr. was told this story by Morris Shuey of the Shuey Dairy.

10. Interview with Mrs. Cyril Chester, Orinda, June 15, 1967; interview with Mrs. E. A. Dawson, and various conversations, 1967–68.

11. *Orinda News*, November, 1950.

12. *Ibid.*, September, 1952.

13. Dawson Interview, see 10.

14. Phone conversation with Mrs. Frank Enos, 1966.

15. Phone conversation with Mr. Werre, Public Relations Department, Standard Oil Company, 1966.

16. Minute Book, Orinda Improvement Association, November 10, 1936, letter from John H. Skeggs, District Engineer to Ralph Sisson, author's possession.

17. *Orinda News*, December, 1952.

18. *Orinda News*, December 2, 1940; *Oakland Tribune*, June 10, 1952.

19. Contra Costa County, Maps, XVIII, 387–88; 400–401; XXI, 588–89, 591–92.

20. *Ibid.*, XVIX, 456–59; XX, 521–23, 536–39, 540–42; Letter from Nathan G. Gray, Attorney, and resident of Oak Springs, 1967.

21. *Walnut Kernal*, Historical and Progress Edition, August 1957, p. 14.

22. Letter and interview with Anthony Cianciarulo, Orinda, February 14, 1967.

23. Telephone conversation with Jack Snow, January 5, 1967.

24. A taped interview with the Domingos family by Brother Dennis is in the Moraga Historical Society collection, St. Mary's College Library.

25. *Contra Costa Gazette*, May 29, 1959.

26. History of the Rancho Laguna de Los Palos Colorados, Moraga Company Letterhead, Item No. 9, copy in author's possession.

CHAPTER IX — *Roads*

1. Slocum, *op. cit.*, p. 663.

2. *Ibid.*, p. 205.

3. *Ibid.*

4. Contra Costa County, Supervisor's Minutes, I, 110, 179.

5. Sherwood Burgess, "The Forgotten Redwoods of the East Bay," *California Historical Society Quarterly*, XXX, No. 1 (March, 1951). See pages 9 and 10 for an interesting story of the development of the lumbering roads.

6. *Contra Costa Gazette*, May 7, 1887.

7. *Ibid.*, May 25, 1861.

8. Contra Costa County, Assessment Book, 1860, Stein Collection.

9. Contra Costa Supervisor's Minutes, III, 47, 59.

10. Date of beginning of stage is mentioned in a case filed November 26, 1862, A. C. Penniman vs. John W. Morris, District Court, 4th Judicial District, Contra Costa County; bills filed in the case show monthly payments to stables in Lafayette. Morris's comments are from this case.

11. *Contra Costa Gazette*, March 30, 1861.

12. *Ibid.*, April 28, 1860.

13. Bayard Taylor, *New Pictures from California* (Oakland: Biobooks, 1951), pp. 53–55. Foreword by Joseph A. Sullivan. In this reprint Mr. Sullivan says he feels that Taylor went over Snake Road, but after carefully following the description of the trip, this author feels quite certain that it was the new Telegraph Road. Morris's stage started to run on the road at this same time.

14. *Contra Costa Gazette*, April 27, 1861.

15. Slocum, *op. cit.*, p. 135.

16. From notes of Louis Stein, Stein Collection.

17. Map, 1870; Papers on Milton J. Rook versus his creditors, filed Contra Costa County, June 11, 1867, Stein Collection; and Memoirs of Anita Miner Macy, possession Mrs. James C. Roos.

18. *Oakland Tribune*, June 21, 1959, "The Knave"; Contra Costa County, Deeds, XXXV, 152, June 13, 1878.

19. Purcell, *op. cit.*, p. 458.

20. *Contra Costa Gazette*, June 24, 1882.

21. *Ibid.*, July 22, 1893.

22. *Oakland Tribune*, May 7, 1952. See page 10 for a history of the Chamber of Commerce.

23. *Oakland Tribune*, June 21, 1959.

24. Purcell, *op. cit.*, p. 458.

25. *Oakland Tribune*, June 21, 1959.

26. *Post Enquirer* (Oakland), November 4, 1903, p. 2.

27. Talk by Eugene Moraga, Moraga Historical Society, May 18, 1967.

28. Information about Winslows, Olives, and Fish Ranch taken from will of Martha Winslow, stipulations and testimonies in the Matter of the Estate of Martha Winslow, John Hanford Olive, deceased, and various other papers, Stein Collection.

29. Contra Costa County, Patents, IV, 350, March 1, 1899.

30. Contra Costa County, Deeds, CI, 364; CXVIII, 434, 436, 449; CXX, 411.

31. *Oakland Tribune*, January 15, 1946. See article on "Days of the Moragas."

32. Letter from Shell Oil Company, April 16, 1968, J. McDougal, District Manager.

33. Telephone interview with Mrs. Basil Perry, March, 1968.

34. *Oakland Tribune*, February 4, 1962, "The Knave."

35. *Ibid.*, October 1, 1887; November 12, 1887.

36. *Ibid.*, April 5, 1890.

37. *Ibid.*, October 17, 1891.

38. *Orinda News*, May 1, 1938.

39. Louis Stein Memoirs, Stein Collection.

40. Letter from E. I. deLaveaga to Frank Bryant, December 12, 1935, author's possession.

41. *Contra Costa Gazette*, December 14, 1912.

42. *Ibid.*, June 28, 1912.

43. *Ibid.*, July 15, 1916.

44. *Post Enquirer* (Oakland), November 4, 1903, p. 2.

45. *Orinda News*, July 7, 1937.

46. *Ibid.*, November 1, 1940.

47. *Ibid.*, February 1, 1941.

48. *Contra Costa Gazette*, April 15, 1893.

49. Letter from Ezra Nelson, March 15, 1969, author's possession.

50. *Ibid.*

CHAPTER X — *The Schools*

1. Contra Costa County, Minutes of Meetings, Board of Supervisors, II, 201, February 4, 1857.

2. *Ibid.*, III, 143, November 5, 1861.

3. Letter from J. H. Wickman, Land Agent, East Bay Municipal Utility District, October 25, 1967, author's possession.

4. *The Sun*, February 18, 1966, Gladys Shally, "Dear Old Golden Rule Days Before 1865," February 25, 1966, "Schools Change—Gripes Don't."

5. *Contra Costa Gazette*, May 20, 1908.

6. *The Sun*, March 1, 1966, Gladys Shally, "Miss Bickerstaff, An Eternal Teacher."

7. *Ibid.*, March 8, 1968, p. 2.

8. *Contra Costa Gazette*, June 11, 1881, Moraga Valley School Report.

9. Phone conversation with Mrs. Giles Crandall, Oakland, February, 1966.

10. Book of Minutes of Meetings of Trustees of Orinda Union School District, September 14, 1924, p. 35.

11. Letter from Ezra Nelson, Orinda, May 18, 1967, author's possession.

12. Minutes of Meetings, Board of Trustees, Orinda Union School District, February 12, 1927, pp. 89–90; Contra Costa County, Deeds, CCCLIV, 231, June 8, 1920.

13. Minute Book, 89–90. See 12.

14. *Ibid.*, pp. 53–54.

15. Contra Costa County, Minutes of Meetings, Board of Supervisors, III, 243; Map of the Rancho El Sobrante accompanying final partition report, 1909, Elam Brown, Surveyor, Stein Collection.

16. *Ibid.*

17. *Orinda News*, September 15, 1947.

18. *Ibid.*

19. *Orinda Sun*, March, 1966, Gladys Shally, " 'General' Wagner Fights for Land."

20. *Orinda News*, September 15, 1947.

21. *Orinda Sun*, March, 1966. See 19.

22. Catalogue of the Public Schools of Contra Costa County, June 30, 1962, Gladys Shally collection.

23. Contra Costa County, Maps, XVII, 363; Letter from Carmel Martinez, January 21, 1968.

24. Several interviews with Florence Sullivan, 1967–68.

25. Letter from Mrs. Grace Kendall, January 21, 1967, author's possession.

26. Minutes of Meetings, Board of Trustees, Orinda Union School District, p. 55.

27. Letter from J. H. Wickman, Land Agent, East Bay Municipal Utility District, October 25, 1967, author's possession.

28. Information about Orinda Union School District from Minutes of Meetings of Board of Trustees, August, 1923 to June, 1928.

29. Letter from E. I. deLaveaga to Orinda Improvement Association, June 15, 1923, author's possession.

30. *Orinda News*, September 15, 1947.

31. *Orinda News*, December 1, 1937, November 1, 1937, May 1, 1938, September 1, 1938, January 1, 1939, March 1, 1939, November 1, 1939.

32. Letter from Orinda Union School District, January 16, 1968, author's possession.

33. From Fontaine Harrington's articles on the schools of Contra Costa County, No. 3, July 30, 1953.

34. *Orinda News*, January 1, 1939, July 1, 1940, April 11, 1941, May 5, 1941, June 2, 1941, April 1, 1942, December 9, 1946, April 1, 1947, September 15, 1947.

35. Service of Dedication—Bulletin, Orinda Community Church Dedication, June 7, 1959.

36. *Orinda News*, December, 1947.

CHAPTER XI— *The Churches of Orinda*

1. Delight deLaveaga, "The History of Santa Maria Church of Orinda, California," December 3, 1939, Edward L. deLaveaga collection.

2. Contra Costa County, Assessment Book, 1882, Stein Collection.

3. Contra Costa Gazette, September 26, 1892.

4. Orinda News, May 1, 1939.

5. E. Geoffrey Banks, *Portals West* (San Francisco: California Historical Society, 1960), Plate 22.

6. Letter from Rev. David Harrington, January 15, 1968, Orinda, author's possession.

7. Orinda Community Church Development: *Orinda News*, July 7, 1937, November 1, 1937, December 1, 1938, December 1, 1947, May 9, 1947; Booklet, "The Service of Dedication of the Orinda Community Church Congregational, Ruth Howe, "The History of the Orinda Community Church," June 7, 1959; Letter from A. W. Elkinton, Carmel, January 16, 1968.

8. Dedication Bulletin of St. Stephen's Episcopal Church, Orinda, California, March 14, 1954.

CHAPTER XII— *Community Services and Utilities*

1. *Orinda News*, July 4, 1947.

2. *Ibid.*

3. *Ibid.*, August 1, 1939.

4. *Ibid.*, June 7, 1947.

5. *Ibid.*

6. *Ibid.*, July 7, 1937.

7. *Contra Costa Gazette*, December 4, 1889.

8. Interview with Mrs. Cyril Chester, June 15, 1967.

9. *Contra Costa Gazette*, Centennial Issue, December 7, 1959, Section 6 gives chronology of county's post offices.

10. *Oakland Tribune*, December 23, 1945, Knave section.

11. *Orinda News*, September 1, 1937.

12. *Orinda News*, September 1, 1937.

13. *Ibid.*, September 1, 1939.

14. *Ibid.*, February 1, 1940.

15. *Ibid.*, November 1, 1941, February 1, 1942.

16. *The Boulevard News*, August 3, 1944.

17. *The Lafayette Sun*, January 22, 1945.

18. *The Walnut Kernal*, 25th Anniversary Edition, August, 1957, p. 86.

19. Minutes of the Orinda Improvement Association, 1935–1936; *Orinda News*, March 1, 1940; Orinda Public Library, Dedication Bulletin, November 14, 1958; Personal interview with Mrs. E. A. Dawson, January 12, 1967; and Orinda Library Chronology prepared by Orinda Library.

20. *Geologic Guidebook of the San Francisco Bay Counties*, No. 154, p. 295, Bureau of Mines, 1951.

21. H. W. Carpentier, R. S. Carpentier, E. R. Carpentier and C. F. Wait, on July 26, 1869, through their agent, John B. Watson, gave a quit claim deed to the Contra Costa Water Company for all waters of the San Pablo Creek, Cordonices, Cerrito, San Leandro and San Lorenzo and the sources and tributaries. The Articles of Incoroporation of the Peoples' Water Company, September 15, 1906, are filed in the office of the County Clerk, Contra Costa County.

22. Abstract of Title to lands described as portion of Ward and Smith League, Rancho El Sobrante, from June 14, 1907 to June 25, 1913. Stein Collection.

23. *Ibid.*

24. *Contra Costa Gazette*, November 16, 1926.

25. Information about early gas and electric service from a letter from Lawrence R. McDonnell, Publicity Director, Pacific Gas and Electric Company, March 19, 1968, author's possession.

26. *Orinda News*, November 1, 1937.

27. Information from Pacific Telephone and Telegraph Company files, Room 1116, 666 Folsom St., San Francisco.

28. *Ibid.*

29. *Contra Costa Gazette*, Centennial Issue, May 29, 1959.

30. *Contra Costa Gazette*, January 14, 1882.

31. William Warren Ferrier, *Berkeley, California* (Berkeley, 1933), p. 165; *Telephone Directory*, 1899. Stein Collection.

CHAPTER XIII — *Community Organizations and Plans*

1. *Orinda News*, July 7, 1947.

2. *Ibid.*, July 1, 1937; January 1, 1938.

3. *Ibid.*

4. *Hayseed Siftings*, Orinda Park, April, 1893, 1, No. 2, Stein Collection.

5. *Orinda News*, Special Edition, February, 1956.

6. *Ibid.*

7. *Ibid.*, February, 1955.

8. *Walnut Kernal*, 25th Anniversary Edition, p. 32.

9. *Orinda News*, September 9, 1946.

10. *Ibid.*, December 9, 1946.

11. Letter to residents of Orinda from the Orinda Union School District, author's possession.

12. Letter from Woodbridge Metcalf, Extension Forester, Emeritus, University of California, January 23, 1969.

13. *Orinda News*, March 1, 1956.

14. Information about Dramateurs from "The Story of Lafayette Town Hall and the Dramateurs," author's possession.

15. *Orinda News*, January 1, 1940; March 1, 1940.

CHAPTER XIV — *Orinda*

1. Smith & Elliott, Illustrations of Contra Costa County with Historical Sketch (Oakland: 1879; Contra Costa Historical Society, 1952), p. 18.

2. *Ibid.*; Jacob Wright Harlan, *California 46' to 88'* (San Francisco: The Bancroft Company, 1888), pp. 214–15.

3. *Orinda News*, May, 1950.

4. *Oakland Tribune*, October 1, 1961; *San Francisco Chronicle*, October 1, 1961.

5. *Contra Costa Gazette*, July 17, 1894.

6. Walter Stalder, "History of Exploration and Development of Gas and Oil in Northern California," *Bulletin 118, California Division of Mines*, p. 75.

7. Gordon B. Oakeshott, "Mineral Fuels of the San Francisco Bay Counties," *Bulletin 154, California Division of Mines*, p. 227.

8. Stalder, *Bulletin 118*, p. 78.

9. Smith & Elliott, *op. cit.*, p. 10.

10. Purcell, *op. cit.*, p. 383.

11. Louis L. Stein, Jr., has a stock certificate for Berkeley Crude Oil Company, 1902. It was evidently located on the Flood Ranch, in the first canyon after entering Happy Valley.

12. *Orinda News*, February 10, 1947.

13. *Ibid.*

14. *Ibid.*

15. *Contra Costa Gazette*, October 17, 1903.

16. Purcell, *op. cit.*, p. 383.

INDEX